WAY

OF THE

DRUID

Published by O Books
O Books is an imprint of The Bothy, John Hunt Publishing Ltd.,
Deershot Lodge, Park Lane, Ropley, Hants, SO24 0BE, UK
office@johnhunt-publishing.com
www.O-books.net

Distribution in:
UK
Orca Book Services
orders@orcabookservices.co.uk
Tel: 01202 665432 Fax: 01202 666219 Int. code (44)

USA and Canada
NBN
custserv@nbnbooks.com
Tel: 1 800 462 6420 Fax: 1 800 338 4550

Australia
Brumby Books
sales@brumbybooks.com
Tel: 61 3 9761 5535 Fax: 61 3 9761 7095

New Zealand
Peaceful Living
books@peaceful-living.co.nz
Tel: 64 7 57 18105 Fax: 64 7 57 18513

Singapore
STP
davidbuckland@tlp.com.sg
Tel: 65 6276 Fax: 65 6276 7119

South Africa
Alternative Books
altbooks@global.co.za
Tel: 27 011 792 7730 Fax: 27 011 972 7787

Graeme K Talboys has asserted his rights under the Copyright, Designs and Patents Act 1988 to be identified as the author of this work.

ISBN 1-905047-23-1

A CIP catalogue record for this book is available from the British Library.

Design: BookDesign™, London

Printed in the USA by Maple-Vail Manufacturing Group

WAY
OF THE
DRUID

THE RENAISSANCE OF A CELTIC RELIGION
AND ITS RELEVANCE FOR TODAY

GRAEME K TALBOYS

BOOKS
**WINCHESTER UK
NEW YORK USA**

This book is dedicated with
much love to the memory of my sister
LORNA JEAN

CONTENTS

ACKNOWLEDGEMENTS

A work of this nature is never accomplished entirely alone. I have drawn ideas, inspiration, and a great deal of strength from many sources – not all of them obvious candidates for such a role.

Of those who have helped, I would like to make especial thanks to Julie White, a dear friend and Druid of great experience who read the book, pointed out errors and exclusions, and let me use some of her own material as a source for sections where she undoubtedly has the greater knowledge and experience.

I would also like to thank Liz Murray, Pauline Kennedy Allan, and Louise Turner Young for looking at an early draft of the book – they made useful suggestions, and ensured that I clarified points that my familiarity with the subject had led me to leave obscure; Eleasaid Ní h'Eibhin for allowing me to look at and quote from her research into the Celtic metaphysic and for highlighting the importance of the structure of language in the unconscious conveyance of ideas and attitudes; Brendan Myers for permission to quote from his recent book, *Dangerous Religion*. Thanks, also, to Catkin and Tilly, whose presence is a joy, despite their odd habits and the strange hours they keep.

Finally, I would like to thank my wife, Barbara, without whom, quite literally, none of this would have been possible. Her strength, companionship, and love have kept me going through the hardest of times. Meeting her was a blessing for which I am ever grateful.

Translations are my own unless otherwise stated, as are any errors.

Graeme K Talboys
Clas Myrddin

INTRODUCTION

INTRODUCTION

This book is about the Druid Way. Most people will have heard of Druids, but their knowledge and understanding of a Druid's religious beliefs and practices is likely to be meagre. Most major religions are sufficiently well known for there to be common terms of reference when they are discussed. And for those who know nothing about them, there is a wealth of information to be found. Minor religions are, perhaps, the preserve of the dedicated student, but there is usually sufficient material available for study to make informed discussion possible. When it comes to obscure or truly exotic religions, there are difficulties. Although adherents may have no problem, for those on the outside there is not enough information in the public domain to enable them to study and understand the religion. In an age when religious understanding is more important than ever, such a situation should be remedied.

The Druid Way is a fast-growing minority pagan religion. Paganism is a worldwide religion with many local variations. Originally, it was the religion everyone practised. Even today, approximately 300 million people[1] are pagan and the numbers are growing. This is particularly so in the Western world where many people feel that comparatively recent religions (such as Christianity) no longer address the concerns of the everyday world. To fill their needs, they look increasingly to those religious traditions that had a particular reverence for the natural world. The Druid Way is just such a tradition, one that is particularly relevant to the Western world as it is not only the West's heritage, but is of direct relevance to the spiritual and material concerns of people today.

Exact numbers of Druids are difficult to come by,[2] but given that the growth rate is greater than that of most other religions,[3] it is important that the Druid Way, along with its wider context of paganism and Celtic discernment, should be understood properly. At present, this is not the case. As a religion, it is rarely treated seriously (particularly on television and in the newspapers), and is often misrepresented. In some cases, this is extreme and deliberate, but overall it is caused by a lack of opportunity to access well-informed and accurate information.

This book was written to fill the gap between basic introductions and the more academic books by Druids that explore the philosophy and theology of their religion in detail. It does not pretend to be a definitive account of all aspects of the Druid Way, not least because of the distinct traditions and the large numbers of Druids who live and work outwith the Orders and other formal groupings. The subject matter discussed herein, however, is common to all Druids and provides a thorough grounding in the history, theology, philosophy, and practices of the Druid Way. There is certainly enough here for the interested reader to become well informed about what Druids are and what they do.

One of the major obstacles to understanding is that the Druid Way is a pagan religion. This fact immediately conjures up a number of disparate and erroneous images, which deter people from further and serious study. The word 'pagan' is often used in a pejorative way to mean 'uncivilized' (a term that is more accurate than most people think) or 'un-Christian'. Indeed, many of those within the Abrahamic tradition[4] are taught to equate 'pagan' with evil or with the devil. Yet pagan religions are entirely distinct from the Abrahamic religions and in most cases predate them.

The term 'pagan' derives from the Latin *paganus,* which as an adjective means 'rural', and as a noun means 'villager' (carrying also the pejorative meaning of 'yokel'). It is also related to the Latin *pagus,* which means 'village' or 'country district'. Roman soldiers posted to out-of-the-way areas tended to use *paganus* as a contemptuous term for a civilian. It was adopted by some very early Christians (who thought of themselves as 'soldiers of Christ') to refer to any non-Christian, but this was a usage that had disappeared before the fourth century AD.[5] It is since that time that 'pagan' seems to have been used in the sense of a person whose spiritual and religious beliefs are associated with the spirit or deity of the countryside (as opposed to those whose religious beliefs are 'civilized' because their deities have a largely urban following).

Paganism is a broad religious movement that encompasses shamanistic, ecstatic, polytheistic, and magical traditions, along with less well-defined but generally pagan attitudes such as nature-centred spirituality, a veneration of female and male deistic principles, personally developed belief systems based on a direct experience of the divine in the world, and an encouragement of tolerance and diversity. Honour, trust, and friendship are also key elements.

It is essential to understand the connection of paganism with the natural world. It is this that makes it a religion in its own right and not a perversion of, or an attack upon, other religions. Indeed, comparatively modern religions such as Christianity have made liberal use of pagan ideology, theology, and myths. Paganism is a religion based on material and spiritual experience of the world rather than on creeds and other affirmations of faith in a transcendent deity. Nature is considered theophanic, the visible manifestation of the divine, which is why a veneration of the natural world is a core expression of pagan religions. This is not a crude worship of trees or stones or rivers or hills. Rather, it is a recognition and reverencing of the divine in the material world (including humanity), using nature as a model for understanding the divine at work in our lives.

Not only is the divine manifest in the world, but aspects of the divine are also made manifest in specific parts of the world. This gives rise to a local emphasis on worship (whilst not denying the universal nature of pagan thought and belief) with certain sites being regarded as concentrations of the divine. It also gives rise to polytheism – the belief in more than one deity. Paganism is not alone in being polytheistic. Indeed, the majority of religions have pantheons of spiritual and deistic beings. Paganism generally has goddesses and gods playing equal roles, often reflecting the social structure of the people who worship them.

As well as having a number of deities, pagans also recognize a female divine principle, often referred to simply as The Goddess, as well as a male divine principle, simply referred to as The God. These are not composites, not all goddesses rolled up into one Goddess and all gods rolled up into one God. Rather, they are the divine principles of life, which we see reflected in the world about us.

Polytheism does not preclude an ultimately monist understanding of the sacred. A number of pagan religions have a monist dimension. Those who belong to these religions believe that there is an ultimate deity or force that is beyond our comprehension, that we are materially and spiritually incapable of perceiving anything but simple manifestations of a single entity, and that one of the reasons for our existence is to mature sufficiently to perceive that ultimate deity. This is rarely stated explicitly (and may, in any case, exist because of monotheistic enculturation) and plays no central part in pagan religion. For the most part, it is the world we live in and the relationship we have with the divine in the here and now that is important. Claiming connection with or understanding of the ultimate seems to pagans to be presumptuous.

The number of deities is not, in any case, important. Rather, it is the nature of deity and the kind of relationship that exists between people and the divine that differentiates paganism from other religions. For a monotheist, deity is transcendent. For a pagan, deity is immanent. Monotheism depends on special messengers conveying the will of deity to people and intervening on their behalf. For pagans there is no historic revelation; they experience their divinity directly and take what teachings they may feel exist from the world around them.

There are, of course, a number of other aspects of paganism that make it distinct from other religions. Many pagans are animists; they see things as cyclical; many believe in reincarnation; most practise some form of magic; and they are often informal in their expression of their belief. This is not because they take their belief casually. Rather, it is because their beliefs are the entire framework of their existence, inseparable from their everyday lives. They also consider their material existence to be as important as, and inextricably linked with, their spiritual existence.

The pagan resurgence in modern Western society is, broadly speaking, a form of nature mysticism that has evolved out of a metaphysical stance that is at odds with the prevailing metaphysic of Western society. Whether by coincidence or as the result of something in the human psyche, this 'new' metaphysic resembles that of peoples who are pagan. Therefore, although the impetus may be modern needs (such as ecological awareness, feminist issues, and political ideology) in search of a spiritual home, it is a re-awakening of latent ways rather than an invention of new ones. This takes on various forms, many of them without any specific tradition. Out of those pagan religions that adhere to a specific ethos, the most popular is Witchcraft (of which there are many varieties). And then there are Druids.

Druids today are pagans whose religion is shaped by a particular view of the world, one that is derived from that of ancestral Celts.[6] Of course, Druids today are not what Druids were two thousand or more years ago. No Druid pretends they are. Being Druid is not some exercise in historical or fantasy role play; it is a deeply spiritual way of life that pays due cognizance to the fact that we are material creatures in a material world. Druids today use the name as an easy way of defining the fact that they live by the metaphysical and spiritual stance of ancestral Celts who had no name for their religion and general outlook on life.

What follows is an explication of the modern Druid Way, along with its historical, theological, and philosophical context. It is intended as a work for the general reader rather than an academic treatise. Most academics approach the Druid Way (and other religions) as a mere matter of history or social science, or by subjecting source material to a form of literary criticism. Yet the Druid Way is a living religious tradition, and such an academic approach, though it has its value, rather misses the point. As well as being factually correct, what follows also attempts to give some flavour of what it is to be Druid in the world today.

1

THE CELTS

THE CELTS

To understand the Druid of today, it is necessary to understand the Druid of the past. And to do that, we have to know about the context in which Druids existed and operated – Celtic society. This in itself presupposes a number of things, not least that we are all agreed on what we are talking about when we use the term Celt.

From the outset, it is important to remember that the Celts are not, nor have they ever been, a 'race' of people. At its very simplest, the Celts are defined as people who speak Celtic languages. This has wider implications, as we shall see later, but for the time being we will stick to this definition, which is the one used by archaeologists. It is not an infallible definition, but it is does provide the major key to understanding how Celtic culture was transmitted. It also allows us access to a wealth of place-name evidence, which reveals a great deal more than the geographical spread of Celtic speaking peoples.

The history of the Celts is extraordinary, yet remains overshadowed by veneration for all things Greek and Roman. At one time, however, the Celts inhabited a huge swathe of the European[7] landmass and its northern islands. Their language, culture, and traditions have survived through three millennia,[8] despite the impact of martial dominance by the Romans, Goths, Huns, Vandals, Saxons, Danes, and Normans – along with many other influences, both cultural and religious. Indeed, despite all of this, Celtic people have left a distinct and indelible – if often deliberately obscured – mark on the world. National borders have come and gone; invaders have come and gone with them. In the end, the Celtic peoples have outlived them all and although the pressures on them continue, they still exist and they still have influence in the world.

Claims for this continuity have not gone unchallenged, especially by some archaeologists.[9] For all the debate, however, it cannot be denied that

Celtic speaking peoples have played an important role in Europe over the last three thousand years. Why they should have survived for so long, especially under such prolonged pressure from so many directions, is hard to tell. Perhaps it is their ability, amply demonstrated through the centuries, to absorb new ideas of worth and remake them in keeping with their own view of the world. The willingness to absorb new ideas in this way speaks of an essential vision of the world that is both robust and vital. Not only is this vitality a strong inner core, its composition is such that wherever Celts and their ideas went they found this vision reflected in what was already there.

It is, of course, a huge leap to argue that a people who share a language also share a metaphysical outlook. Huge, but far from outrageous, for language and thought are not separable. How we think about things at a fundamental level is expressed in our language, for those thoughts must be communicated. How we think about things at a fundamental level is also expressed in social organization, in our relationship with the rest of the world, in personal behaviour, and the expressive arts.

At this point, we stray beyond the material certainties of archaeology for archaeology, inevitably, can only provide part of the picture. Material or physical culture, however, goes hand in hand with metaphysical and spiritual culture. We can intellectualize about both, but the way in which the Celts saw the world and the many ways in which they expressed their vision have the ability to touch us directly at an emotional level.

Moreover, there is something else to be taken into account. The way in which ancestral Celts viewed the world was very different from the way in which we now see it. Not different in the minor details inevitable when considering a culture from the past, but different in its very essentials. Just how, we shall see later, but it should be borne in mind that the baseline from which we interpret the past can make interpretation extremely difficult, even erroneous – like using calculus as a means of understanding the nonsense poems of Edward Lear.

PROTO-CELTS

Although the earliest examples of fully developed Celtic culture are associated with the working and use of iron, this culture did not come into being overnight. No culture does – even if some are created quickly under pressure. Three thousand and more years ago, society was relatively stable and developed extremely slowly by today's standards. We are so used to social and technological change that it is hard to imagine a society where generations could pass without the need or the desire for the new.

Metal-working skills, for example, had existed for fifteen hundred years before iron came into use. No doubt the techniques had become more highly refined over the centuries (as Late Bronze Age implements readily testify), but they would not have changed greatly in all that time. Similarly, iron working remained largely unchanged from 700 BC, when it was taken up by the Celts, until the industrial revolution nearly two and a half thousand years later. Indeed, the old ways, tried and well tested, were in common use even as recently as the last fifty years. Some of my earlier memories are of my grandfather's forge.

Archaeological evidence now dates the earliest phase of Celtic culture to around 1200 BC, well back into the Bronze Age. The Celtic peoples were descended from a people we call the Urnfield culture.[10] These people in their turn had became a distinct culture from the more generalized Bronze Age culture of the period, which included the peoples of Britain who built the megalithic monuments and other landscape features.

This notion of continuity is important. At one time it was thought that changes of culture were occasioned by social upheaval (revolution, invasion, and mass migration) as well as widespread environmental problems. Although these have no doubt played their part, it is now thought that the major driving force for cultural change in the past was trade and the accompanying transmission of ideas.

The Bronze Age as a whole was one of increasing settlement and improved agriculture. By 1500 BC, there is evidence of successful mixed farming, crop rotation, and a pattern of social complexity. The Indo-European language[11] was beginning to fragment into distinct dialects and an early form of Celtic was probably being spoken. This move towards a new cultural identity was consolidated by external forces. Around 1200 BC, events in what we now call Russia caused a movement of peoples across Urnfield territory. Not only did this put pressure on Urnfield peoples, it upset many of the societies around the eastern Mediterranean, which is where these itinerant peoples finally came to rest.

Egypt was temporarily taken over; the Hittite Empire in Anatolia collapsed; Mycenae never recovered and began its descent into obscurity; Philistines overran Palestine. As we are so often reminded, however, it is an ill wind... The collapse of these old orders broke down barriers and allowed new ideas to flow north and west. New trade routes opened along which these ideas flowed with the wine. Perhaps the most important things to move were new bronze-working techniques that led to the heavy bronze sword and, following that (in a roundabout fashion), the secrets of iron working that had long been a monopoly of the Hittites and a reason for their dominance.

It was Urnfield peoples who benefited most from the changes. Hillforts spread and along with them there developed a warrior society equipped with armour, shields, and those heavy swords. This was probably defensive as much as it was aggressive. Their own people needed protecting from the social unrest that rippled through the continent and the new trading routes needed to be kept safe.

A warrior class needs more than weapons, however. It also requires a society capable of supporting it. Urnfield peoples were extremely successful farmers. Their development of crop rotation improved field fertility and thus increased yields. It also had the added bonus of reducing the risk of crop disease and pests. They were a prosperous people who wanted to ensure that their standard of living remained high.

These developments are now regarded as the beginning of Celtic culture. Yet there was one element left, which, when added, would see the transformation complete. During the period in which the Urnfield warrior class developed, other peoples were reaping the benefits of the breaking of the Hittite monopoly on iron-smelting technology. These were the Cimmerians, a people who lived to the north of the Caucasus.

During the eighth century BC, unrest in their own lands began to push some of the Cimmerians westward toward the Danube basin. With them they brought two things of enormous importance. The first was their horses. The horse was already important to the early Celtic peoples, but new breeds and new skills invigorated the stock and its use, and led to the horse taking a central role in the life of all classes of Celt.

The second important thing that the Cimmerians introduced was, of course, iron, along with the skills to smelt and work it. The already prosperous and strong early Celtic culture did what it has always been good at – it absorbed these skills and the ideas that came with them, enhancing itself in the process.

HALLSTATT

Archaeologists divide Celtic culture into two distinct periods. The earlier of these is known as the Hallstatt, named after a village in the Austrian Salzkammergut. It was there, in 1846, that a cemetery was discovered with evidence of a distinct cultural type. The name should not be taken to imply that this was the birthplace of the Celts, nor that it was the centre of their world. It is simply the place where evidence was first discovered of a distinct culture.

The Hallstatt is divided into four phases. Phases A and B correspond with the Late Bronze Age developments described above. With the introduction of iron, we see the beginning of phase C – a comparatively short period of enormous change. Hallstatt D, which was also comparatively short, marks a shift westward of the Celtic heartland to the Rhône, the Loire, and the headwaters of the Seine.

So what is it about those graves in Hallstatt that provides evidence of a distinct culture? And why the shift westward? It is that whereas in the Urnfield culture, people cremated all their dead, the Hallstatt shows a marked difference. Although the change was not complete, the elite of the new culture were being inhumed with considerable amounts of grave goods. Cremation still continued, but tended to be the practice for ordinary members of society.

What occasioned this particular change is not known, but it does mark a shift in thinking about the afterlife. The change was gradual, suggesting that the new ideas were adopted by those who had greatest contact with outside influences. This is only speculation, however, as the changes may have come entirely from within. Whatever the case, they are indicative of major shifts in thought and outlook.

Although the name Hallstatt cannot be used to indicate origin or importance, it is significant that the area is rich in salt. Salt had been extracted here (by mining) for centuries before the emergence of Celtic culture, but there is no doubt that it was instrumental in the rise of the Celts to prominence. Being essential to food preservation, salt was both widely traded and used locally to preserve fish and meat. Not only did this improve living conditions (and increase winter survival rates), but it also increased the distance that people could travel without the need to take time hunting for food along the way.

When the working of iron was added to the equation, along with improved horse stock, the balance was tipped even further in favour of this vigorous people. Along with the salt, iron became a major currency. Yet although these commodities produced a surplus of wealth and increased the amount of trade, it has to be remembered that the mainstay of the Celtic economy was farming.

Farming in the region, already advanced in many of its techniques, was greatly enhanced in quality by the introduction of iron. There were no radical changes to method, but those methods already in use were made more effective. Fields, for example, were more easily and more deeply ploughed. Not only did this make existing fields easier to work, but it enabled new areas, with heavier soils, to be opened up to cultivation and soil improvement. Iron tools, which lasted longer and held their edge better, meant that levels of productivity could be maintained whilst less work needed to be done.

Woodland could also be worked more efficiently. This did not mean an increase in felling. Just as Hallstatt people were efficient farmers who worked the land in a sustainable fashion, so they were also efficient stewards of woodland. The value and use of different timbers was well understood and woodland was coppiced and otherwise harvested on various rotations to ensure a lasting supply of timber for building and for making wagons and tools, as well as a supply of other woods and underbrush for fuel, and for charcoal making – essential to the smelting of iron.

Farming became immensely productive. More land was worked and yields were increased. Livestock products, along with other goods, could be traded farther afield. Now that agriculture was able to support a larger proportion of the population not working on the land, other forms of artisanship could flourish. The area became increasingly prosperous and the Celts thrived.

The increase in material culture was matched by an increasingly sophisticated non-material culture. This has already been hinted at with a change in burial practice. There was an increasingly complex social order, as well as the development of a distinctive art form in the decorating of all artefacts. This was not yet the elaborate knotwork and spiral designs we generally associate with the Celts, but the precursors of this are now visible in delicate patterning. Moreover, the standard of workmanship is breathtaking. All this bespeaks an increasingly coherent and sophisticated way of viewing the world.

Increasing prosperity and leisure brought with them two things – greater life expectancy and a drop in infant mortality. That, in turn, meant a growth in population. This pressure, along with an increase in trade and the inevitable move of settlements toward the major trade routes, resulted in an expansion of the area in which the Hallstatt Celts lived. Yet this is more complex than a mere expansion of population. There were undoubtedly movements of people, not least because the elites would wish to keep control of trade, but making new land available for agriculture did not cause the problems that would have resulted if the area had already been crowded. More important was the movement of ideas and of language.

Trade is not just the passing of goods from one place to another. Traders must share language, make contacts, and develop relationships with trading partners. Moreover, the objects that were moved were not the throwaway items of today's world – mass produced, shipped halfway across the planet, and yet still cheaper than can be produced in the country where they are bought. Traders grew rich and guarded their markets carefully, but those who made the objects also travelled back and forth along the trade routes. Why pay a high price for all those things that are not quite to your taste when the person who makes them can be hired and can create them exactly as you want? And when traders and manufacturers moved, their families moved with them – extended families who brought along their whole way of life.

By the time that Hallstatt Celts were well established in the area we now call Austria, Celtic culture had spread into most of western Europe, including the south-eastern corner of Britain. This is a remarkable achievement, showing how vigorous and attractive were this way of life and this way of viewing the world. The trading links along which this cultural expansion occurred were already long established, having been in use since the Mesolithic. These links did not bring much in the way of strife or conflict and when a new prosperity and vision appeared, it spread readily.

The expansion and movement of the Hallstatt centre of power meant that by the sixth century BC the headlands of the Danube were part of a much larger territory. The upper Rhine, with its links all the way to the North Sea, encompassed southern Germany. The Rhône, with its access to the western Mediterranean, brought in Burgundy, which also opened on to the Loire and the Atlantic coast.

This expansion firmed up the trading links and greatly increased, the power and influence, not just of the elite, but also of the ideas of these people. These strong links and the intellectual cross-fertilization set the stage for the development of a new period of Celtic culture. However, it was events beyond the control of the Celts that were to prompt the change.

LA TÈNE

The middle of the fifth century BC saw a marked change in political geography across Europe. The precise chronology and the exact reasons are uncertain, though the nature of the change provides us with possible answers. Whatever the case, throughout much of the Hallstatt heartland rich burials ceased and the hillforts were abandoned. Something drastic had happened to deprive the elite of their wealth and power. At the same time, smaller power centres around the northern and eastern peripheries of the Hallstatt region came into their own and flourished. Although having much in common with the Hallstatt, these new centres also differed in ways significant enough for us to consider it a new period of Celtic culture.

We call this new period La Tène after an archaeological site in the shallows of Lake Neuchâtel in the west of Switzerland where excavations between 1906 and 1917 uncovered a mass of iron swords and other weapons, along with other ironwork, woodwork (including an entire wheel), as well as skeletons. The place was clearly of great significance and the items disposed of must have been given as offerings. We do not know the state of the bodies when they entered the water, but there is no evidence of human sacrifice. Further discoveries throughout the region, stretching from the Marne, through to Moselle, and on to Bohemia, showed a shift not just in power but also in ways of thinking, doing, and making.

The events that brought about these changes were probably linked, in part at least, to trade. The Hallstatt peoples had grown prosperous on their trade with Greek and Phoenician colonies along the western Mediterranean shore. At Massalia (Marseilles), the Greeks in particular began to dominate trade traffic in the region. With the south and west controlled by powerful groups, it was to the north and east that there would have lived those tribes and peoples who benefited only indirectly from the flow of wealth. They may have been Hallstatt peoples or neighbouring peoples who came under their influence. They may have been waiting for the first opportunity to exploit any weakness in their neighbours or they may just have been in the right place at the right time. Whatever the case, they were ideally positioned for what happened next.

The world of the eastern Mediterranean was now in turmoil with wars, one after the other, between different states and groups. As ever in such situations, trade suffered. The flow of goods into the western Mediterranean faltered. The Hallstatt elite lost access to that which had kept them in power and their people content. Within a period of two generations at most, the old order had gone. The new order, though still definitely Celtic, reflected the immense changes that had taken place in the world.

La Tène culture differs from Hallstatt in two major respects. The first of these is burial practice, which clearly reflects a change in social structure. Hallstatt Celts buried their elite in rustic wagons with other grave goods. Any weapons were largely those used for hunting or for ceremonial display – an indication that farmers and traders were also chieftains. La Tène Celts buried their elite with two-wheeled chariots and weapons of war. The leaders of society were now warriors.

This change probably does not mark a shift to outright aggression as much as it displays a clearer demarcation of the roles of people in society, along with the need for those who are warriors to make decisions on behalf of others. Today we might see that as sinister, but times were different. The La Tène period was more turbulent, as we shall see, but this was true for most peoples at that time. And at such times warrior elites come to the fore – they take the risks on behalf of others in their tribe (in ways that modern leaders do not in militaristic societies) and they reap the rewards.

As well as this shift in social organization, there was, secondly, a major development of artisanship. As before, this was not so much a change of method as a development of style. There was, however, another factor at play. With the diminution of trade, there were fewer imported goods. This meant that much more had to be produced locally, the slack probably being taken up by those who normally produced for export. Now no longer having to please outside markets, they could concentrate on developing what they wanted. It is entirely possible that the skills to do this had become moribund within the Hallstatt heartland and that sudden demands on the peoples to the north and east stimulated this new flowering of skill and design.

The flourishing of new skills is amply displayed in the chariots found as grave goods. These magnificently constructed vehicles were in all respects far superior to any other form of chariot in existence at that time. And so it remained for a number of centuries. Modern reconstructions of similar (if later) models show that they were light, sturdy, manoeuvrable, capable of crossing rough pasture (although the Celts were great road builders), comfortable because of an effective system of suspension, and adaptable ? a vehicle that was used to take the family on a picnic one day could be converted in a matter of minutes into a highly effective war chariot. In combination with the spear and the Celtic long sword, the chariot was part of a flexible and formidable armoury.

Design, too, came to the fore. What we now consider the classical form of Celtic art was developed during this period. Delicate metalwork, knotwork and spiral designs, ceramics, jewellery, and statuary all abound. This, if nothing else, is evidence that the change in leadership, with warriors now being in charge, had done nothing to stifle the creativity and skills of the ordinary people.

Such vitality and creativity could not be contained. Hallstatt culture, perhaps, had grown complacent and too dependent on imported goods. The shift of power to a new elite unleashed a new and vigorous attitude. La Tène influence soon began to spread. Moreover, this time it was not just ideas and skills that were on the move. In a complex story of expansions and migrations, the reasons for which are still not clearly understood, along with military opportunism, whole tribes and peoples migrated. As a result, the Celtic world expanded enormously.

Whereas Hallstatt remains are found in central Europe as far south as the Alps and into south-east Britain, La Tène culture very soon expanded well beyond those boundaries. In some cases, this was down to wholesale migration of tribes,[12] but much of it was owing to the influence of ideas whose time had clearly come. Eventually, by the third and second centuries BC, La Tène Celts were to be found in what we now know as Ireland, Britain, northern and western Spain, virtually the whole of France, northern Italy, Switzerland, Belgium, the Netherlands, western Germany, the Czech and Slovak Republics, Romania, Bulgaria, and the Republics of the former Yugoslavia as far south as the northern borders of Macedonia. They even colonized a large part of central Turkey, which became known as Galatia after its people. Moreover, they traded well beyond these areas and played an important role in the histories of other peoples.

It is no coincidence that it is at this time that Celts first appear in written accounts from the classical world.[13] These accounts are brief, but show both respect and a degree of anxiety. The respect derived from the fact that the authors recognized that Celts were every bit their equals in all aspects of life.

The anxiety was because the authors recognized that there was no effective means by which to prevent Celtic expansion into their territories.

Of all these movements, perhaps the one with the most far-reaching consequences took place in the fourth century BC. It began when Celts moved southward through the Alps and down into the Po valley, where they settled. They did not stay there, however. In 387 BC, under the leadership of Brennus,[14] Celts marched on Rome. They sacked most of the city and left only after the Romans paid them to go. So began the Roman obsession with creating a buffer zone between themselves and the rest of world, along with their abiding hatred and mistrust of the Celtic peoples.

For all their drive, martial prowess, and skills as farmers and artisans, the Celtic peoples were not empire builders in the same sense as others, especially the Romans. It is often claimed that they were too fragmented to create an empire, too inclined to argue amongst themselves to form the lasting and disciplined armies that such an enterprise demanded. This is true to a point, but it neglects to explain why – taking it as a given that a people would *want* to impose their will on others by force and create a vast martial empire. As we shall see, the Celts did not view the world in this way; their views on ownership of land in particular were very different from those of other people.

The tide eventually began to turn, although the change was barely perceptible. In 295 BC, the Romans began their long expansion. It was to be a slow process. Seventy years passed before they gained control of northern Italy, and another generation before they had sufficient control of their home territory to embark on empire building. And whereas the Celts had expanded as opportunists, the Romans were far more systematic in their approach. This is not to say there was some master plan to dominate the known world, merely that each step was one of consolidation with an eye to the resources that could be annexed for the greater glory and wealth of Rome.

This did not stop the Celtic world expanding in other directions. As Rome fought westward and northward, Celts moved through Greece and into the Balkans. In 279 BC, they even entered Macedonia, taking the hub of what had been Alexander's vast and short-lived empire.

The martial prowess and other skills of the Celts, along with their ever-growing contact with other peoples, increased the demand on their services. It was this that led to the founding of Galatia. Celtic mercenaries were also to be found in the Syria of the Seleucid kings, in the Judea of Herod the

Great, in Carthage until its impending defeat by Rome (guiding Hannibal across the Alps being one their more notable accomplishments), and even in the Egypt of the Ptolemy pharaohs. The Celtic troops of Ptolemy II actually attempted a *coup d'état*. The *coup* was unsuccessful, although one has to wonder what turn history might have taken had they succeeded. Despite that, Ptolemy II and his successors continued to use Celts. Indeed, Cleopatra VII (the last of the Ptolemies) had a bodyguard of 400 Celtic warriors. It was this unit that was gifted to Herod by Octavian. Recent archaeological evidence also offers a tantalizing hint that some Celts (traders, warriors, or settlers – we do not know) may have reached as far as China.

The expansion of Celtic peoples and their cultural influence ended in the second century BC when countries in the eastern Mediterranean began to reassert their independence and push back their boundaries. The Cimbri of Jutland joined forces with the Teutones in harrying the Celtic tribes of north-eastern Europe. And the Romans moved out of their Italian heartland.

Roman techniques for conquest were sophisticated, and are still in use today. Trade is generally the first step, with increasingly stringent and monopolistic treaties being enforced. Some groups are picked out for favourable treatment, creating civil discontent. Training and weapons are provided for malcontents who would otherwise have little impact on their own society. If challenged about this, any imperial power will usually either deny any involvement or will talk about support for the oppressed and a desire to bring freedom and political enlightenment to barbarians who, despite their uncouth ways and lack of the benefits of civilized society, are always painted as a threat.

Thus weakened, any society becomes wide open to military or economic domination by outside forces. It certainly happened like this in Gaul, with Gaius Julius Caesar using the situation to his personal advantage. With Gaul caught in Rome's web and unable to present a united front, Caesar was able to tear the country apart piece by piece. Gaul, however, was no walkover. Caesar's ambitions cost many tens of thousands of lives on both sides of the conflict and left the country in turmoil. Famine, homelessness, and the movement of refugees, along with the fear of conquest and occupation, may have undermined the confidence of some, but for others the sight of their world so damaged was a spur. Caesar's intelligence had clearly underestimated the strength of any resistance, especially when a number of tribes put aside their differences and accepted Vercingetorix as their war leader. Only Rome's ability to draw on the resources of already conquered territories outwith Gaul allowed Caesar to prevail in the seven-year campaign.

When Caesar was assassinated in 44 BC, Gaul was still not wholly under Roman control and the much-vaunted invasion of Britain had been little more than a flag-waving exercise. We know very well from recent events what happens when a superior power moves into a so-called less-developed country. Winning the war is usually the easy part. Winning the peace is far more costly and takes much longer. In the end, it comes down to how much money and how many lives the conquerors are prepared to lose.

Throughout central Europe, trade with and occupation by Rome increasingly diluted Celtic culture. The last remaining strongholds of the La Tène, and the places where it had its greatest flowering, were Britain and Ireland. Ironically, it was increasing Roman dominance of continental Europe, prompting the final large-scale migration of Celtic peoples, that had caused this vitality in these islands. These Celts, the Belgae, had crossed the Channel and reinvigorated insular culture, at the same time opening up trading links with Rome.

There is uncertainty about the nature of the movement of the Belgae into Britain. Some still consider it to have been an invasion. But though it undoubtedly caused unrest, as any large-scale influx of people to an area will, it is more sensible to consider it a migration. There was a great deal of movement of peoples throughout the La Tène period and such an influx would not have been entirely unexpected or completely unheard of. A common (if by now fragmenting) language and a common culture, along with a fertile and lightly populated countryside, would have made absorption of a people possible.

An invigorated culture, first-hand knowledge of the Romans, and the fact that several generations had had a chance to observe what was happening across the Channel, all combined to make Britain an even tougher prospect than Gaul. There were tribes that accepted Rome, having built up lucrative trading relationships. But the tribes that did not want Rome made life precarious for the invaders. Of twenty-eight Legions deployed throughout the Roman Empire at its height, four were required for the part of Britain that was considered Roman territory.

In the event, that number was barely sufficient. From the outset, there was unrest. Perhaps the best known of the early rebellions against Roman rule was that of the Iceni and the Trinovantes under the leadership of the

Iceni queen now known to us by her battle cry *boudicca*, meaning 'victory'. And victory it so nearly was. An entire Legion slaughtered, cities razed to the ground, and the much-vaunted efficiency of the Roman army shown up for what it really was. The defeat of this rebellion is traditionally put down to the undisciplined Celts' inability to face up to the might of the Roman military machine. It was more likely down to bad luck and a leader dying of septicaemia. Whatever the case, the Roman retribution was relentless. Towns and villages were destroyed, fields salted, and those who were not killed were driven from their homelands or sold into slavery. It was the first real taste in Britain of the *pax Romana.*

It did little to quell the Celtic spirit. There was trouble and there were rebellions throughout the 350 years that Britain was counted part of the Roman Empire.[15] It is one reason why the Romans never established themselves fully beyond the south-eastern corner of the island. Hadrian's Wall famously marks the northernmost extent of Roman control. To the west, Cornwall and most of Wales occasionally saw Roman troops, whilst the Isle of Man and Ireland remained altogether free of a Roman presence.

HISTORICAL PERIOD

It is during the period of the Roman occupation that most accounts of the Celts come to an end, as if they somehow faded away. Yet Celtic people continued to live and work as they always had. Only the south-eastern corner of Britain became Romanized in any significant way and even there only a minority of the population wholeheartedly embraced the new culture and the new language. Indeed, the greatest change to Celtic culture came about as the result of the spread of Christianity.

During the fifth century AD, Rome abandoned Britain. Already military strength had slowly been withdrawn as the Roman Empire came under pressure on the Continent. When appeals were sent in AD 410 for help against increasing raids by Saxons, the response was that Britain must look to its own defence. Much of the wealth that Britain generated was consumed in rebuilding hillforts and other defensive works, as well as training warriors and hiring mercenaries. Although much of this work would have been undertaken by those once close to or part of the Roman military establishment, it does not seem that any attempt was made to reproduce Roman methods. As always with the Celts, they took what suited them best and made it their own.

Whatever the eventual form of the Celtic military defence, it was effective – which is especially impressive when you remember that the country was emerging from centuries of colonial rule. Invading Saxons were fought, their presence being initially confined to the south-east, and for several generations their power was broken. The Saxon peoples, however, like the Romans, were unremittingly warlike – without the pretence of being civilized. Yet even after they resumed their conquest, they were never able to occupy more territory than the Romans. The western extremities of Britain, and much of the north, remained Celtic.

The difference, however, was that, unlike the Romans, the Saxons were not interested in assimilation. They drove Celts from their lands or slaughtered them where they stood. There was no middle way unless you count slavery. Archaeologists and historians who try to argue for a gentle migration are increasingly in a minority. The Celts as a cultural grouping are defined, as we have seen, by their language. Place-name and language evidence are very clear – nearly everything Celtic was expunged from the land that is now England. A few place names survived, but the few Celtic words in use in the English language were introduced in the seventeenth and eighteenth centuries.

Bloody battles between Celt and Saxon were fought through the following centuries, with internal Saxon strife, and Danish raids from the ninth century onward, complicating the story. Things finally came to a head in AD 937 at the Battle of Brunanburh (somewhere near Chester). This turned out to be the last attempt of the Celts to drive the Saxons from Britain. The Saxon name of the battle tells us the result. From this time forward, the borders we are familiar with come into being and England ceases to have any claim to being Celtic.

On the fringes of all this, and throughout the battles for sovereignty, a new flowering of Celtic culture was under way, principally in Ireland. This was, in part, driven by the arrival of Christianity. Whilst the old social orders remained and traditional Celtic beliefs and motifs continued in use, a new dynamic was introduced which viewed the past through fresh eyes. Universities and monasteries flourished. Books that contained what previously had been passed orally from generation to generation were written and copied.

This revival was not confined to Celtic lands. Missionaries and teachers from the shrinking Celtic realms travelled throughout Europe, establishing monasteries, setting up schools, and keeping alive the Celtic worldview. At one stage, what we now call Celtic Christianity looked set to rival Rome in its dominance of Europe. The Roman Church declared many Celtic teachings to be heretical and slowly suppressed them, often by force. Monasteries and schools founded by Celts were taken over and their histories re-written to cast favourable light on Rome.

With England now established and Celts pushed out to the very fringes of what had once been a pan-European culture, the Normans invaded and set about the further subjugation of the Celtic world. They planted castles, annexed land, engineered famines... The litany is depressingly familiar and continued through the next thousand years with Celtic countries being the first to be annexed by England into what has now become known as the British Empire. Yet whatever else all this may have achieved, it singularly failed to destroy Celtic culture. Celtic peoples and their distinctive languages and view of the world still exist and are now enjoying something of a revival.

2

CELTIC CULTURE

CELTIC CULTURE

Much was made in the preceding chapter of the term 'Celtic culture', and the Celts themselves were defined as 'people who speak Celtic languages'. But this takes us only so far. Though language might be considered a major element in the definition (and the one most useful for archaeologists and historians) it is by no means the only element. Many Celts were also fluent in Latin and Greek without adopting other aspects of Roman or Greek culture – just as Romans and Greeks learnt Celtic without becoming Celts.

Along with its other functions, language is the expression of thoughts and ideas. Those thoughts and ideas do not pop into our heads at random, but are shaped by an underlying pattern. They possess a degree of coherence of which we are often unaware. The underlying pattern is the particular metaphysic or worldview by which we understand the world. This will be discussed in more depth in Chapter 5. For the moment, it is enough to know that language is not the only overt sign of an underlying pattern. Indeed, culture is properly defined as *all* the ways in which a people perceive, make intelligible, and organize their being.

In our present and hugely disarticulated society, the term 'culture' has come to refer to a much narrower expression of thought and activity. That is, 'culture' has become more or less synonymous with 'aesthetics' – encompassing painting, music, poetry, literature, drama, opera, dance, sculpture, and so on. Any suggestion today that culture should include farming, manufacturing, or the legal system would be met with little understanding.

Quite aside from this narrowed focus, there is also the fact that the arts are now often seen as separate entities that exist within society without having concern for or direct relevance to our everyday lives, to science, technology, politics, or any of the other aspects of our being. To most people, the arts are a matter of leisure, a pastime, something with which to idle away a few hours before getting back to the serious business of real life.

This notion (that aesthetic pursuits can be separated from the rest of life) is derived from the metaphysic on which modern Western society is founded. Ancestral Celts would have found this modern attitude to the arts and the aesthetic dimension of our culture incomprehensible. Indeed, they would find our whole way of life strange – built as it is on ideas about the world that are alien to the ones they held. For them, all aspects of life were connected and derived from a single source. Each aspect was reflected in the other.

Of course, ancestral Celts had art, music, architecture, and all the rest – in these areas they had distinctive forms of expression that we can identify and study. However, where modern thought disarticulates the differing facets of our life, ancestral Celtic thought unified them. Nor is it just modern thought that differs in this way from that of ancestral Celts. The seeds of the way in which people of modern Western society think are to be found partly in the Greece of classical antiquity, but mostly in the burgeoning Roman culture that absorbed it. This goes a long way to explaining the antipathy between Celts and Romans. It also goes a long way to explaining why most people today, in the face of considerable evidence to the contrary, regard Greece and Rome as models of civilization and democracy and Celts as uncouth barbarians.

It is clear, then, that in talking of Celtic culture, we are not confined to the arts any more than we are confined to language – even if we use language as the parameter for deciding what is and what is not Celtic. Such an all-encompassing, holistic approach to life is difficult to portray in an approach that is analytical. However, if we look at the role of certain individuals within society, we might begin to see something of what this means.

Bards, for example, were not poets as we understand them today. Whilst we clearly recognize the worth of poetry and its ability to prize open and illuminate the more complex recesses of human nature, and whilst we recognize the skill of the poet who can use language to accomplish this task, we still set poets apart. We study them at school and college and some of us even read their work thereafter. But on the whole, few of us see them as essential to society. For ancestral Celts, however, this is exactly what Bards were – integral and essential. They were certainly capable of all that we have described of the modern poet, but they also applied these skills to functions that were crucial to the good running of Celtic society. They were historians, genealogists, law keepers (they literally kept it in their heads), as well as arbiters in disputes, philosophers, theologians, elegists, and entertainers.

It was the same with Druids. They were not an isolated parasitical elite who went their own way in pursuit of some vaguely defined esoteric knowledge. Rather, they were doctors, teachers, lawyers, diplomats, priests, surgeons, judges – what we might now call the professional class of society. Their role was also overarching. They held the picture of society in their heads, carrying out all their duties in accord with their understanding of the world. The fact that they trained in colleges to what may have been a common curriculum meant they were also uniquely placed to reach beyond the normal tribal divisions and act as a cohering force in Celtic society.

That the Celts recognized the need for, and the importance of an intellectual class, did not mean they believed it or its members were in any way superior. Warriors were also integral to society. Although the structure varied from tribe to tribe, a chieftain normally had a full-time bodyguard that was expected to police and defend the tribal area. Nor was this a male preserve. Celtic women had the right to bear arms, could become warriors, and were known to have been involved in training warriors in the martial arts. Other members of the tribe, again including women, would be called upon to bear arms if and when it became necessary. Conflicts were rare, however, and normally only involved the professional warriors whose main role was as the executive arm of the legal system.

Farming was the mainstay of Celtic life, the powerhouse of its economy. For all there were Druids and warriors, the majority of people, including most of those selfsame warriors and Druids, worked on the land – especially during the harvest. There may have been some whose role prevented them from participating (perhaps even those who thought it was beneath their dignity), but the majority were members of the tribe and this carried weight beyond the needs or desires of the individual.

It has already been mentioned that for the Celt, working the land was not a matter simply of producing maximum yield no matter what the consequences for its long-term health. Each tribe worked the land knowing that it was held in sacred trust; knowing that if they abused that trust, its bounty would be denied them. They developed sustainable techniques of arable farming, the harvesting of timber, and animal husbandry. They did all this with reverence and with guidance – not as superstitious yokels, but as a people who knew that you could not fight the natural world and win.

Even as an intellectual concept, this attitude is difficult for most people brought up in modern Western society to grasp. Yet for ancestral Celts it was not an intellectual exercise, it was the way of things. It was a way so deeply ingrained that it was second nature. It was a way that produced a vibrant culture that, at its height, was as sophisticated as any other on the planet – past or present.

One way to gain something of an insight into Celtic culture and to see how it differed from classical Greek and Roman culture (and, by implication, our own) is to look at the way in which Celts decorated the things they made. Celtic decoration as it is commonly recognized – curvilinear patterns and intricate knotwork – is La Tène. This is, however, the result of centuries of development. Hallstatt artisans were just as skilled as La Tène and worked designs that were every bit as intricate. Moreover, in whatever age they lived, these artisans made things that were eminently functional, elegantly designed, and always decorated with subtlety. Jewellery, weapons and armour, pots and plate, caskets, horse and vehicle harness – these things were rarely plain. Everything was made to last, even (if not especially) items that were made to be given as offerings in religious rites.

Nothing, beautiful as it may have been, was produced for its own sake. Everything had a purpose – even jewellery. Whereas we largely use jewellery for purely decorative purposes, ancestral Celts rarely made decorative items that did not also have a specific symbolic or practical function. Whatever the reason – be it for fastening clothes, as a sign of status, for an offering in sacred ritual, even in payment of a fine – a reason was always there. Ancestral Celts, overall, may have been prosperous, but the idea of making something to serve no purpose other than to sit on a shelf (a souvenir of Camulodunum?) would probably have vexed them.

Of all the designs used to decorate items, those most easily recognized are the sinuous knotwork borders and panels. As anyone who has tried to produce their own will know, even the simplest knot requires a great deal of planning and an understanding of geometry and perspective. Moreover, sketching on paper with a pencil, a ruler, and an eraser is difficult enough; imagine carving the design into wood or laying it out on metal and preparing it for enamelling.

It is often said that Celts would not depict the human form or produce images of their gods and goddesses. Although it is true that, until the late La Tène, depiction of the human form (both mortal and divine) was relatively rare, there are plenty of examples. Of these, however, many are quite abstract. The most common form of naturalistic depiction is to be found on coins.[16] Which raises a question. If ancestral Celts were capable of accurate portraiture, why were depictions of people rare?

There are a number of possible answers, but the simplest is that there was some form of taboo. This was by no means absolute, but perhaps a feeling inherent in the Celtic view of the world was that to depict something accurately was to become involved in that thing at some magical level – not just in the act of creation but also in the life of the object. We cannot ever know, but such an idea could rise from a belief in the unity of all things. It may also be that ancestral Celts recognized that the natural world was beyond imitation, that it was not the role of people to try to reproduce something that was quite capable of reproducing itself, and that representations of animate beings would always lack vitality.

Whatever the case, it was not until the coming of Christianity and the production of books that we see widespread representations of people, and even then, they quite often continued to be abstract forms, which were woven into the increasingly complex designs of fine lines and many colours that could be worked on flat vellum. Such designs have become popular in recent years, but all too often they are divorced from the wider context to which they once belonged and are shorn of any specific symbolic value they may once have had.

And therein lies the point. The decoration of an object was integral to its overall design – not just as a visual effect, but also at a much deeper level. The consistency of design embedded it within the culture from whence it was derived, since it was a product of the metaphysic held in common by Celtic peoples. Even if only at an instinctive level, such design would have spoken of much more than just a pretty pattern that pleased the eye.

The widespread nature of the basics of design and decoration also had the effect of creating anonymity. Undoubtedly, there were artisans better at what they did than others, but it was the efficacy of the item that was important, not the ego of the artisan. This was not a conscious decision on anyone's part; it, too, was an aspect of the way in which ancestral Celts viewed the world. It may well be that just as archaeologists now can determine where certain things were made, cognoscenti then could look at a sword or a shield and know that if it had not been made locally it was the product of this, that, or the other tribe. The cult of the individual is a relatively recent development.

It would be tempting to say that perhaps every object was produced as an act of worship. Commentators both ancient and modern have attested to the fact that ancestral Celts were a religious people. However, that would be to look through modern eyes. All life was an ongoing act of worship, a participation in the ongoing creation of the world. Belief and action reflected not only the unity of all things, but also that all things were sacred and imbued with spirit. This was not just a universal spirit, but also the spirit of the artisan, the spirit of the person who owned the object, as well as the spirit of the object itself. This is readily illustrated by the flowing lines and sinuous forms of the pattern. These speak of the way in which the natural world flows and curves, and of an understanding of the cyclical nature of existence. Moreover, it is a sophisticated interpretation of the visible world as well as a symbolic representation of the forces at play within the world.

It is also worth noting the scale of the objects in question. Ancestral Celts were undoubtedly skilled engineers when it came to large-scale projects – Maiden Castle in Dorset, the brochs in Scotland, and the *oppidum* of Los Cogotas,[17] to name but a very few, are all evidence of that. Yet impressive as these works are, they retain a human scale. What is more, the majority of material remains are relatively small, personal, and portable. Ancestral Celts knew that, in a sense, they could take these with them to the next world. They also knew that they would live on in this world in the memories of loved ones and of the tribe. There was no need to leave behind them vast monuments to their own egos. Contrast this with Greek and Roman artistic expression, which is idealistic, linear, large scale, and invested in things they hoped would survive after they had died, gaudy tombstones to remind those still alive of their existence.

RELIGION

It would be impossible to conduct any discussion of ancestral Celtic culture without at least a mention of religious belief and spiritual life. Given that the purpose of this book is to explicate what claims to be a modern development of that belief, it is imperative that we do so. This is no easy task. The primary sources one normally associates with religion, such as ritual, sacred writings, prayers, and commentaries, are all lost to us. If such things existed in any distinguishable form, they were transmitted orally. Much of what we do know is derived from secondary sources. These include the myths, wonder tales, poetry, teachings, and other texts that were transcriptions made in later centuries. Archaeology, history, and comparative philology have also helped to cast light on what time has obscured.

In venturing into this area, we must tread warily. A certain amount of light has been cast but the ground beneath our feet is uncertain. The maps still have their equivalent of 'here be monsters'. To begin with, we cannot talk of the 'religion of the Celts' as if it were a geographical and temporal constant. The beliefs of insular Celts, the gods and goddesses to whom they paid respect, the rites they performed, may all have differed considerably from those of, for example, the Galatians.

There is a degree of evidence that, as in so many other aspects of Celtic life, there were underlying principles common to all, along with some deities and myths that were universal. It is likely that there was a shared bedrock of belief, which, however, each tribe or confederation expressed in their own ways in keeping with their own history and the locale in which they lived. Thus, each tribe had its own deities, its own totems, and its own ways of worship, which were usually kept private.

Another reason why we must be careful is that the life of ancestral Celts was religious in a sense lost to much of modern Western society. They were not pious, nor were they zealots or evangelists (to borrow words from other traditions). As we have seen, they did not separate religion out from the rest of their existence. Such an idea would have been foreign to them. Their religion, like everything else, was derived from the metaphysic common to them all. And this metaphysic was, ultimately, spiritual.

It would be sensible at this stage to dispel some of the more foolish notions that have been put forward about ancestral Celtic religion. The first of these is that their beliefs were primitive in the disparaging sense of being the crude superstitions of barbarians. The Hallstatt people were not barbarians. Over the centuries, their culture had become highly sophisticated. Their belief system would have been equally sophisticated. They did not, for example, worship the sun or the trees. To claim so would be as absurd as to claim that Christians worship crosses.

One particular piece of evidence that is commonly cited as proof of the primitive nature of Celtic religion is its lack of organization. To begin with, we do not know for certain that that is the case —although it would go against the idea of personal and tribal autonomy that was so important to Celtic people. But lack of a hierarchy or the absence of a centralized authority is not evidence that the religion was primitive. It merely shows that a single authoritarian source did not determine belief and practice. There was no charismatic, revelatory teacher; there was no holy book which needed defending against dilution and distortion. Instead, there seems to have been an all-pervading understanding of the world and all therein as sacred. Whether this went as far as to be pantheism or panentheism is open to debate, not least because such a stance relies heavily on monotheism.

For all that the religion itself was not organized, there was an organizing principle involved in the practice of public rites. Druids officiated at public religious ceremonies, presumably to ensure they were carried out correctly as well as to act as reliable and trusted witnesses. They were taught these procedures (along with much else) in colleges[18] and were, in general terms, considered a unifying force within society. This is not the same, however, as an organized religion.

What Druids presided over were the rites and ceremonies of a highly religious people. Life for ancestral Celts was a spiritual journey. Every thought and every action had a spiritual and religious dimension. Everything was done in reference to the gods and goddesses who were part of the family and part of the tribe. There existed an intimate relationship with the sacred in which everyone could participate as the sacred was there in the everyday world.

There appears to be no name for the religious beliefs of the Celts. This in itself is indicative of the degree to which religion was integral to their lives: you only name something that can be distinguished from other things. Of one point we can be sure, the religion was not called Druidry or Druidism. Some Druids acted as priests and they certainly shared the beliefs of all other Celts, but their 'teachings'[19] did not constitute a religion any more than they constituted a separate cult. They were far too much a part of the structure of society to engage in such practices. Of all people, they would have adhered most strongly to the mores of society for they were the keepers of the law.

In common with most religions of the ancient world, and many today, Celtic religion was polytheistic. The names of more than four hundred Celtic deities have survived. These are male, female, animal, and of uncertain form. Many of the 'human' deities are related in family groups or can be grouped loosely into tribes or peoples. Of those known to us, about three-quarters are local, specific to certain regions or tribes. The rest are to be found throughout the Celtic world.

Depictions of Cernunnos, to take one example, have been found in various sites dating back to the fourth century BC. He seems to have been a major deity and there are convincing arguments that Cernunnos is a personal or variant name for The Dagda (the Good God – father of all deities). If this is so, he is a complex character with a multi-faceted nature. As Cernunnos, he is normally depicted with antlers, making him a lord of animals (most famously depicted on the Gundestrup Cauldron[20]). Yet as The Dagda, he would also bear a club that could kill with one end and restore life with the other. This triune nature (Creator, Preserver, and Destroyer) is not uncommon in Celtic deities.

For all that this figure looms large in the Celtic pantheon, and for all that he has a role as creator, it is clear that the Celts believed their origins lay with a Mother Goddess, Danu (or variations thereof – Anna, Anu, Don). She is the mother of The Dagda and is sometimes also known as Brigid, but whether this name is because of a late conflation of goddesses is not known. The name Danu, which means 'divine water of heaven', is to be found as the stem of Danuvius (Danube), the river whose headwaters saw the development of Celtic culture. She fell, as rain, and nurtured Bíle, the sacred oak, which produced acorns. Out of each acorn the gods and goddesses grew – the children of Danu.

In essence, Danu was water that fell from the sky to the earth. This act of creation shows both the virtue and the importance of the number three in Celtic thought and belief. From the Sky, the Land, and the Sea ('Sea' often being given as a generic term for water) all other things are born and derive their sustenance. Most of the major and many of the minor deities had a triune form – three aspects, each sometimes with its own name, reflecting the complex nature of their being. In some cases, deities were depicted as single individuals with three faces or heads; in others, specific deities were shown as three distinct individuals.

A god who was recognized in one form or another throughout much, or perhaps the entire, Celtic world was Lug. He is the quintessential Celt whose skills encompass all aspects of Celtic culture – a great warrior as well as a master of crafts from smithing and farming to harping and games playing. His name means 'light' or 'brightness' and this is often equated with the sun, but it goes further than that for his presence is both physically and spiritually illuminating. His wide-ranging skills and his ability to illuminate made him especially important to Druids – a connection that is underpinned by a number of similarities between Lug and Myrddin.

Goddesses also figure strongly. Brigid, for example, was so firmly fixed in the Celtic psyche that she survived the transformation to Christianity and is still beloved by many as St Bridget, the foster mother of the Christ.[21] As Brigid, she had three aspects – fertility, healing, and smithing. She is also often cited as a Bardic muse. The range of her attributes suggests that the crafts practised by Celts were not gender-specific. We know that women trained some of the great warriors of history and legend, as well as going to war in their own right. It seems likely, therefore, that women were also smiths, doctors, and farmers.

From the very beginning, animals also played an important part in Celtic religious life. They are widely depicted in carvings, decorations, and as statuettes. They also figure extensively in the poems and tales that have come down to us, often connected with religious rites and quests. They are also seen as sources of wisdom. Hardly surprising, then, that they were considered to be endowed with spirit.

There is no surprise in the importance of animals. Celts were much more reliant on their domesticated creatures than we are today, and they were no doubt much more aware of wild creatures in their environment. This is reflected in the range of creatures depicted – from cattle, sheep, pigs, dogs, and cats, to badgers, foxes, bears, otters, deer, and birds of all kinds. Pride of place, however, must go to the wild boar. This powerful creature was found across the whole Celtic world and was probably the most dangerous wild animal a person was likely to encounter (as both wolves and bears will avoid people if at all possible). *Ard* (pronounced 'arth' – the 'th' as in 'this') seems to be a root word for boar in continental Europe and Arthur is sometimes known as the Boar of Cornwall. In Irish and Gaelic, however, the word for boar is *torc*, which has led to the suggestion that the neck ornament of the same name was once worn only by warriors.

The otherworldly nature of animals and their role in religious belief can be seen in the many tales of shapeshifting. There are a number of elements to this, but most of them involve teaching and initiation. Celts believed that not only did the natural world have much to teach them, but also that human beings were entirely a part of that world. They also believed that the boundaries between humans, animals, plants, and the mineral world were nowhere near as fixed as we now believe.

The names of deities, animals, and trees can be found as elements of personal, place, and tribal names. Cunobelinus (the Cymbeline of

Shakespeare) means 'hound of Belinus' (the Shining One); Camulodunum is 'fortress of Camulos' (a Gaulish god of war); there are many rivers named for Danu or Don; the Brigantes are the 'people of Brigantia' (a goddess of victory); Biliomagus (a Gaulish place name) is 'Plain of the Sacred Tree'; and Drunemeton (the meeting place of the Galatian council) means 'sacred oak grove'.

Religion, however, was not just about ritual and deities. Religious beliefs encompassed and permeated all aspects of Celtic life, shaping behaviour, institutions, and the way things were done. We have already seen, for example, that the number three is significant in understanding the complexity of deity. However, it goes much further than that, for the number is found in the very structure of Celtic understanding of the world. The Celts considered people to have three distinct aspects – body, spirit, and soul. Nature was divided into animal, vegetable, and mineral realms. The elements were threefold – the Land, the Sea, and the Sky. Celts knew the primary colours as red, yellow, and blue, and ascribed the colours of red, black, and white to the mysteries of life, love, and death.[22] Even teaching made use of threes. The triads of Britain and of Ireland[23] are powerful poetic forms, even now, when they exist only in corrupt form and without much of the material to which they acted as pointers.

Other numbers were also important to the Celts for their symbolic value. These numbers, however, tended to be derived from and were directly relevant to the material world, whereas the number three was more closely associated with non-material aspects of life. We should not conclude from this, however, that Celts were obsessive numerologists. They knew the value of number and of mathematics, and saw how it helped them to understand the world, but they were realistic enough to accept that the world was far too complex to be bound by simple formulae.

Another important and widespread aspect of the religious sensibility of Celts was their fascination with the head. They believed that the head was the seat and source of all that defined human beings, that it was the home of the soul. The head was venerated – but veneration is not the same as worship, far from it. Celts were too sophisticated to believe that deity resided in inanimate objects, even if they believed deity could be manifested through such symbols. It was simply considered a mark of respect to keep and embalm the head of a person who had been admired in life – be that a friend or an enemy. Some have interpreted this as evidence that Celts were headhunters. This is nonsense. They did not seek out others and kill them simply to get their heads. Heads were taken only after a person had died – naturally or in battle – and then only if they had been held in respect.

Heads feature in wonder tales and myths, sometimes remaining alive in disembodied form. Bran the Blessed (Bendigeid Fran) is one such. Mortally poisoned, he entreats his companions to sever his head from his body before the poison can reach it. This they do, and on their long journey home the head of Bran talks, gives advice, even tells jokes. Another well-known tale featuring decapitation is *Sir Gawain and the Green Knight*, a Middle English poem that contains unmistakable parallels with episodes from the life of Cúchulainn. The piece is vibrant with mysticism and important in understanding the cyclical structure of the year.

Beheading, and stories of the disembodied existence of the head, are indicative of the Celtic belief that the soul was indestructible. Being immortal, it passed, on the death of the body, to a new life in the Otherworld, a place of wonder and ease. But life in the Otherworld would also end, with the soul then returning to this world. The death of a person here was both mourned and celebrated – in recognition both of the loss and the certainty that the departed had gone to a better place. The celebration of birth in this world acknowledged the death and sorrow that must have occurred in the Otherworld in order to allow the soul to travel here.

When the dead were buried, grave goods fitting their status and wealth were buried with them. These were often personal items, imbued by constant use with the spirit of the person. So strong was this belief in another life that, as Valerius Maximus wrote in the first century AD, Celts 'lent sums of money to each other that are repayable in the next world, so firmly convinced are they that the souls of men are immortal'.[24] This was not common practice, but serves to illustrate the point.

The Otherworld also had a physical, if somewhat peripatetic, location. The Celts believed that it was a place the living could visit and from whence, if they were careful, they could return. Arthur went raiding there in search of a magic cauldron; Bran the Blessed travelled to islands in the west by boat; Cúchulainn journeyed to Hy-Falga; Oisín dwelt there for three hundred years.

There were many names for the Otherworld, and not all referred to the place to which the soul migrated. The boundaries between these worlds are elastic. In some will be found the gods; in others the faerie folk. Many of the names were euphemistic terms that spoke of things that touched the Celtic heart. Annwfn (*an,* meaning 'not'; *dwfn,* meaning 'the world') is the traditional Cymric name, although it is also known as Caer Feddwid (the Court of Intoxication) and Caer Siddi (the Court of the Gods). In Ireland the name may be Hy-Breasail (Breasail's Island); Dún Scaith (the Fortress of Shadows); Mag Dá Cheó (the Plain of two Mists – a real place with strong Otherworldly connections); or Tír na tSamraidh (the Summer Land). Many other names exist. Most evoke an image of an earthly paradise, a land of warmth and plenty; others are darker and tinged with sadness. All seem to be reflections of this world and the human experience.

The journey to the Otherworld (by the living or the dead) involved a voyage into the west. The living had to undergo dangerous adventures and required considerable skill and wisdom if they were to survive. The dead had an easier time of it. Their souls gathered at special places and were ferried into the sunset. In Irish myth (which has remained least affected by later redactions), the gatekeepers of the Otherworld, appropriately enough, are those from whom our first ancestors sprang – Danu and Bíle.

There was one day of the year when the way between the worlds was open to all – though still perilous for the unwary. This was at Samhain, conventionally celebrated after the sun sets on 31 October.[25] Much debased now as Hallowe'en, it was a time to remember, and pay tribute to, those who had died during the past year. It was also a time when the dead who had been wronged by the living could return to rebalance the scales.

A great deal has been made of the similarity between these beliefs and those of the Pythagoreans. Indeed, over the years there has been a great deal of sterile debate as to whether Druids took their beliefs from Pythagoras, or Pythagoras learned of them from the Druids. In all likelihood, given that the differences between the ideologies far outweigh the similarities, they were parallel developments of the basic notion of the immortality of the soul.

The ideas of Pythagoras (as far as we can know them from second-hand sources, which is why it is more accurate to impute them to the Pythagorean School) were a form of karmic metempsychosis. That is, the soul was given a new body and a new life in accord with how well the previous life had been lived. A bad life was punished, and the punishment was to be born again into a life of poverty, or as an animal. A good life was rewarded with a life free of problems. The ethical standards by which good and bad, reward and punishment, were set are uncertain.

Celts did not believe in reward for, or punishment of, this life in the next. This was due in part to their highly developed sense of moral and legal justice in the present life. Their idea of immortality stood apart from that. Rather, it reflects the idea that the world is cyclical in nature. They knew that death occasioned new life; was, in fact, essential to the constant revitalization of the world. To Celts, this was how the world was and it could not be co-opted as a system of reward and punishment for what they did or did not do with their lives.

The religious beliefs of any people invariably have a moral or ethical dimension. What we know of the moral stance of the Celts is sufficient for us to tell that morality stood at the very heart of their vision of the world. Good was something you did for its own sake. According to Diogenes Laertius, the central principles of Celtic life – expressed appropriately in triadic form – were that they 'should worship the gods, do no evil, and exercise courage'.[26]

These tenets were underpinned by the absolute importance of truth. Truth was fundamental to Celtic thought and to the position of Druids within society. Their word, after all, was law. It was, however, much deeper than that for the notion of truth goes well beyond the veracity of language. Out of truth comes the world and it is truth by which it is sustained. Its importance as a concept can be seen in Celtic languages, where the word for 'truth' shares its roots with words such as 'holiness', 'faithfulness', and 'reality'. It also has linguistic connections with the idea of free will and responsibility. Another name for the Otherworld was the Place of Truth.

A number of other ideals can be found in early texts. Druids taught, for example, that people should aspire to live in harmony with the natural world. They saw spirit in all things – a unifying force. To damage part was to damage the whole. This harmony also applied to human relations. Quarrelling and fighting were frowned on (despite the picture of the Celts presented to us by the Romans and Greeks). Such behaviour reflected badly on the whole tribe and unruly behaviour would result in a fine being levied. Disputants were expected to settle their differences peacefully and if they could not do it themselves, they were to do it through their very advanced legal system. Equally, excessive litigiousness was frowned upon.

Celts had a highly developed sense of what was right and what was wrong. Although much of this was encoded in complex law systems and teachings, reinforced by the use of taboos, it was not inflexible. Much of the legal expertise of Druids would have been applied to judging cases on their merits. Tribal living helped to reinforce standards and was a moral pressure of its own. In the end, however, individuals were held responsible and accountable for their own actions. Offences against religious, moral, or civil law could not be forgiven. The transgression had to be paid for –through fines, community service, or by being bound over to work for someone else for a given length of time. The ultimate punishment was exile from the tribe as that removed the transgressor from both the material and spiritual community.

The notion of free will, with its concomitant of personal responsibility for one's actions and moral welfare, was deeply embedded in the Celtic psyche. In the fourth century AD, the Christian theologian Pelagius (a Celt from Britain or Ireland) was accused of reviving Druidic philosophy on nature and free will. His writings were a rebuttal of the teachings of Augustine of Hippo on preordination, an idea that Pelagius considered responsible for moral decline in the Christian Church. Quite what Pelagius had to say is uncertain. His two major works, *On Nature* and *On Free Will* are lost to us, perhaps deliberately rooted out and destroyed after his death – for he was condemned as a heretic. We only know his arguments from his opponents' record of them. Whatever the case of the specific arguments made by Pelagius, it is clear that the metaphysic on which they were based was extant in the sixth century AD. Pelagians in Britain and semi-Pelagians in Gaul were still being condemned for their views.

All of this is now worth bearing in mind as it would not be possible to conclude this brief introduction to Celtic culture and belief without mentioning sacrifice. We know that Celts sacrificed inanimate objects: torcs, swords, armour, jewellery, chariots, statues, and even severed heads. We know also that animals were sacrificed, using methods in common use for the slaughter of all animals at that time. Celts may not have feared death, but they did not delight in it and found cruelty abhorrent.

The first references to human sacrifice in Celtic worship are by Caesar and Strabo, both of whom appear to use Poseidonius[27] as their source. Neither these, nor any of the later passages, are first-hand accounts, and many are merely quotations, or elaborations on earlier reports. All are written by people who make no distinction between what they have seen for themselves and hearsay; between fact and propaganda. Their accounts (some quite absurd) have to be approached with extreme caution.

Within Celtic tradition itself and the extensive Celtic literature, there is no mention of the practice of human sacrifice. Given that this literature was collected and written by Christian monks, who took every opportunity to highlight and attack the pagan ways of their forebears, it is curious that, if it existed, they should have found no hint of it. The same is the case with the *Confession* of Patrick. He never misses a chance to criticize strongly the pagan practices of the Irish and their Druids, but there is no reference in his writings to human sacrifice.

Archaeological finds that are said to offer evidence do no such thing. The best we can say, in the absence of reliable first-hand accounts, is that someone did not die of natural causes. This man or woman might have died in battle, have been the victim of violent crime, have had an accident, or even been the subject of voluntary euthanasia on learning of a painful and terminal illness. Indeed, everything that we know of Celtic beliefs, along with the absence in extant law codes of a death penalty, would suggest that human sacrifice was not practised.

3

THE DRUIDS

THE DRUIDS

THE MEANING OF THE WORD 'DRUID'

For many, the search for the meaning of a word can seem a dry exercise, redolent of the schoolroom. And it is true that a word derives its meaning in large part from current context and use. Nevertheless, seeking out the origins of a name does help to illuminate the origins of that which bears the name. This is particularly useful when those origins are lost in the hoary old mists of antiquity.

Particular care has to be taken in such an exercise. The distance at which we work is great and it is all too easy to see what we want to see. Much better that we use only natural light and make do with what is revealed. The minute we start using artificial light, be that via rose-tinted lenses or generated by the heat of fantasy or prejudice, we run into serious trouble. The temptations (if nothing else) are clear. When a goal is elusive, the desire to attain it can sometimes cloud objectivity. Our judgement is even more likely to be clouded if we approach our goal with any sort of preconceived notion of what form it should take and why.

With a word as elusive of fixed meaning as that under scrutiny, it is little wonder that all manner of meanings should have been suggested. These have ranged from genuine, if misguided, attempts to make sense of the word to the truly bizarre. In particular, those who have attempted, in various ways, to connect the Druids with the Abrahamic tradition have found many spurious connections between the Welsh and Hebrew languages, as well as the respective mythologies of these peoples. Thus we have the Hebrew *Drusim* (a Persian Magi) cited, along with *derulsim*, meaning 'mediators'[28] as possible origins for the word 'druid'.

Others have looked closer to home and to less contrived readings of the word to elicit a meaning. Davies derived 'Druid' from the British *dar*, which he gives as 'superior' and *gwydd*, which he gives as 'a priest'. This was presumably in an attempt to provide a meaning for and connection with *gowydd* or *ovydd*, 'a subordinate priest'. Toland thought that the word *drud* (in old British), signified 'a discreet or learned person'. The basis for these particular interpretations is obscure. Less contrived still is the derivation suggested by Pezron. He offers the idea that 'Druid' is from the Celtic *deru*, 'oak', and *hud*, 'enchantment' – citing Pliny on the Druids' attachment to performing rituals in the presence of the oak.

One of the problems in arriving at a meaning is that Druids have been the focus of intense cultural scrutiny, particularly during the last three hundred years. Competing claims on their origin, their function, and their spiritual and religious significance have been put forward, with those proposing them all trying to make their mark. It might be said that Druids today are equally guilty of cultural claim staking. However, there is a difference in that claims made by Druids today must be in accord with what is said by independent experts if they are to retain any vestige of credibility.

It was in the second century BC that the word *Druidae* first began to appear. Instances of the use of this word by classical Greek writers have come down to us as sourced quotes in a work called *Lives and Opinions of Eminent Philosophers* written by the Greek, Diogenes Laertius (fl. AD 225-250). There had been earlier references to *sacerdotes, antistites, gutuartos,* and the like, but it was not until Poseidonius (c.135-c.50 BC) travelled through Gaul that there was a realization that all intellectual functionaries in Celtic society were known collectively as Druids.

Speculation on the origin and meaning of the word began at an early date. Pliny the Elder, in his *Natural History*, made the connection between the word *druid* and the Greek word *drus*, which means 'oak'.[29] He thought it possible that *druid* was taken from the Greek. The meaning of his text, however, is not altogether clear. He could be saying that he believed the Celts to have adopted a Greek word as the name of their intellectual class. Equally, he could be stating that the word in general circulation amongst Greeks and Romans was of Greek origin. Neither is particularly likely although, as we shall see, he may have been partly right for the wrong reasons.

The connection of the Druids with the oak in particular and with trees in general is pervasive. Lucan refers to them as *dryadae*, which may be an attempt to link them with Greek wood spirits. Equally, the word *dryadae* could be a scribal error introduced when copying the text. Other aberrant forms also appear, including *drasidae* and *drysidae*.

Although words from one language are adopted into another, it is highly unlikely that a well-established and integral institution of Celtic society would have been known by anything other than a native name. Indeed, the Greek *druidai* and the Latin *druidae* and *druides* are consistent with a Celtic form *druvis*, from *druvids.*[30] As this word does not appear in any known Romano-Celtic inscription, the existence of such a word can only remain conjectural, but it is consistent with known words.

Other etymological evidence strengthens the likelihood of this suggestion, both elements of the word *druvis* being widely accepted Celtic and Indo-European root words. Unfortunately, this does little to fix a precise meaning for *druid*, as root words have a tendency to produce many branches. This being the case, we will begin with that element about which there is the greatest consensus.

The word *druid* splits easily into two elements, *dru* and *wid*. *Wid* we can confidently dispose of straight away as most authorities agree that it is a root word meaning 'to know' or 'to see'. From this, we get such words as the Latin *video*, with the same meaning, and *videlicet*, which means 'clearly'. To see or to know encompasses the whole idea of understanding – of great importance to a class of society responsible for all aspects of the intellect.

But what is it that is seen, known, or understood? It has already been remarked that Pliny considered the whole word to be derived from the Greek for 'oak'. Moreover, we have already said that this is unlikely. Celtic languages, however, all have similar words for 'oak' and they are strongly evocative of the Greek. It is entirely possible that they all have a common root, an Indo-European word *deru*. The Gallic (one of the few words we know for certain) is *dervo*. Other early forms are *daur* (Gaelic), *derw* (Welsh), and *derv* (Breton). Modern versions are similar – *dair* (Irish), *darach* (Gaelic), *daragh* (Manx), *derwen* and *dâr* (Welsh), *derowen* (Cornish), and *dervenn* (Breton).

If this is correct and *dru* can be taken to mean 'oak', then *druid* would mean something like 'one who sees/knows/understands the oak' – perhaps more comfortably rendered as 'oak-seer' or 'oak-knower'. This is not entirely beyond the realms of plausibility, especially if we accept a long development of the class, starting in a time when hunter-gatherers were still prevalent.[31] Those who had knowledge of the oak (and, by extension, the oak forests) would have played an important role in society.

Some leading Celtic etymologists (Thurneysen, Pederson, de Jubainville, and Stokes among them) originally considered *dru* to be an intensive. The meaning of *druid* would therefore be something like 'all-seeing' or 'all-knowing'. Although there some plausibility about such a meaning, it is not one that has stayed in favour.

Dru has also been interpreted as *dreo*, meaning 'truth'. Given that the root of both words is probably the same and that truth is a central tenet of ancestral Celtic thought and belief, there is a strong degree of plausibility in this interpretation. A Druid as one who sees, knows, and understands the truth certainly reflects accurately the function of Druids in society.

This is important. Names are not arbitrary. They serve a distinct purpose: that of identifying an individual or group in a useful way. Thus, personal names were once descriptive of a person's trade, location, or status. My own ancestors were Norman foresters (*taille*, 'to cut'; *bois*, 'wood'). Over time, such names become fixed and lose their original significance. In some cases, where a word still serves actively to identify a person or group, its meaning evolves.

Druids, then, may originally have been knowers of the oak, but over time, changes took place. The idea of the oak remained central, but the meaning broadened as the role of the oak-knower increased in complexity. The wise men and women of the proto-Celtic peoples may have been shamanistic in nature, guiding their people through the forests of this world and the spirit world. With the settled existence brought about by the introduction of farming, the role of the oak-knowers would have had either to change or become irrelevant.

The Bronze Age was one of slow, but increasing social sophistication. You cannot build ritual sites on the scale of Avebury and Stonehenge without social continuity and cohesion. Nor can you achieve that without good communication, careful organization, and a social system that can spare the people involved and provide them with food and shelter. Finally, it cannot be achieved without intellectual vision and ability.

By the Iron Age, society (now Celtic) was every bit as complex as our own. The cohesive element was the Druid class – 'oak-knowers' who had evolved into 'truth-knowers'. Yet although their role developed and became more complex, their core function did not. Knowing the forest and being able to guide their people would have meant knowing the truth of all things. This fundamental aspect remained at the same time as its application adapted in response to a changing social environment. Just how accurate this is as a description of ancestral Druids will be discussed below. Just how relevant it is today depends on how much that function has remained at the core of what Druids are.

ORIGINS

History is silent on the origin of the Druids, other than a statement by Caesar that 'it is thought the discipline was devised in Britain and from there brought across to Gaul...'[32]

This is a subject that has occasioned much debate amongst scholars over the decades. Until recently, much of the discussion was posited on the erroneous beliefs that Druids were nothing more than priests and that the Celts were a distinct racial group. We now know, of course, that neither of these beliefs is true.

At its most basic, the debate was largely about whether Druids were wholly Celtic or whether they originally belonged in some way to some other culture (real or imagined). This then spawned a sub-debate on whether Celts had subsumed this other culture and adopted their priesthood, or whether Druids had arrived from elsewhere and taken over the Celts. Much of this was driven by doubtful scholarship and in some cases by a desire to prove pet theories. It is now clear that Druids were Celts, and that the name denoted a class of people within Celtic society and wholly part of Celtic culture. This, however, is only true as far as it goes. It gives no indication as to the origin of Druids, nor of the complexities inherent in the development of a group of people with such a wide-ranging set of skills and interests.

The previous chapter on the history of the Celts made it clear that although Celtic culture as we now recognize it, is defined by certain markers (primarily linguistic) and went through two distinct phases, there was never a distinct 'racial' group. This was not a people who went rampaging through Europe, conquering everyone in sight, and imposing their culture on others. Rather, there was a culture (the ways in which a people perceive, make intelligible, and organize their being) that first developed a distinct form in the peoples who lived around the headwaters of the Danube.

Linguistic and genetic studies, along with advances in archaeological understanding, have given us in recent years a better understanding of the movement of peoples through the millennia. Despite a number of migrations, many of which we know about from other sources, the population of the area inhabited by Celts was static. The people who became Celts were already there, and had been there for millennia.

Evidence of this continuity is clearly indicated in a number of genetic studies, along with analysis of the chemical and mineral content of bones and teeth. One dramatic example is the 9,000-year-old remains found in the west of England, genetic and other indicators from which were compared with those of people living in the village adjacent to the archaeological site. These showed that people alive today could be direct descendants of those later Mesolithic people. The gene pool, in that area at least, has barely been muddied in all that time.[33]

It cannot be stressed often enough that genetic and other indicators have nothing to do with race. They simply serve to tell us where people originated in a geographical sense. They can also indicate general lines of descent. And on the whole, the peoples of Europe were, in antiquity at least, extremely settled. That said, we also know from some exceptions to the general rule that trade routes were extensive and that people as well as goods moved hundreds and sometimes thousands of miles.

Celtic culture, therefore, developed in a population that had been native to the Danube headwaters for millennia and spread through peoples who were equally settled. These pre- and proto-Celtic cultures were equally as widespread as Celtic culture was to become. There were, of course, regional variations, but the underlying ethos was sufficiently similar for us to realize that communication of goods and ideas was widespread.

Our perspective (looking back over thousands of years), along with the terminology we use to discuss these things, can often obscure the gradual nature of change. Celtic culture did not come fully formed out of a big box. Urnfield culture simply altered fraction by fraction over the generations until we, from our great distance, can say that one culture is distinct from another. People at the time would not have seen much change in their lives.

We can step back even farther, for Urnfield culture was but one development from earlier cultures to be found in prehistoric Europe. All of the people in these cultures were trading across vast distances, although not necessarily directly, from the Shetland Islands to Anatolia and beyond. The Iberian Peninsula no doubt had connections with north-west Africa. The sea was not an obstacle. It was the major highway.

This point has been laboured for a purpose. For just as Celtic culture and the social structures of the Celts did not come out of a box, nor did the Druids. If we accept that they are fundamentally Celtic (and all the available evidence supports this), then we have to accept that they came into being in the same way as Celtic culture. That is, they were a development of something that already existed. The evidence already presented in discussing the meaning of the word *druid* certainly supports this view. The evolving dialect of the Indo-European language that became Celtic already contained some of the root words that are associated with the name. It follows that the class of society that fulfilled the role of Druids was already there in some form prior to the Hallstatt period.

How far back in time we can go with this is moot. It has become fashionable again of late to attempt to construct a direct line of descent between the Neolithic and Bronze Age megalith builders of north-western Europe and the Celts and, thus, the Druids. There is a superficial case to be made. The peoples who directed the construction of the stone circles and the sculpting of the landscape were highly organized and extremely skilled. The mathematics, engineering, and logistics involved in making concrete a vision of the world are all evidence of an intellectual class that wielded a high degree of power within a complex social structure.

It is tempting to make the leap and claim that these people were direct antecedents of the Druids. The problem is that the area in which the megalithic and landscape structures were created does not coincide with the area in which Celtic culture developed. Celtic culture, however, found extremely fertile soil in the north-western reaches of Europe and flourished there. So, although there may not have been a direct line of descent from the astronomer priests of the Late Neolithic and Early Bronze Age to the Druids, they probably came of common metaphysical stock. No wonder, then, that as Celtic culture developed, it took the shape it did. It was growing out of a people who already had a well-established social structure, one that may have been in place for millennia. And within this structure was to be found a class of people whose role was based to some degree on intellectual endeavour.

How well developed this class was at the beginning of the Hallstatt is impossible to say with any certainty. However, we can hazard an educated guess, for we know that there was a ruling elite, that farming was well established, and that artisanship was highly advanced. For all this to function smoothly and vigorously there would have had to be well-established laws and administration. Social structures of such complexity would also have required teachers, historians, healers, priests, and so forth.

The more complex a society becomes, the greater its need for specialists. These are inevitably grouped through similarities. Those that make and produce become one group, those that rule and defend another. The third are those whose specialisms require an intellectual training. In the Celtic culture, these were the Druids. To begin with, it is possible that their role was limited to one or two functions evolved from the earlier 'oak-knowers', although there is no reason why these earlier Druids were not fulfilling a great number of functions within society. Whatever the case, the kinship between certain roles was retained. This may have been due in part to a common basic education, but it was also no doubt due to the perceived role first of 'oak-knowers' and then of Druids as a cohesive force within and throughout Celtic society.

ORGANIZATION AND ROLE OF DRUIDS

It is often asserted that the intellectual class of the Celts was divided into three distinct groups. These are usually given as Bard, Vate, and Druid. A close examination of the source material, however, does not support this contention. It is true that Strabo, in his *Geographia*, writes:

> ...there are three classes of men held in special honour: the Bards, the Vates, and the Druids. The Bards are singers and poets; the Vates are the interpreters of sacrifice and natural philosophers; whilst Druids, in addition to the science of nature, study also moral philosophy. They are believed to be the most just of men, and are therefore entrusted with the decision of cases affecting either individuals or the public...[34]

Although it is the case that Strabo writes that three classes were held in special honour, he does not say that *only* three were held in honour, any more than he states that these three particular groups are what constitute the whole of the Druid class. In fact, he seems to be saying that in addition to Druids two other groups are held in high esteem.

The same holds true for what is written by Ammianus Marcellinus in surviving extracts from his lost account of the Gauls.[35] This work was produced from first-hand observation and would no doubt have helped to clarify many of the mysteries that existed in respect of the Celts and their Druids. In one of the extracts we do still have, he talks of Bards, Euhages (Vates), and Druids as if they were separate classes of people rather than divisions of a single class. Diodorus Siculus does little to clarify the situation for he states that Druids are treated with honour by the Celts who *further* make use of seers.[36]

Of course, it can be argued (and has been) that classical sources are not the most reliable when it comes to the Celts. Yet native sources are no less confusing on this point. In the Middle Ages, we have references in groups of three to Bards, Vates, and Druids, but it could be argued that these words are used in their medieval sense (which have slightly different meanings) and there is no certainty that they reflect the position as it was over a thousand years before the terms were written down. Indeed, the uncertain use of the title *fili* (see below) suggests that the confusion of classical authors was being perpetuated.

Whilst some texts use *fili* and *fáith* (Vate) as interchangeable terms, others make it clear that they belong to different classes of person. A *fili* is a poet, the lowest rank of which is known as *bard*, and the highest as *ollam*. It is why native texts sometimes state that Bards were held in lower regard than Druids. Given the length of training that a poet undertook (twelve years[37]) a *bard* was the fifth former (eleventh grader) to the *ollam's* postdoctoral researcher and practitioner. This is not to say that a *fili* could not also be a *fáith*. No doubt there was a great deal of overlap. What is important is that we are careful with what are, after all, technical terms.

Even though the threefold division of the Druid caste is uncertain, we cannot deny that these three groups were considered important. If we look at the classical sources, we are told that Bards are singers and poets (the scope of which has been made apparent); that Vates are interpreters of sacrifice and natural philosophers; and that the talents of the Druid apparently know no boundary. They are natural philosophers, moral philosophers, judges, arbitrators, law officers, priests, teachers, lawyers, adjudicators, astronomers, theologians, logicians, and political advisers. The native texts agree with this, and also add that Druids are historians, physicians, and magicians. No wonder they were exempt from military service!

It is becoming clear, perhaps, that two particular species of mistake are being made here, not just by classical authors, but also by native redactors, and by some modern authorities. Dion Chrysostum sheds some light on this in his *Orations* when he writes:

> ...the Celts have men called Druids, who concern themselves with divination and all branches of wisdom.[38]

This makes it clear that seers are Druids. However, what it does not say is that all Druids are seers. This is where the first mistake has occurred. In the past, some people have assumed that as all priests are Druids, then all Druids must be priests. This has no basis in logic.

The second mistake is that of the man who, having been shown all the different colleges in Oxford, then asked, 'But where is the University?' Having been shown all the poets, seers, priests, judges, teachers, historians, physicians, and so on, it makes no sense to ask to see the Druids. And if that is the case, then it makes no sense to continue to entertain the idea that the Druid class was divided into three. It was a single class comprised of many different members of society who had it in common that their roles were based principally on the use of the intellect.

That having been said, it is clear that Druids were highly organized. We know that in Gaul, a chief Druid was elected by a convocation of Druids. They also met annually to discuss affairs, to review laws in the light of precedents set in recent times, and perhaps to discuss political issues. There is evidence to suggest that this practice also occurred elsewhere in the Celtic world. No doubt any major decisions were swiftly passed on to those who were unable to attend.

There must also have been a high degree of organization when it came to education. The training of a Bard took twelve years; that of a Druid took up to twenty years. Even if some of the primary education took place within tribal communities, specialist centres would still have been needed for the proper training and assessment of students.

We know nothing of the curriculum, although the Bardic course is probably highly indicative of the rigours involved. In addition, we can speculate that to become proficient in whatever profession one eventually chose, it was first necessary to become proficient in the basics of Bardic knowledge. The fully qualified Bard was a virtuoso in the use of words and music and it was through these media that all else was accomplished. Indeed, the notion of specializing was probably not entertained until one had achieved this 'basic' level of education.

Druids (no matter what they specialized in), had to memorize everything, as the writing down of their teachings was proscribed. We should not take this to mean that either Celts in general or Druids in particular were illiterate. Far from it. Many Druids were known as polyglots and there are plenty of references to books and writings being made and kept by Celts. It was only the teachings of the Druids that were kept orally. A number of reasons have been put forward for this. The idea that there was some arcane knowledge that must be kept from others seems the least likely explanation, as that implies a secret sect or cult. The most obvious reason is that in the long run, it is far easier for a lawyer, for example, to know the whole of the law than it is to be reliant on a set of large and very expensive to produce books. Druids carried their knowledge with them.

Someone going to see a lawyer or historian may have found the consultation a little strange. No doubt, with so much stored in the memory, various mnemonic keys were required to access specific information. The sight of someone chanting under their breath, perhaps with their eyes closed, or adopting a particular physical stance (the one used when learning the material), may have given the impression – especially to a non-Celt unused to such a sight – that magic was being worked. And in a way, it was.

The memorization of huge amounts of information over a long period may strike us as a superhuman feat. Those of us fortunate enough to live in the wealthy countries of the world have become used to printed text that is mass-produced. Newspapers are generated by the million every day (and then thrown away). Books are published by the million every year. Why bother to remember something when it can be looked up – especially when so many facts change on an almost daily basis? Ours is a different world. Even so, there are still societies and cultures that have strong oral traditions in which people memorize vast quantities of material and recall it accurately.

We can speculate, on no real evidence at all, that if there ever was a threefold division of the Druid class in ancestral times, it actually referred to levels of competence rather than division of labour. Completing the first seven years of Bardic training may have been something equivalent to obtaining a first degree. Having learnt the basics, one could then go on to an advanced degree and follow this with a research degree. The awarding of branches (quite literally a small branch from a tree, possibly giving rise to the modern idea of a wand) tends to suggest that levels of competence were rewarded and that these branches were displayed or paraded much in the way modern doctors or lawyers might hang their degree certificates where clients can see them.

The nature and structure of Druid colleges is unknown to us other than through folklore, which must be taken with more than a pinch of salt. Talk of extensive campuses where thousands gathered to study is fanciful. The population of Britain was only about three million at the time of the Claudian invasion. Besides which, the majority of Druids worked in the everyday world of Celtic society. Specialist instruction undoubtedly took place in out of the way places where students could concentrate on the prodigious amounts of material they had to memorize and understand. These, however, were unlikely to have been larger than a village.

Even in the colleges, students would not have been completely isolated from everyday concerns. Druids, no matter what they specialized in, were an integral part of Celtic society. Whereas some may have had their services paid for in kind, and others may have been in the employ of chieftains, the majority would have seen to all the everyday needs of their lives. This has led to some speculation that the Druid colleges were models for later Christian monastic communities.

It is unlikely that the whole of the twenty years it took to become qualified was spent in special school or colleges. The Celts as a whole were an educated people. Even those who had no formal schooling were probably 'literate' in the terms of an oral culture, as well as being aware of their social responsibilities and legal obligations. Children who were to receive formal schooling generally started at the age of seven. As children had no legal responsibility until they were fourteen, it is unlikely they went away before that age unless they were fostered (often with a neighbouring chieftain or local Druid). Even then, the basics would be learnt within the community.

If we assume that the first seven years of a Druid's education were common to all those who received an education, and that they then followed a course analogous to that taken by early medieval Bards, we arrive at a period of education lasting nineteen years. Although only speculation, this is a much more satisfying figure than twenty years. Celts used a lunar calendar for mundane life and a solar calendar to measure spiritual cycles. The nearest these two reckonings come to coinciding is once every nineteen years.[39] Myrddin speaks of his nineteen apple trees[40] lost to him in his madness, as if they, perhaps, represented his learning. That he had nineteen branches or wands, no doubt reflects his preeminent position as a Druid.

So far, the implication has been that being Druid was a male preserve. Most classical texts refer to Druids as men. There are, however, occasional references to Dryades, or Druidesses, and Celtic sources readily confirm this. In both myth and history, women have leading roles in society. As rulers and warriors, we need look no further for an example than Boudicca, who may also have been a Druid since she is recorded as fulfilling a priestly function. Other rulers include Cartimandua of the Brigantes and a Gaulish chieftainess called Onomaris, along with many powerful wives of tribal rulers who clearly took an active role in political life.

Celtic women were appointed as diplomats, and engaged in negotiations not just between tribes, but also with non-Celtic peoples, to whom they were sent as emissaries to discuss treaties and other matters. They were judges of renown, physicians, bards, teachers, seers... Indeed, they filled all the roles that come under the collective heading of Druid and did so on an equal basis with men. Furthermore, they fulfilled other roles that have become obscure with the passing of time. A large number of references are made to sisterhoods, usually of nine women, who often lived on an island or in a remote place close to water. Such groups often feature in myth as the teachers of heroes, instructing them in all the skills they required – including the martial arts. These sisterhoods also seemed to keep shrines, as if the places in which they resided (and where they offered healing and teaching) connected them directly with the Otherworld.

This last observation directs us to a further aspect of the role of Druids. So far, for the most part, a somewhat prosaic picture has been painted. However, over and above their individual roles, Druids were the cohesive force of what otherwise might well have been a fragmented society. Their studies and their intimate understanding of the metaphysic on which Celtic culture was based would have made them aware of the less tangible dimensions of existence.

As 'oak-knowers' they knew that they were integral to society and an integral part of the natural world. Their 'knowledge of the oak' can also be taken as meaning that they perceived and understood the world as it is perceived and understood by the oak. That would mean being part of the forest, taking a long view of life, taking a slow view. It would mean adopting wood-sense.

Druids, then, were the oaks of human society. They emerged as the 'forest' became sufficiently complex, mature, and stable enough to support them. In turn, they provided the structure for society, provided the continuity, the heart of oak. They nurtured all living beings and in so doing allowed the other 'trees' (for some people are birches, others are yews, some hazel, and others still are willows) to flourish and to coexist.

4

THE CELTIC
METAPHYSIC

THE CELTIC METAPHYSIC

It has already been stated that the Celtic metaphysic is the linking factor between ancestral Celtic practice and the Druids of today. We have so far had a brief introduction to the Celts and their history, as well as the Druids, who were so important to Celtic society. Up to this point, we have been looking at what can be gleaned from archaeology and from written records. And although these paint for us a fairly comprehensive picture, they can only hint at what lies beneath the surface.

We know *how* Celts behaved. If we are to go any further with this investigation, however, we must also know *why* they behaved as they did. Why was their society structured as it was? Why did they devise the law codes that they did? Why were their beliefs as they were? These questions raise issues that are much more tenuous than the bare facts, and archaeologists and historians tend to fight shy of exploring them. However, that does not mean that answers are not there to be found. We can derive a great deal about thought processes from observing behaviour and from studying the beliefs of a people.

Reconstructing the way a people thinks, especially a people from the past, is fraught with difficulty. Sources of information, because of the very nature of the subject, are never explicit. Everything must be scrutinized with a careful eye and a good deal of caution exercised. Attitudes and trends derived from one source must be checked against others to ensure there is congruity. In addition, attitudes themselves must be consistent one with another. We may not construct our metaphysic in any conscious fashion, but it is nonetheless internally consistent.

Because of this, everything must be considered and all sources scoured. Laws, myths, history, architectural design, methods of construction, agriculture... all are shaped by the underlying metaphysic, as is the language by which ideas are communicated. And just as we can accurately surmise the optimal shape of the foundation of a building by studying its structure, so we can reconstruct the metaphysic of a culture by studying that culture's shape and how it changed in response to pressure.

This is not as far-fetched as it might at first seem. We know, for example, that Islamic art eschews the depiction of human and animal forms and that its floral designs are abstract. If we had no written or living source to explain this, we might, at the very least, reasonably assume that even though such depictions were not forbidden, they were considered inappropriate. And to decide how strong that consideration was, we would look at other aspects of Islamic culture.

It is the same with the Celts. By studying their artefacts, the way they are made and decorated, we can make certain assumptions. We can see that there were underlying concepts of design and decoration that were universal to Celtic peoples, even though there were many localized variations. If nothing else, this tells us that there was a high degree of identity with the culture (even if this was not overtly displayed by the wearing of 'Proud to be Celtic' badges).

Myth also provides this sense of a cohesive society. The same themes are widespread, but in common with all other aspects of Celtic culture, they are adapted to local conditions. We see from the myths that the very land in and from which the Celts lived was part of their being. The deities, heroes, and other wonderful beings that inhabit the Celtic world reflect this bond. They also reflect the culture itself in that their exploits and behaviour sit within the codes of conduct expected of ordinary folk in everyday life.

Historical texts are perhaps the clearest, most overt, indicators of the way in which Celts thought. This is especially so with law texts. The laws that we know of are based on the concepts of honour and responsibility and, in the case of criminal law, of the need for the perpetrator to compensate the victim. The duties inherent in various relationships (within families and foster families, for example, or between tenant and landholder) as well as the fees that can be charged by professionals, are carefully set out. All of which is universally applied – with bonded folk having the same rights and protection under the law as a High King.

It is in language, however, that we find the most powerful indicators of what the Celtic metaphysic consisted in. Both the structure of the language and its use, particularly in poetic forms (which are often the most vivid expression of how a person sees the world), give clear indication of attitudes and ideas. We do not have access to very ancient forms of the Celtic language, but study of early, middle, and modern forms of the two major branches (Goidelic and Brythonic) make it clear that the ideas discussed here were stronger in the past than they are now.

Perhaps the clearest example of this is in the notion of possession. In Welsh, there is no verb that corresponds with the English 'to have' or 'to possess'. Rather, one has to use the preposition *gan* ('with') and talk about something being *with* something else. Thus, 'They have a garden', translates as, *Y mae gardd ganddynt hwy* (literally 'There is a garden with them'). In Irish, it is possible to express a difference of relationship between those things that are innate (like one's head or hand) and those that are not (like a dog or a garden).[41] This is just a tiny proportion of the language, but it is indicative of what readily becomes apparent to anyone who learns a Celtic language – that the structure and the vocabulary strongly reflect a particular way of viewing the world.

Thus, the sources by which we might elicit the metaphysic are clear. Yet that still leaves us with a number of major problems. To begin with, reconstruction and discussion of this metaphysic must be done with reference to the metaphysic of our own culture, which is quite alien to that of most people of two or three thousand years ago. This has nothing to do with technical and scientific advances per se, although the development of science does play its part. It is just that during the last two millennia our very way of understanding the world has been turned round, pulled inside out, and stood on its head.

Another problem is that our way of looking at the world is so deeply ingrained in our psyches that the majority of people have trouble identifying it. Indeed, we have trouble accepting that there might be other ways of viewing the world and interpreting what we see. This is largely because the means by which we learn about the world (as well as the content of what we learn) are determined by the precepts of that metaphysic. Each reinforces the other.

A third problem is that the metaphysic prevalent in modern Western society is such that an attempt to reconstruct a 'lost' metaphysic would be considered, at the very least, to be nonsensical. This is especially so if the purpose is to demonstrate the basis and ancient pedigree of a 'modern' pagan religion.

Notwithstanding all this, it is possible to look at a culture and tease out something of the basic patterns of thought that underlie the way in which its peoples behaved as they did. A metaphysic is learned, but not in the way we might learn mathematics or history. Rather, we acquire it from the way the world around us is ordered and from how those around us behave. This is what sets the standards, not just for our own behaviour, but also for the way in which we learn to think. This is not absolute. We are all capable of breaking the patterns, although it is far easier if enquiry, sensible thought, and personal responsibility are part of what we learn. However, the attitudes and behaviours we learn at an early age are generally the ones that shape us for the rest of our lives. What is more, they are often reinforced (and sometimes magnified) in our own children.

Our immediate families, where we learn the basics, are, of course, part of wider society. There are enormous variations within and between various sections of any society, but overall, the people of a given culture will have a common view of the world. The dynamics involved are obscure. Few societies consciously adopt a ready-made metaphysical stance that is then taught in special classes at school. Those that have tried this approach soon lose control of the beast. It escapes and it evolves or dies. Our stance is, for the most part, unconsciously held. Few of us are equipped or encouraged to work out the prevailing metaphysic in which we are raised and make critical decisions about it and our personal attachment to its precepts.

A given metaphysic, therefore, will evolve as a result of influences over which we have no control. This lack control is not because we would be unable to make changes if we so wished, but because we are largely unaware of the metaphysic, of the pressures to which it is subjected, and of the forces that work to keep us unaware. In most cases, there is nothing sinister in this. There is no controlling cabal, merely a collective ignorance of the way in which these things work, an ignorance that is born of the very metaphysic to which our society currently adheres.

Although what follows is the exploration of a particular metaphysic that was self-contained, in order to make clear certain meanings, it will at times be necessary to compare and contrast this metaphysic with that of modern Western society. It is important to note that comparisons are not being made in order to claim superiority or correctness; they are being made for the sake of clarity and understanding. That something is different does not make it better or worse than that from which it differs. It simply makes it different.

It is also important to remember that what follows, although it appears to be a 'system', is simply a description of some strands of metaphysical thought that have been teased from the available sources. It is neither complete nor organized, other than for the ease of readers. This is not least because too rigid a system of thought would have been counter to the metaphysic with which Celts were raised.

Celts, then, viewed the world as synthetic, organicistic, and holistic. This was the basis of everything else for their concern was with the interconnectedness of things and with an understanding of the real world and their place within it. Many of the laws that have come down to us are concerned with relationships. Many of the tales and myths explore the consequences of broken relationships. And these are relationships at all levels, between people, animals, plants, the wider world, and the deities of the Celtic pantheon.

Synthetic

By synthetic is meant the combining of distinct things and concepts to form a complex whole. Implicit in synthesis is an understanding of the parts, so that analysis has a part to play, but only a part. Synthesis is about knowing the world. It is about knowing materials, about making, about building, and about growth – and not simply in physical or material terms, for it reaches into the realm of spirit as well. It is about bringing things together that have been parted as well as not placing obstacles between things that should be together. It is also a recognition of the fact that, though things might be distinct one from another, they are not actually separate.

Synthesis today has become in some degree synonymous with artificiality – with abstracting and creating things that would not occur naturally (and which might even be considered as violence against the natural order). All technology does this. However, there is a fine line between things produced for need and those produced for greed; there is an even finer line between those things that enhance the world and those that do damage. That line is not always clear or readily agreed upon, but the existence of the line was something of which the Celts were well aware. They considered everything a gift that could swiftly be removed if they transgressed, if they crossed that line.

Primarily, however, synthesis is about natural processes and learning to work with those processes. It was considered an essential of physical and spiritual evolution. Indeed, in specific terms, we can see this notion at work in the idea that the spiritual side of life is as important as, and inextricably linked with, the material side of life. A person was not considered complete if both aspects were not equally treated. That is why exile from clan or tribe was the ultimate punishment as it divorced a person from both material *and* spiritual connection and sustenance.

However, the notion of synthesis went further. As far as Celts were concerned, creation was not a fixed and long past event, but an ongoing process. They considered everything to be in a constant state of renewal and believed that all things were working together toward some future synthesis. Synthesis was a recognition that nothing is truly independent in this world. All things are related, all things combine, all things are constantly born anew.

ORGANICISTIC

In a situation where a set of entities combine to compose a greater entity, which then combines with similar entities to compose yet greater entities, and so on, it is inevitable that an overview develops. With the development of technology this has tended to be mechanistic – the brain is seen as a computer, the body as a machine, organizations are charted as if they were electrical circuits, and so on. In the past, however, before technology took a disproportionate place in our thinking, the overview would have been in organic terms, in terms of viewing things as living entities.

Organicism, therefore, means that the parts of a whole can only be understood properly in relation to their functions within the complex and evolving whole, with the whole envisioned as a living entity. Thus, a meadow flower can only be properly understood in relation to its function in any given whole to which it belongs – be that a meadow, a food web, the life cycle of an insect, the inspiration of a poet, and so on. The same is true with people. Their behaviour can only be understood in relation to all the people about them, the structure of the society in which they live, and so on. Such an attitude accounts for what is often wrongly taken as the egocentric boasting of Celtic warriors. A claim to be the best warrior has little or nothing to do with ego, and almost everything to do with lauding the fact that only such a wonderful tribe with such a wonderful chief could produce and maintain such a wonderful warrior.

The complexities of such an attitude are readily apparent. Of course, we cannot ever hope to know all the connections. However, Celts were aware at all times that these complex relationships existed and that any relationship is as important as the things that are related. As with people and animals, things are defined as much by their connection with others as by what they are within themselves. Thus, a meadow flower being studied on a laboratory bench is not fully a meadow flower.

There is also an awareness that an ill-considered action may lead, through complex networks, to quite unforeseen and disastrous consequences. This notion is quite often the theme of the myths and legends of the Celtic peoples.

HOLISTIC

Holistic means that in terms of systems and living things (their organization, relations, cultures, and so on), the whole is greater than the sum of its parts. The concern of the Celtic metaphysic is with life and with things as dynamic entities. It exists as a positive force through thought and action in both spiritual and material realms in the maintenance of life. It is concerned with all living things as living things, not as objects, statistics, or sociological models. Furthermore, it accepts a much wider definition of life than we are used to in the present day.

This wider definition of life is apparent in the way Celts talked about and treated their world. The very land on which they lived was endowed with life. This view was made manifest in a number of ways. At an ultimate level, it was in considering the land as a goddess, usually a goddess of sovereignty. The right to the land, to work it and live from it, was not a right simply because people were people. It had to be earned. The goddess would bestow this right, but she could just as easily remove it. Where some see this as the idolatry of savages, it is in fact a sophisticated understanding of how the world works and the place of people within it. The Celts did not think that human beings were the pinnacle of all creation any more than they thought that they had the right to do as they wished with the world and all to be found therein.

At a less exalted level, evidence of this attitude can be found in the relationship of the person to the tribe. The tribe itself was considered a living entity that had its own sentience, its own behaviour, and its own relationships. The individual was cared for by the tribe (and there is plenty of evidence of highly advanced forms of social welfare) and, in return, the individual cared for the tribe. A tribe often had its own gods and totems, which would all have been shaped by the environment in which the tribe evolved.

Living by these three major precepts was not, as already mentioned, a conscious thing. Celts did not spend their time seeing how they could apply these concepts to their world. It was simply how they understood the world to be. There may well, however, have been some Druids who explored these ideas, for we know that Druids were accounted great philosophers and theologians. Their role as a cohesive force in society would certainly suggest that they had some understanding, not just of the main structure of their metaphysic, but of the more specific aspects discussed below.

CONCORDANT

Celts lived in and with the world. This means that whereas they undoubtedly had a complex society, it was directly connected with the land on which they lived. Neither their social structure, nor the technology they employed, acted as a barrier to isolate them from a very real understanding of how the world worked and their place in that working.

This way of life was not the result of a conscious choice. Although they were, for example, technologically advanced, they had yet to produce anything with the intention of replacing people. Whether they had the skill to do that, is open to question. Much more important was that they would not have considered it acceptable. A Celt simply would not do things that would disconnect others from something of which they were a part.

This concept of unity was a strong and overarching element of the Celtic metaphysic. Yet their feeling of connection with the land was not just spiritual; it was also pragmatic. When the mainstay of your economy is agriculture, it is vital that you should be at one with the land. It is all too easy to view this cynically (or to assume that it is a modern gloss) in an era that has witnessed the mechanization and industrialization of food production. In the past, however, there was (and still is in many communities worldwide) an understanding that people were part of the world rather than separate from it.

All things, all aspects of being, were connected. They may have been distinct, but only in the sense that facets of a crystal are distinct. In a crystal, each facet is made by the others and has no meaning or existence if separated from them (which is, in any case, an impossibility). Some have taken this as evidence that Celts were monist in outlook. Although it is true that they did not subscribe to a dualist view, it is far from certain that they regarded the world as being one and only one substance.

It is far more likely, given what evidence can be gleaned from texts and traditions, that Celts held to a form of pluralism – but a pluralism more attributive than substantival. That is, they believed that the distinctions between discrete objects were due to particular attributes of a single underlying essence. This would certainly accommodate the notion of shapeshifting and of the movement of the soul from one world to the next. It would also account for other aspects of a generally concordant view – that balance, harmony, and order are essential elements not just of society but also of the world as a whole. We are used to Celts being portrayed as anarchic and argumentative, but this is a false picture. They were certainly a self-contained people, who elected their leaders and accepted them on sufferance, but Celtic society was well ordered (which is not the same as highly structured) and Druids were renowned for their role as mediators in the settling of disputes both small and large.

Celtic society could not have survived without a sense of order. No society can. But there are many ways in which order can be manifest. Indeed, studying and devising such ways was a major preoccupation of classical Greek philosophers. It says a great deal for the essential nature and importance of the concept of cohesion in Celtic thought that, whilst there were local variations, the way in which society was organized was fairly consistent throughout the Celtic world.

This occurred because the sense of unity (and its concomitant sense of order and balance) was innate. Every Celt grew up learning that this was the way of the world, and not just because they were told it was so, but also because they lived in a society that was based on such principles and in which people acted accordingly. When different forms of order were imposed upon them, they did not take very kindly either to the ideas or the reality.

CYCLICAL

The Celts lived in a part of the world that has distinct and ever-changing seasons. As an agricultural people, they would have been highly conscious of the annual round and of how this was merely part of a much wider cyclical pattern to life. Crops and livestock would be born, grow, flourish, and die. Celts would measure their time by circadian and lunar rhythms. Every nineteen years the lunar and solar cycles would coincide. Everywhere there was evidence of the cyclical nature of things. We have evolved over millions of years against this cyclical background, and this way of looking at the world was deeply ingrained in all people. No wonder, then, that it features so strongly in Celtic thinking and belief.

The most obvious manifestation of this is in decorative handiwork that features knotwork and spiral motifs. The circle is also important, however, as it symbolizes cycles in their purest form and relates to major cyclic elements in the world. Buildings and other built features are often circular in plan (although by no means exclusively so). Fires were centrally placed so that families and other gatherings sat round them – not only symbolizing the cyclical in life but also equality and unity.

The concept of the cyclical was not confined to the material world. Indeed, given the acceptance of an attributive pluralism, it could not be. Thus, the spiritual journey of the Celts was also seen in cyclic terms with death leading to rebirth in the Otherworld, where the next cycle was played out before the soul returned to this world. Initiations found in myths and poetry are frequently cyclical in nature, involving changes of form before a return to the original. This is entirely appropriate for something that represented a rebirth.

Yet this was not seen as the turning of circles, each cycle a repeat of the previous one. Rather, there was an understanding from the example of nature that things move on. No seed produces an exact replica of the plant that formed it, just as no child is an exact replica of its parents. Lessons are learned and carried forward – a concept that applies as much to evolutionary theory as it does to spiritual growth and wisdom.

REALISTIC

For all that Celts loved tales of wonder and viewed the world in a way radically different from most people in modern Western society, they were firmly attached to reality. Their whole lives were lived in intimate relationship with the world about them – a world that had horizons far wider than the material world that is immediately apparent. They tended not to build the sort of barriers that prevent direct contact with and experience of the world. They faced the realities of everyday life without hiding them away or letting someone else deal with them. For example, even though there were specialist healers and facilities, the elderly and sick were cared for within the community. Death was a cause of sorrow, but it was accepted as a natural part of the cycle of life.

Technological items were viewed as what they were – tools. They were the means to an end. So, too, were language, beliefs, and ideas. They were used, and if better ones were found, those were used instead. The Celts were not so wedded to or dependent upon their tools that their preservation was considered more important than the basic realities of life.

Life, after all, was something in which ancestral Celts participated. The idea of withdrawing from contact with the world would have been puzzling to them. They may even have considered it a sickness and have done what they could to care for the person. This is not to say they did not have hermits and other solitary folk (although they were few and far between). However, these were people who had made a conscious choice to eschew human contact in order to have closer contact with the rest of the world.

This can be regarded as a form of naturalism, with Celts making no distinction between the natural and the supernatural. The distinction they did make was between what they could and could not understand. What was ugly or difficult was neither hidden nor idealized, simply accepted as part of the world. Deities and 'magical' events were part of the natural order. Above all, they lived life as it was without the need to theorize or spin webs of wishful thinking about themselves.

This realism was possible in large part because of the balanced relationship Celts had with time. There was a tendency to leave the past in its place. In one sense, it had gone and was lost to them. Yet they also realized that it was an ever-open storehouse of example and wisdom that they could examine and from which they could learn. They also recognized that their immediate future was their children – in whom they invested a great deal of love and time. Beyond that, they did not know nor care over much. They knew they would be back to see for themselves. Their immediate concern was with the here and now. That is where they lived their lives and that is the basis on which they conducted society. It was not that they had no concern about the future, simply that they recognized that the future was made in the present. If they lived their lives properly now, the future was assured.

MAGICAL

Celts had an excellent grasp of science and technology. You do not carry out successful brain surgery, smelt iron, create exquisite enamels, or construct complex stone buildings to heights of 30 feet (10 metres) or more without it. Their lives and their thinking, however, were not governed by a scientific paradigm. Rather, they saw the world as magical.

We should not be confused by this term into thinking of some vague and superstitious nonsense. A definition of magic given today might talk of using supernatural power to manipulate natural forces. We know, however, that such a definition would have no meaning for ancient Celts as they did not believe in the supernatural. The world was one. Magic was a study of the world so that what was unknown could be understood.

Some would argue that this is science. Science, however, concerns itself only with the material world, with the relation between physical objects and the physical forces that influence them. But there is much more to the world than that and it is through this broader approach that the world can be fully understood. This also applies to technology. The technology of magic makes use of both material and spiritual understanding of the world to provide tools to manipulate the world to provide for sustenance and comfort. On the one hand, that might be a better plough, on the other, it might be a more effective form of fertility ritual; it might even be a safer form of pain control. In all cases, as part of the general metaphysic that governed the lives of Celts, these were subject to its innate morality.

To direct life in this way, to study and perform magically, requires a different view of what constitutes knowledge, as well as of its ultimate value. As with other aspects of the Celtic metaphysic, knowledge was seen as having intrinsic worth. It was considered sufficient in itself for being. People cannot help but know things. It is part of what it is for us to be. Indeed, knowledge cannot logically be divorced from that which knows. However, knowledge was recognized also as having extrinsic worth, for knowledge is yet another tool, infinitely adaptable if it is used well. Whilst recognizing that knowledge had intrinsic worth (in that it was a condition of human existence), Celts were not interested in it for its own sake. It was there to be used for a better understanding the world. Ultimately, knowledge was an attempt to get at the truth that lay at the heart of all creation.

The means by which this understanding could be achieved were many. Today, we know the world in so many different ways, and, equally, we can express that knowledge in so many different ways, that the standards we now apply would be inadequate to assess the veracity of knowledge as understood by the Celts. Empirical study would have been considered too restricting since it simply did not address the aspects of the world that are beyond the material and experimentally verifiable – aspects that the Celts knew to exist.

Druids (at least, those who were philosophers) were much concerned with understanding the nature of the universe and the place of humanity within it. Judging by Old Irish texts, the central concept of this search was that of the truth. Although we cannot assume that the preoccupations of Irish Druid philosophers were shared universally, it does seem that the concept of truth is so basic to an understanding of the world that it was common to all Celts.

This is evident when looked at from a number of disparate perspectives, all of which seem to be underpinned by, or reliant upon, a notion of truth. As an example, we know that the dualistic concept of good and evil was foreign to pre-Christian Celts. Yet they still led moral lives and had sophisticated systems of civil and criminal law. This would only work if truth were an essential of both thought and action.

Truth, however, was considered to be important to much more than just human affairs. And, as we have seen, it meant much more than veracity of language. In fact, truth was regarded by Celts as the sustaining power of all creation. In the myths, an act of truth (be that by word, thought, or deed) was endowed with power. Cormac mac Airt was given a golden cup that could be shattered if a lie was told over it and made whole if a truth was told. Similar tales concerning swords that will shatter if those who wield them are unjust can also be found.

The concept is not only to be found in myth. Feradach Finn Fachtnach is advised by the Druid Morann mac Cairbre (in his will) that 'through the ruler's truth all the land is fruitful and every child born worthy'.[42] Other references to truth in the same text refer to its power to avert disaster, bring tranquillity, increase knowledge, and preserve life. This idea of truth as an essential power has ancient roots. Its Indo-European origins are evidenced in its importance (in almost identical form) in Hindu culture.

Language, too, displays the essential nature of truth. In both branches of the Celtic language, the root of the word for 'truth' is shared by words that mean 'real', 'pure', 'fact', 'verdict', 'fulfilment' (as of prophecy), 'knowledge', 'investigation', and 'justice'.

Other evidence suggests that truth was regarded in much the same light in the Stoic school of philosophy. That is, that truth is the controlling principle of the universe, what we might call the law of Nature. Truth, if not quite the ultimate source of all being, is to be found at the source. There are many tales that tell of the hazelnuts of wisdom and truth that are to be found in pools and springs that are the source of watercourses. Hazel wands were a badge of the poets' art and, thus, connected with the use of words. Words and names are endowed, therefore, with great power if given in accord with the truth.

Since truth is the controlling principle of the universe, it follows that whatever happens in the universe, happens in accord with truth. The natural world is a place of truth. The only exception is as the result of the gift with which human beings are endowed – free will. We cannot know, but it is reasonable to speculate that Celtic philosophers saw this gift as being endowed by the use of language, which gives people a degree of control over the truth. It also gives them the ability to act against truth.

Ignoring truth has a cost. In Celtic myth, this usually results in the person who commits a false act being blemished with spots or an illness. The consequences, however, can be far more severe. If, as suggested by Morann mac Cairbre, truth makes the land fruitful, then the opposite must also be the case. Rulers who have responsibility for the land and their people can bring disaster and famine to the land if they are untruthful or allow deceit to flourish. The whole of the Grail cycle of tales (despite its later Christian embroidery) is predicated on this basic idea.

The requirement to live by the truth affected all aspects of Celtic culture and may well have been one of the reasons why the Celtic world could not withstand the pressures of Roman expansion. To Celts, the truth was so fundamental to their dealings with other people that they found it difficult to adjust to the idea that others would deliberately lie, that they would act dishonourably, or that they would work against the very thing that sustained the world.

ETHICAL

The Celtic metaphysic was inherently moral. Truth was paramount. Life was seen as the real wealth, and the purpose of society seems to have been to enhance that life. Not only were there many laws enshrining what was considered right, and setting out a system of fines for those who transgressed these laws, but the very attitude to life encapsulated a highly ethical stance. Honour and responsibility are mentioned repeatedly in Celtic literature, and Celts were no doubt imbued with these concepts from a very early age.

Of course, one can only be truly responsible if one has freedom – of action and of will. It is true that certain obligations were placed on members of society, and these constrained them in some ways, but on the whole, Celtic society was free and highly egalitarian – even by today's standards. We know that the concept of free will figured strongly in the Celtic metaphysic. Not only is it apparent in the literature, where tales often hang on the choice made by individuals, but, as we have seen, it also played a large part in what is known as the Pelagian 'heresy'. The 'British heresy', as it was also known, was regarded by the Christian Church as Druidic philosophy, which thus had to be repressed.

Free will on its own does not make for a moral philosophy. Any freedom, as the Celts recognized, must be balanced by responsibility. Nor is any freedom absolute – it is freedom, not licence. Living in a close-knit tribal society would demonstrate that the freedom to do things and to make whatever choices one wishes is relative to everyone else's freedom. Decisions and actions all have an effect on others and on the environment that sustains them.

Without the concomitant concepts of honour and responsibility, there could be no society. Honour (that is, a sense of justice) derives in part from seeing the world as unified, of seeing that balance and harmony are essential. This quite naturally extends to human relationships with the wider world. Celts, however, recognized that people are shaped largely by their relationship with other people. A society in which everyone treats everyone else in a just fashion is not only easier to live in, but it is one that requires far fewer rigid rules and methods of enforcement.

Responsibility was also a very personal thing. Each person was responsible for their own thoughts and deeds. What is more, the legal system ensured that people were responsible for repairing any damage they caused. This was standardized by the setting of an honour price for people and for transgressions against people. This could be paid in money or by working off the debt. Perhaps the best-known example of this is the tale of Sétanta, who was invited to a feast when he was playing a game with his fellows. He accepted the invitation, but, being honourable, would not leave the game until it was finished in order not to let down his team mates. Arriving late, he found that everyone had gone indoors and his host, Culann, had let his prized watchdog loose in the compound. The hound, a huge and ferocious beast, attacked Sétanta, who killed it. Culann was distraught as it was his favourite hound and an excellent watchdog. Sétanta saw that Culann now had no means of guarding his house and his cattle, and although he had done nothing wrong in defending himself, he took responsibility for the situation. Acting with great honour, Sétanta offered to act as a watchdog until a new hound could be trained.

The importance of this episode in Celtic mythology is reflected in the fact that Sétanta is thereafter always known as the Hound of Culann – Cúchulainn. The wisdom, rightness, and truth of the reparation that he offered were applauded and have stood as an example through the ages.

DYNAMIC

Life is innately creative. It constantly engages with the world to make it favourable for itself. The Celts knew this and saw creation itself as ongoing. The world, therefore, and everything in it, is actively engaged in life. This vigour is an essential of Celtic life and not just in simplistic terms of relation to physical vigour. Their whole culture – physical, mental, and spiritual – was bursting at the seams with life.

A consequence of this positive attitude to life was that Celts were extremely assertive and would defend themselves fiercely. They felt no need to justify or apologize for their existence. Nor did they believe any other culture to be superior to their own. This did not mean, on the other hand, that they believed any other culture to be inferior. They recognized the need for variety. Such assertiveness can seem aggressive to some and Celts past and present have a reputation for being quick tempered – even though this has much to do with being a people who will not be downtrodden. Sadly, however, the history of the Celts has mostly been written by non-Celts.

In tandem with this vigour was a recognition of the essential balancing factor – quiescence. The two went together as naturally as waking and sleeping, summer and winter, day and night. One without the other is unhealthy and unsustainable. Quiescence itself can have a dynamic aspect in that it is a life-enhancing state. It also means knowing when to stop (which is not the same thing as knowing how far you can go). It speaks of an acute awareness of a world beyond the ego and the need to lead a balanced life.

PERSONALIST

By all the measures we have so far encountered, we have to say that the Celtic metaphysic was a form of personalism. Although this philosophical theory only found formal expression in the twentieth century, it is clear that it applies to Celtic thought.

Personalism considers the person ontologically fundamental. This simply means that the person should be the starting point of philosophy and therefore of an understanding of the world. This is not to place the person at the centre of the universe and make all other things subordinate. It merely points out that as it is the person who does the understanding, it is the person that is the reference point for that understanding (rather than *a priori* truths or empirical scientific facts).

Precisely what constitutes a person has long been a matter of debate – probably amongst philosophically inclined Druids and certainly amongst Personalists, who have drawn on many schools of thought in this matter. On two things, however, Personalists are all agreed – as were the Celts. The first is that the fundamental structure of the person is both matter and spirit. The second is that the person is not an atomistic individual, but a being whose nature is formed by and implies community.

These points have already been mentioned from other perspectives. They have further implications, however, not least of which is the influence of such thought on the shape of a culture and the structure of society. If the starting point of enquiry and understanding is the person, it is inevitable that how the person is understood per se will affect the way in which each person lives in the world. For example, we have said that the person is seen as a being whose nature is formed by and implies community: that is, people are shaped by the community in which they live and are diminished if they become divorced from that community. It is part of their identity.

For this to work effectively, the community must be of an optimum size. For young people, this would be the extended family. As they grow older, it needs to be the clan (a group of related extended families). However, this only works in the larger context of a tribe, which provides overall cohesion and identity. There is a biological imperative here as well as a psychological one. The basic social structure is thus governed by this personalist view (although, in truth, the structure and the view probably grew in tandem). The scale is set by the degree to which the person can engage meaningfully with and understand the workings of the system. The whole of Celtic society was arranged to this human scale.

Material structures were also built to this same scale. The Celts certainly had large buildings and cities, but they never exceeded a size that could be easily encompassed by the human mind. The concept of the state, for example, was alien to Celts. It had no human scale and could not be connected with, whereas chieftains and Druids, kings and queens, could. So, too, could the land and local deities (which is why Celts had them as well as universal deities).

This view made for strong social cohesion. When people are formed by community and derive part of their identity from it, their needs and the needs of their social group (be it family, clan, or tribe) are rarely at odds. What is good for the person is good for the group. What is good for both is good for the place in which they live - for this, too, was part of the community and contributed to the identity of person. Yet this was never a denial of the person. The community was not the whole of a person's identity, just the fertile soil in which each person could flourish. The place where they lived was home and an integral part of their being, which is why early Celtic Christian monks considered it a form of martyrdom (the 'White Martyrdom' because no blood was shed) to move away from their home on a permanent basis.

Everything – material and spiritual environment, material and spiritual culture – used the person as the base unit of measure. The wellbeing of the person was the starting point of all endeavours and the final measure of success. Economics, politics, philosophy, agriculture, art, science, religion, education, technology... all began with the needs of the person, with their communal and ecological existence, and was used to satisfy their needs by doing the most with the least. All of these things, attached to the reality of human life in and of the world, were vastly enriched and enriching through the personalist approach to existence.

SACRED

Celts were well aware that we each have an inner life. Given the way in which they viewed the world, however, it will be clear that they did not regard this as something that made us separate, either one from another or from the rest of the world. Rather, it was what joined each of us with the others, all with the world, and all with the ineffable. This recognition that being ensouled is part of the shared experience of personhood is further evidence of the Celts' personalist stance.

Being aware of this communion was important. We know already that the evidence suggests that Celts viewed the world from a pluralist perspective – one that regarded distinct entities as attributes of an underlying unity. However, the spiritual aspect of life was especially important to the Celts.

They felt a direct link with the sacred – not because they regarded themselves as a chosen people, but because they knew they were an integral part of the world. They were connected because all things were connected. Moreover, that being the case, they knew that if just one thing was sacred then all things must be sacred. And one thing we can be certain of is that Celts regarded some things as sacred.

Place name evidence alone provides us with an abundance of examples of inhabited sites that have connection with deity. Other sites (particularly rivers and lakes) not only bear the names of deities, but have also produced hoards of materials that appear to have been given as offerings. Furthermore, what we know of Celtic religious rites speak of a deep connection between agriculture and the sacred. We also have many hymns and incantations that suggest a pre-Christian origin[43] and deal, not with the great mysteries, but with the everyday.

Indeed, the whole of Celtic culture reflects the idea that the entire universe is ensouled and therefore sacred. There may have been differences in emphasis, but Celts lived in a sacred environment, their whole lives being an act of communion with spirit and with deity. And true to the way in which they viewed the world, their perspective was very personal. The sacred was in the everyday, in the tasks of ordinary life, in relationships with other people and the land. This was reflected even in their great religious festivals, with the everyday transactions of the market place and personal relationships being given special force at these times of year. Yet the high days and holy days marked the public face of their belief. At the personal level, they believed that if they acted honourably and responsibly in the everyday things, the cycles of their lives would eventually bring them to an understanding of the greater things that were currently beyond their comprehension.

Of necessity, this has been a very brief look at the way in which ancestral Celts viewed the world. Some of these themes will be taken up again later when we consider how they relate to modern Druid thought and practice. The rest are ripe for careful exploration.[44]

5

SURVIVAL AND REVIVAL

SURVIVAL AND REVIVAL

The question of survival and revival is both complex and controversial. Is it possible that pagan Celtic religious and spiritual belief and practice can have survived through the last two millennia? Academics are certainly divided[45] and it is likely that debate will continue for a long time to come. Of course, the answer to the question depends in large part on what definition you give to the term 'pagan' and the specific relationship of that to the Celtic speaking peoples. One thing is clear, however, and that is that there was no survival of something called 'Druidry' simply because, as preceding chapters have made clear, there was no such thing to begin with. What has survived, however, are both the worldview of the Celts and certain of their rites and practices.

Most people, if they think about it at all, assume that the Romans destroyed the Druids. This idea relates to the notion of Druids as a priesthood scheming to bring down the Roman Empire. Many Druids (in common with the majority of Celtic peoples) did not like being taken over by a foreign power. Some, no doubt, were involved in rebellion. But the Romans did not destroy the Druids or even contemplate such a task as that would have meant destroying the entire intellectual class of the Celtic peoples – teachers, doctors, engineers, historians, priests, and so on. Pol Pot's murderous regime and the brutalities of Mao Zedong's 'Cultural Revolution' would have seemed slight by comparison. Such a campaign, if it had taken place, would have been mentioned somewhere in the historical record, especially if it had been successful.

This is not to say that individual Druids were not a problem to Roman expansion. After all, Druids did have a cohesive role within Celtic society as well as the authority to ensure the alliance of tribes and peoples who might otherwise be at odds. A classic example of this is Julius Caesar's campaign in Gaul. It took him eight long and bloody years to 'conquer' the territory. The main opposition came when Vercingetorix was elected leader of the resistance by the people (his appointment having been opposed by chieftains). This could not have happened without the support, tacit or otherwise, of the Druids. Although his campaign nearly succeeded, it was too little and too late.

Despite the ultimate failure of Vercingetorix, it was another ninety years before Rome felt that Gaul was sufficiently under their control to be able to launch the invasion of Britain. It was a decision dictated by politics rather than military necessity. As such, it was only ever a partial success. It tied up a large proportion of Rome's military strength and resulted in bloody battles, rebellions, and seething discontent that lasted for centuries.

The campaign of Gaius Suetonius Paulinus from AD 58 to AD 60, in what is now northern Wales, is often cited as the main evidence for the theory that the Romans wiped out the Druids in Britain. It is, of course, no such thing. There is no evidence of Druids other than Tacitus' mention of their presence in the resisting army, where they provided moral support and used a form of psychological warfare. The subsequent destruction of sacred groves on Anglesey was a common Roman tactic, one of the ways in which they brought the *pax Romana* to the natives. It seems more likely that Suetonius' was after the training camps of the guerrilla fighters who had been plaguing the western border of the Roman occupation, his conquest of the local tribes clearly having failed to quell the hit and run warfare that was being waged.

It was whilst this was going on that the Iceni and several other tribes (most notably the Trinovantes) rose against the Romans after the Queen of the Iceni was flogged and her daughters raped (for Roman law would not allow virgin women to be executed). We have already referred to the fact that during her campaign Boudicca officiated over rites normally associated with Druids, which may well indicate that she was a Druid in her own right. Whether or not that was the case, as we have seen, she nearly succeeded in destroying the Legions and driving Rome from Britain. She probably failed through a combination of misfortune and failing health rather than poor tactics.[46]

For all the bloody retribution meted out by the Romans for those who had dared to resist the might of Rome, Druids were not considered a particular or special target of the military authorities. Moreover, in civil matters, the power of the Druids was simply superseded by Roman bureaucracy in south-east Britain and was never touched elsewhere either in Britain or in Ireland.

When Rome formally withdrew its protection of Britain in AD 410, the structure of Celtic society was largely intact, including the presence of the Druids. This meant that the schools still existed, which, in turn, meant that both the Celtic metaphysic and Celtic beliefs and religious practices also still existed. Romanization had been just skin deep, often just wineskin deep.

Where the Romans failed, Christianity is supposed to have triumphed. Christianity became tolerated during the reign of the Emperor Constantine. Following the Edict of Milan (AD 313), State persecution of Christians ceased, Christianity was made legal, and Christians were no longer barred from holding official positions within the empire. It was not long before they were in positions of authority and accelerating the acceptance of the new religion. The situation was far from clear-cut, as succeeding emperors held differing standpoints. Nevertheless, from the fourth century onwards, Christianity grew in strength and influence. Nor was it backward in spreading the good word. Martin of Tours, for example, set about converting the people of Gaul, leading a mob that destroyed pagan groves and shrines wherever they found them, as well as attacking Druids who even at that early stage were being regarded solely as priests and keepers of the old ways.

The situation is even less clear-cut when it comes to Britain and Ireland. This is due in large part to the fact that the whole of Ireland and large parts of Britain never came under Roman rule. This meant that the beliefs and practices of the Celts in these areas were carried on without the admixture of Graeco-Roman deities, but at the same time it also meant the possibility of safe haven for persecuted Christians.

Quite when Christianity reached Britain and Ireland is not known. Distinctly Christian buildings appear in the archaeological record in the late third century AD, but that suggests a settled Christian presence perhaps as early as the middle of the second century. Tales of Joseph of Arimathea arriving some thirty years after the crucifixion are part of Christian mythology, but mythology often has some basis in fact and this may represent a tradition of people fleeing persecution in Palestine and other parts of the Middle East that had come under Roman rule.

The question of acceptance is one that is yet to be made clear (if that is at all possible). There are no Christian martyrs from this period other than the three who died because of Roman persecution. Celts may not have cared for the new religion, but their sense of hospitality would not have allowed them to do anything other than shelter their guests and eventually send them on their way to look elsewhere for a new home. The influx of refugees is, however, unlikely to have been the main way in which Christianity arrived. The population of the Roman Empire and its outlying lands was extremely mobile, as were ideas. We already encountered this when discussing the diffusion of Celtic culture.

That there were no martyrs does not mean, however, that Christianity was universally welcomed. Indeed, by the fifth century, in spite of most historians suggesting that Christianity was widespread and firmly rooted, paganism still seems to have been the norm. Not just Celtic paganism, but the darker vision of the Saxon invaders who were already casting their bloody shadow on the land. When Germanus visited Britain in AD 429, it was to dispose of the Pelagian heresy (the attempt to 'revive' the philosophy of the Druids), which was considered such a threat to the Church. What he discovered was that many Britons still adhered to their pagan religion and were officially sanctioned in this by chieftains and kings.

In Ireland, a real and lasting effort was made to accommodate both paganism and Christianity. This was not simply a matter of tolerance, but one of integration. In AD 438, High King Lóegaire mac Néill appointed a commission of nine eminent persons to study, revise, and commit to writing the laws of Ireland. The nine were comprised of three *breitheamh* (Brehon), three Christians, and three kings. The resultant law code, based firmly in Celtic culture and preserving the concepts of responsibility and honour rather than that of retribution, survived until the mid-seventeenth century when Oliver Cromwell devastated the country and its population. Although these laws are frequently cited as a triumph of Christianity, they actually carried forward a pagan metaphysic for many centuries.

All through the fifth and sixth centuries, Celtic paganism flourished. In the mid-sixth century, Kentigern[47] found that it was strong in the south of Strathclyde, taught by Bards and officially recognized. The Battle of Arderydd (AD 573), at which Myrddin is said to have gone mad at the sight of so much slaughter, was fought between Christian and pagan kingdoms. Whether or not this was a religious dispute is not known,[48] but it does demonstrate that paganism still existed in the late sixth century.

At the same time, the High King of Ireland was inviting Gildas and other monks to travel to his lands to help revive Christianity, which was falling out of favour. This was largely because of its antagonistic stance over matters of doctrine, which the Church claimed should apply universally rather than just to Christians. On the Continent, the Third Council of Toledo had declared against the sacrilegious idolatry that was firmly rooted and widespread throughout Iberia and Gaul. All of which sounds very much as if pagans were still using their shrines and sacred places for worship, despite Christian attempts either to destroy them or use them solely for Christianity.

In other respects, the appropriation of pagan ways by the Christian Church was far more successful. One suspects that this has more to do with the ordinary person's ability to stay true to what they believed than any innate superiority of one system over another. So it was, for example, that the goddess Brigid became the Christian Saint Bridget, her story, customs, and significance intact. Indeed, the sacred flame kept at Brigid's shrine in Kildare (which means 'Church of the Oak') was kept alight until AD 1220.

Many other pagan ideas and practices were absorbed wholesale into Christianity. These did not all come from Celtic paganism, although Augustine's second question of Pope Gregory[49] suggests that there were local and regional variations in Christian practice not only in the English parts of Britain, but also in the Celtic lands. Major solar festivals were incorporated into Church usage and lost their uniquely Celtic character and name. Pagan gods and goddesses were either condemned as demons and devils or converted hastily into local saints. Many of the 'saints' associated with Cornwall, for example, predate Christianity and are likely to have been local deities.

Though officially sanctioned Celtic paganism began to fade, it still flourished unofficially. And alongside it, a distinct form of Christianity evolved as the official religion. This was marked not just by outward appearance (such as the retaining of the Druidic tonsure by monks[50]) but by the continuity of the Celtic metaphysic, through which the Christian message was transmitted. These days, to refer to Celtic Christianity is to draw down the wrath of sections of the academic community, but it cannot be denied that Rome considered the British Church (as they called it) not only to be distinct but also as seriously 'infected' by Druidic philosophy.

Yet for all the advance of Christianity, of whatever flavour or taint, Celtic paganism persisted. Druidic schools continued to train Druids who fulfilled their normal functions within Celtic society. Nor did successive waves of Saxon invaders do much to alter this. The maps changed, with Celtic territories squeezed closer and closer to the Atlantic fringes; Christianity spread; but this did little to diminish the Celtic vision of the world. Indeed, the first shoots of Celtic nationalism can now be seen, with the consequent entrenchment of ways and ideas along with a determination to see them survive.

When the priestly function was forbidden to any but Christians, and the Druid schools were outlawed, Druids continued to exist. Nor did the Druid schools disappear. With the simple expediency of calling themselves Bardic schools and with judicious minor alterations to their syllabuses, they continued much as before. Indeed, many Druids also played safe by taking on a dual role, remaining Druids and keeping to the old ways whilst also being ordained as Christian priests. Many saw no real conflict of beliefs. It has been suggested that the *Céli Dé* (commonly known as Culdees), formed in Ireland in the eighth century, were just such a movement with their particular ascetic derived from the Celtic notion of rights and duties. They are also said to have favoured the Druid or Celtic tonsure. Mention is still made of their existence in Scotland as late as the fourteenth century.

Even though dispersed and their schools officially closed, Druids survived and helped keep alive the Celtic metaphysic. In the tenth century AD, and possibly later, the Kings of Cashel in Ireland were still being gifted Druids. Welsh Bards in the twelfth century AD wrote openly of the Druids who still lived, practised, and taught in their country. Gerald of Wales mentions the existence of Vates or soothsayers,[51] giving a vivid description of their methods as well as offering scriptural support for what they did and the way in which it was accomplished.

With most of the Druid schools gone, and the role of Bardic schools reduced, a possible crisis was averted by a sudden found enthusiasm by monastic communities for writing down all they could of the vernacular. Although the Druidic embargo on writing applied only to their very specific teachings, fewer people were carrying forward the old learning and the old tales. The growth of nationalism ensured that some, at least, of the native tales and poems were recorded. Although many of the texts have Christian additions and glosses, they retain their pagan character and it is clear that these tales were considered a vital part of Celtic identity.

From the seventh to the eleventh centuries, the poems by and attributed to Aneirin, Myrddin, and Taliesin were set down, as were the tales we now know as *The Mabinogion*.[52] Most of the great Irish epics were also written down during this period. All these texts contain densely packed and multi-layered tales, which suggests that they are of great antiquity. They may well have been transmitted orally for centuries, maybe even a whole millennia, before being written down – part of much larger cycles of myth and legend now lost to us. They have helped to keep alive the Celtic metaphysic and Celtic paganism and are a treasure trove for careful and thoughtful explorers.

Whilst this aspect of the past was being preserved, pagan practices were continuing. Although no longer formal, and certainly frowned upon by the Church, paganism had found refuge in a place where it could not be destroyed as long as the native languages of the people were preserved – folklore. Preservation of teachings and practice cannot be assured in such a situation. There are no formal means by which to check whether ideas and practices remain 'correct' – although Celtic thought and practice were always under review. It is therefore surprising to see how accurately such things can pass from generation to generation.

In Ireland and Scotland, the Bardic schools survived as formal institutions until the early eighteenth century, and would have helped to sustain the folkloric element of both metaphysic and pagan belief by providing an authoritative source for genealogy, history, myth, and legend, whilst also keeping the record alive and transmitting current news. The changing political scene saw the patronage of these schools destroyed by the sword or lured to London. Yet even then, into the late eighteenth century there were clansmen in the Highlands and Islands of Scotland who were sending their sons to be trained as Bards. To be sure, these were not Druids, but the link with the past was still strong and these Bards fulfilled many of the functions of their Druid forebears.

Elsewhere there can be found examples of pagan practice that suggest it was still widespread. In 1538, an image of Darvel Gadarn, to which locals paid their respects, was removed from Llandarfel in Merionethshire and taken to London. There it was burned at Smithfield. Clearly, from its name, it was a local deity that provided protection and strength to the village or parish of Darfel. The burning of idols, however, was an ineffective means of stamping out pagan practice. Fifty years later, there are still reports from Wales of bullocks being sacrificed to Beino – which may be a corrupt form of the deity Belinus.

In Brittany, we find a similar transformation to that undergone by Brigid. There, however, it is Anu who remained firmly fixed in the hearts of the people and gained acceptance as St Ana. Also revered in Brittany at many shrines was Gwen Teirbron,[53] a deity who protected nursing mothers and their offspring. Her cult survived until the latter part of the nineteenth century when Christian priests finally stamped it out and destroyed her shrines.

The Highlands of Scotland were also an area where pagan practices persisted. The church in Dingwall, near Inverness, makes report in 1656 of bulls being sacrificed to St Mourie – a thinly disguised *Mór Rí*, which translates as 'Great King'. Some have attempted to explain this as a reference to the Christian God, but sacrificing bulls is hardly an orthodox act of Christian worship any more than is referring to God as a mere saint. These rites were attended by locals, by strangers (that is, Scots from other parts of the country), and by visitors from foreign countries. Clearly something more than a local folk custom is taking place here. Attempts to suppress this practice clearly failed since in 1678 members of the Mackenzie clan were called to the church at Dingwall to give account of themselves. They had, it seems, sacrificed a bull in the hope of restoring an ailing member of their clan to health.

Such persistence of belief and practice is remarkable, not least because it was known of far and wide and people were apparently prepared to travel overseas to attend certain rites. More astonishing is that a century later, in 1774, there are still reports of people in the Highlands honouring places associated with the *Mór Rí* by leaving small gifts. That would suggest mere folk custom were it not also for the fact that that we have reports of a pagan priesthood still in operation toward the end of the eighteenth century. On the island of Maelrubha in Loch Maree (*Mór Rí?*), which is in Wester Ross, there was a sacred oak attended by priests, along with a well said to have healing properties. Sacred wells and trees were not uncommon, but that there were priests who tended them and officiated at rites speaks of some level of organization and the transmission of knowledge, even if it was by that time restricted to a particular clan or family.

Sacred or holy wells and springs could (and still can) be found throughout the lands once inhabited by Celtic-speaking peoples. Many had healing properties and others were the focus of rites that were either banned (usually fertility rites) or incorporated into Christian ritual, often by dedicating the well to a saint. Some of these are clearly pre-Christian in origin and even contained sacred fish that were cared for down the centuries and replaced when they died. That a fish is a symbol of Christianity no doubt aided in their preservation.

All this survived, despite the many attempts that had been made to suppress paganism and impose a Christian orthodoxy on the people. Celtic and (latterly) Saxon pagan practices and beliefs were simply too deeply ingrained. Even the Protestant Reformation, which made a deliberate and concerted effort to stamp out pagan practice, did little to change the way in which people thought and acted in their everyday lives. The period of the Long Parliament in England and Wales (1642-1653) saw a systematic effort to destroy folk customs, especially May Day celebrations, which had a particular association with fertility. Although maypoles may have disappeared in large numbers, the people simply learned to make their devotions more discretely or in private.

The eighteenth century was witness to a new element to this tale. Partly as a backlash against the austerities of Puritanism, but also because of a growing interest in British heritage, antiquaries turned their eyes away from sun-baked Olympus and began to look at the green fields and hedgerows of home. Even today in the Western world, Graeco-Roman culture and languages are considered in some way superior to all others. Most people in Celtic countries (and emigrant populations elsewhere that originated in the Celtic world) will know more about Graeco-Roman history, myth, and institutions than those of their native lands. In the eighteenth century, the first steps in redressing the balance were taken. This was only partially out of purely scholarly concerns. Fashion and the search for a new paradigm played their part in this development, and it was very much an aspect of the times.

One of the earliest to turn his attention to the Druids in particular was the architect John Wood (1704-1754). Convinced that both Bath and Stonehenge had been important Druid centres, he based his designs for Bath Circus on the geometrical studies of Stonehenge that had been made earlier by Inigo Jones. Stonehenge, of course, pre-dates the Celts by many centuries, but at the beginning of the eighteenth century, it became almost de rigueur to ascribe any pre-Roman antiquity to the Druids.

With more enthusiasm than accuracy, large numbers of scholarly gentlemen began to expound on the Druids, their practices, dress, origins, and their teachings. The paganism associated with the native peoples of the Celtic lands was seen as acceptable – no doubt because of the efforts of these scholars (many of whom were Christian clerics) to link Celtic paganism with the religion of the Jewish patriarchs and, by association, with Christianity.

The integrity and veracity of the work of these Druid revivalists has long since been called into question and found severely wanting. It cannot, however, be dismissed out of hand. To begin with, we cannot deny that there was a genuine belief by these men that they were reviving a living tradition, part of which was Bardism. They were educated people and some were truly inspired poets and visionaries. Although some of them (in particular, Edward Williams, known more commonly by his self-anointed Bardic name of Iolo Morgannwg) have muddied our academic pool by inventing what did not exist and by 'adapting' what did, we can condemn them no more than we can condemn the early hagiographers of Christian tradition.

Although these men may have failed to attain standards we now find acceptable, they did manage to make three important contributions, albeit inadvertently. The first was that they made Celtic studies acceptable to people who had previously dismissed Celts both past and present as mere barbarians. Although their approach to the subject was haphazard, they had taken a step in the right direction and in so doing also laid the foundations for making Celtic studies respectable.

Secondly, they made paganism acceptable. Whereas ordinary folk faced with persecution had little option but to abandon their practices (in public at least), these were men who could and did fight legal battles to protect their ways.[54] Furthermore, they helped to keep paganism alive at a time when traditional practices in the countryside were fading as a large proportion of the population migrated to the towns and cities or to far distant shores.

Their third achievement is more tenuous, but perhaps the most important. Whilst the accuracy of their facts and the strength of their arguments are now open to question, they did much to keep alive the Celtic metaphysic. This was an indirect consequence of their work, but at a time when scientific materialism was growing in strength and influence, these eccentrics and pseudo-scholars kept alive the idea that there are many ways of looking at and understanding the world.

The history of the so-called Druid revival is so well documented and so complex that it is not worth attempting to lay it out here.[55] That the Revivalists had a great impact on modern Druidry is without question. That their influence has been superseded is also without question. Even as they were making their studies and forming the first Druid Orders, compiling their books and discussing the finer points of sacred geometry, the other strand of pagan survival was continuing unobtrusively. After all, being Druid (in any age) has little to do with book learning. It is a way of conducting the self in accord with a particular way of viewing the world.

Tracing the survival of the Celtic metaphysic from the late seventeenth century to the present day is not easy, but we do catch glimpses of its existence if we know where to look. In that search, it is important to remember that this was not a conscious dispersal of ideas. Rather it was a reaction of ordinary folk to changes that a minority of society attempted to impose on them. They may have paid lip service to new ways and ideas (those that filtered out from the centres of so-called civilization), but they stuck with those that they knew would work.

This does not mean that Druid teachings, the rites and beliefs of Celtic paganism, or the Celtic metaphysic have come down to us intact. Far from it. However, the same is true for all religions. The world changes, things get lost, others get changed, new ideas flower. Yet sufficient has survived to mark the long path over the centuries, enabling Druids today to remain in touch with their roots whilst also living in the world of the twenty-first century.

Many of the large Druid Orders trace their roots back by sometimes convoluted routes to the Revivalists of the eighteenth century. Some of the links are tenuous and there have been breaks, but on the whole, there is a genuine line of descent. The rituals of some of these groups, as well as their organization and aims, admittedly reflected a hierarchical approach that had more than a slight colouring of Freemasonry about it. The end of the twentieth century therefore saw a number of changes within the Orders with conscious attempts to honour their roots whilst stepping out from the patriarchal shadow.

At the same time, a new trend was emerging outside of the Orders, especially where they were dormant or were seen by those who knew they existed (as they tended to be closed groups in those days) as part of the establishment. This aspect of the Druid Way found itself again in the counter-culture of the 1960s as a general pagan metaphysic found new expression – especially in the environmental movement. This has led to derogatory remarks by some that the Druid Way is the Green movement at prayer. This is, for many reasons, inaccurate, but the awareness that gave birth to the counter-culture[56] also woke the pagan metaphysic in general and the Celtic metaphysic in particular in that part of the world that had seen them moribund for so long.

Once this new way of looking at the world began to flower again, it was not long before the Druid Way became reinvigorated. Many individual adherents (sometimes known as Hedge Druids) began to explore their new-found understanding of the world and began to use the term Druid as a useful label to identify themselves. Some gravitated toward each another, joining the reviving Orders or forming new ones. Many, however, have stayed outwith the formal structures and formed Fellowships and Groves simply for companionship and the exchange of ideas and experiences.

The path from ancestral times through to today is long, complex, sometimes hard to find, but undeniably there. Druids today have every right to claim a link with their ancestors, although they cannot claim direct descent or an accurate reproduction of ritual practice. The link is far less concrete. It is the survival and revival of a way of viewing the world that may not have been unique to pagan Celts, but was certainly expressed in a unique way. Pagans today who live in accord with that metaphysic and who express their apprehension of the divine uniquely through Celtic forms are Druid.

6

IS THE DRUID WAY A RELIGION?

Is the Druid Way a Religion?

It is all very well talking about the Druid Way as a religion and basing this claim on a self-proclaimed connection with paganism as a worldwide religion of great antiquity. The claim to be a religion, however, needs to be tested against criteria that are generally accepted and recognized for non-pagan religions as well – criteria that have been set by someone outwith the pagan community.

This question is not as clear as it may seem. It is an issue upon which even Druids cannot agree. There are some Druids who assert that the Druid Way *is* a religion and there are others who assert that it is *not*. This would, on the face of it, seem to be a classic dilemma – an either/or situation that inevitably leads to some form of conflict. Furthermore, there are those who say it does not matter one way or the other. Yet the question must at least be asked. People cannot commit themselves to such a way of life without having some idea of why they are taking this path. They may not have reasoned it out. Very few people make a religious or spiritual commitment on that basis. They are drawn to a path because they feel the need for a shape to, or direction for, their spiritual life and are (when they have any choice in the matter) attracted to a way that suits their temperament and understanding of the world.

The question also needs to be confronted because of the public conception of Druids and their beliefs. This, quite naturally, is formulated from the public face of the Druid Way, which is seldom seen and somewhat allusive. One of the many roles of a Druid is to know and preside over the eight ceremonies that mark the inner and outer stations of the year. In form, these ceremonies resemble what most people would regard as religious activity. As some of these ceremonies are conducted in public, the question of religion is one that is most commonly raised by non-Druids, and the most frequent assumption is that the Druid Way is a religion.

This matter is complicated by the fact that many of the public ceremonies ascribed to Druids are often seen – especially in Britain and Ireland – as being conducted by eccentrics at controversial places.[57] The picture presented to non-Druids is therefore false and biased by the activities of the minority who enjoy ostentatious ceremonial.

However, these are, in a sense, side issues to the main reason for considering this question – which is the attitude of some factions within the 'established' religions. These tend to be the groups that are most critical of pagans and pagan activity. They often display an appalling degree of ignorance of paganism in general and its many different forms in particular. They deny that the Druid Way (or any other pagan belief) can be a religion or in any way spiritual, much as they deny that any creed or sect but their own can be a religion. They often go much farther, however, and falsely equate the likes of the Druid Way with the unsavoury practices of the personified evil of their own theology. Such denigration has been going on for many centuries and if for no other reason, it is important to consider this issue in order that the ignorance (wilful or otherwise) that fuels such accusations might be countered.

Pagan theology is a relatively new discipline. Rather, it is an ancient discipline that is now being rediscovered. At one time, even to discuss the idea of paganism openly would have put a person at risk of accusations of heresy. The gradual change in climate that has allowed discussion was occasioned by the rise of so-called rational thought. Discussion has become acceptable; the subject has become sidelined. However, because a subject is neither wholly or partly within the realms of the rational does not mean it should be dismissed – otherwise we would have to dismiss the reality and impact of love, music, art, and all other non-rational aspects of our life and being.

On a personal level, there are also many reasons why we avoid discussing or, if we do discuss, avoid reaching conclusions on such issues. Two, in particular, are common to us all. The first is that we are often (and validly so) wary of committing ourselves outright to a particular position. What if we are wrong? Failure, after all, is something our society and its education system has taught us to despise.

The other reason (which is really the same reason stated positively), is that we tend to believe that it is far better to be well informed, and develop a wisdom that will allow us to react to and work in the real world, than pervert things to conform to a specific creed. Unfortunately, this frequently results in a frustrating attitude of non-committal. Commitment is not necessarily bad. It is possible to hold on to something tightly as long as we are equally prepared, if necessary, to let go lightly.

There is also a curious phenomenon associated with many such difficult topics. That is, that we think we know what the answer is. And believing that, we never go any further. It is not until we actually have to articulate what we think we know that we realize how deficient is our understanding. Words seem to be inadequate for the task. They are not *wholly* inadequate. Indeed, a careful choice of words can readily express the many-layered meaning of challenging concepts and open our minds to what lies beyond. They are but symbols and that is their function. It is just that we often lack practice in their use. Most people today are consumers of words rather than producers.

To make the task easier, it is sometimes better to look at a question and consider whether it can be answered in a less complicated fashion. In the case of the question before us, two other questions become immediately apparent and before we can begin to answer the original question, we need to address these. The first is, 'What is religion?' and the second is, 'What is the Druid Way?'

WHAT IS RELIGION?

In discussing religion, it is important to be clear that we are not discussing religions. That is, we are considering an abstract, rather than actual and particular systems of religious belief. This is not a clear-cut distinction because the notion of religion is inextricably bound up with actual religions. Indeed, there is a very real sense in which religion per se does not exist. There is not a perfect religion; there is not a concept, an abstract, or an idea that pre-existed actual religions of which individual religions are but examples or realizations. Religions came first, born of our desire to understand the mysteries of being. Religion came later, born of a desire to understand the desire to understand the mysteries of being.

To say that a religion exists to satisfy our desire to understand the mysteries of being does not fully convey its role in our lives. A religion does not exist simply in order to explain the world. A religion exists to provide a means of integrating the world, bringing together the whole realm of experience and understanding in a unified whole. This does not mean that any religion has succeeded, notwithstanding the claims of many adherents through the millennia. Religion may provide the means of integration, but it also reveals that there is a great deal of mystery in the world, and it is right that this should be so. We need mystery in our lives. It provides the dynamic that moves us to explore. It is also a constant reminder that there are things far greater than us, things that we cannot understand, things that we cannot control. Without that, we lose all sense of proportion, we become arrogant, and we become dangerous.

This element of mystery (and there are others) is sufficient to explain why any discussion of religion is fraught with difficulty. It is not simply a matter of discussing a set of concrete propositions. Religion encompasses much that goes beyond normal experience and understanding. This is not because it is difficult or open only to a select group. It is simply that our approach to the world today, the way in which we are taught to look at things, is biased against anything that is not material or analysable; against anything that cannot be bought, possessed, and consumed. Religion is none of those things. Rather, it is an absolute and unifying experience of the world that transfigures human existence from that of self-centred destructiveness to creative immanence.

Such transfiguration exists in potential within us all. It cannot be encompassed within the rational world, as the rational is a partial form of understanding. Religion, however, can and does encompass the rational. It is, after all, a mark of religious experience that we become enlightened to a greater or lesser degree. Enlightenment is a form of gnosis – a knowing – and knowledge of the world needs to be assimilated into our understanding. This is a form of rationalization, especially when it involves discussion with other people. Enlightenment is rarely complete and instantaneous. For most people it is a gradual process achieved through study, meditation, and work in the world.

Rationalization plays its part in the social cohesion of a religion as well as in its evolution. Religion is, after all, a shared experience of the world, one that is transmitted from person to person and generation to generation. The world changes. People change. If a religion cannot have its central beliefs clearly expressed, then they cannot be conveyed to others. Without that, those beliefs have no chance of reaching fruition as the fully developed metaphysical notions that guide our actions.

Within contemporary Western society, however, there has been an increasing trend toward the analysis of religion – a trend that has developed out of the strange schism that exists between religious and secular life. Those who are truly religious understand religion. However, it is civil society that is predominant and that constantly tries to understand religious belief and its persistence in the face of what secular society claims is overwhelming evidence of the purely material.

Proponents of secular society and of materialistic thought are engaged in a constant search for certainty. When it comes to religion, they demand incontrovertible proof of its claims. But that is to misunderstand what religion is (a misunderstanding that is also not uncommon amongst those who claim to be religious). The error is inherent in using the wrong tools for the job (science) or misusing the correct tools (philosophy). Certain aspects of religion *are* open to empirical investigation, of course. One can study its history, its social impact, and its artefacts. However, they are peripherals, distinct forms of expression of what lies at the mysterious heart. And that is well beyond the rational, beyond proof, beyond empirical certainty.

Religion is also extremely personal. No matter that it may have a commonly agreed core and derive from outwith the person, we each react to it in ways appropriate to our own understanding and level of development. This is not open to empirical assessment, for all that some claim it must be.[58] There comes a point in any spiritual search where it is necessary to leave behind the safe and familiar world.

At this point, those wedded to rationalism begin to get a little irrational themselves. Those that do not stoop to insult, usually spend an inordinate amount of time trying to sideline religion. Why this should so obsess them is itself something of a mystery. After all, it is not unreasonable to go beyond reason and allow our emotions and intuitive faculties to play a central and creative role in exploring and learning about the vast unknown that surrounds us. We have these gifts, so why not use them?

Religion cannot be bounded by empirical thought or a material approach. Nor can it be considered an intellectual exercise. This is simply because religion is deeply rooted in emotional experience. The closest that rationalism can come is in discussing the experiences that we have had. Rationalism works as a descriptive exercise. It can never be successfully prescriptive. Even then, the descriptive exercise is fraught with problems. What is being discussed is a flash of insight, an understanding so comprehensive that it is overwhelming. The desire to share is enormous because the religious experience is invariably of unity. However, this takes us back to one of the problems we started with. Understanding something and describing that understanding are two distinct things. When the understanding is so wholly inclusive, it is difficult to know where to begin. And while there is a feeling that it must be shared, there is also a very strong sense that to analyse it is to lose the very essence of the experience.

A religious experience is one that has a profound effect on us, not just transforming our whole understanding of the universe, but also completing that understanding. After such an experience people realize who they are, what life is all about, their place in the scheme of things, the unity of all being. Exactly how the experience (or set of experiences) is interpreted depends on the culture, ideas, and language of each person involved.

Such an experience breaks down all the barriers that we have been taught to build between the external world and ourselves. It takes us beyond ourselves and makes evident the underlying unity of all things. The normal limitations of time and space, along with the physical senses, are dissolved to the point where there is no longer any definable difference between the self and the rest of creation. The distinction between subject and object is broken down. However, although the barriers dissolve and there is an overwhelming sense of unity with all things, the self is never lost. Religion, therefore, is as much about the self as it is about the divine, as much about the relationship between the two as it is about either.

With this change of perspective comes a sense of joy and of having returned home. There, one becomes aware of the ultimate truth – a knowledge so profound and absolute it simply cannot be put into words. This means that the experience itself cannot become a religion. It is far too personal and certainly not open to being conventionalized and organized. It is the changed person and that person's need to live in accordance with their vision that gives rise to religion. It becomes a means by which the experience can be transmitted to others, no matter how imperfectly, and by which others can be brought toward an understanding of the experience, if not the experience itself. The differences between particular religions derive from the cultural interpretation of the experience.

The formalized expression of the religious experience is what becomes a religion. Whereas the core experience is intensely personal, religion is social. It takes that ineffable vision as a model of existence, setting up formal structures within which people can live in such a way that their every action is an expression of that vision. At the same time, the structures provide the means by which people can be brought, under guidance, to a state in which they also are open to such experience.

Religion is, therefore, 'an organism of many dimensions typically encompassing doctrines, myths, ethical teachings, rituals, and social institutions, all of which are animated by religious experiences of various kinds'. This definition, adapted from that given by Ninian Smart (1969),[59] helps us along our way, but it does have obvious problems in that one of the terms used to define religion is religious experience. Religious experience only has meaning as a concept when we know what religion is. There needs to be something more.

For the moment, however, we will consider the definition that has been offered. Smart suggests that there are six essential dimensions to the organism. These are the ritual (pragmatic and sacred), mythological, doctrinal, ethical, social, and experiential dimensions. To these might be added three others: the charismatic, the historical/traditional and the artistic. These last three are important elements in specific religions, but are not essential to religion itself.

Ritual is one of the ways in which religion tends to express itself. Established forms of worship – prayer, ceremonial, festivals, offerings and the like – are features common to all religions, no matter how informal they may appear to an outsider. Ritual need not be elaborate any more than it need be derived directly from doctrine. Yet whatever its nature and origin, its purpose is quite clear. Through solemn and customary acts or systems, the intention is to create both a space and a moment that transcend time and place in which there can be an apprehension of or communion with the divine. This is sacred ritual.

There is another, distinct form of ritual – pragmatic ritual – that has roughly the same ends as sacred ritual, but which belongs in those religions that do not aspire to direct communion with the divine. The techniques of training and self-discipline involved are analogous to those of sacred ritual, but rather than creating a transcendent place for communion, pragmatic ritual is directed toward attaining states of consciousness that will move the practitioner from worldly experience to mystical experience. The intention is to bring practitioners closer to their goal of nirvana.

Pragmatic ritual may be distinct from sacred ritual, but they do have much in common. This is particularly so in that they both require outer and inner working as well as being aimed toward creating a place in space and time that is outside both. Nor are sacred and pragmatic ritual mutually exclusive. There are, after all, well-established traditions of mysticism within religions that aspire to communion with the divine as well as religions that aspire to different and appropriate levels of the divine.

Whatever its content, ritual is exceedingly important to religious expression. In a field of experience where there is a distinct lack of certainty, it provides a degree of stability. Furthermore, the repetition involved, provided it does not become mere habit, forms a bond between person and belief that is constantly reinforced. Of course, physical or outer ritual is insufficient on its own to create this bond. It must be accompanied by, and be in harmony with, an inner, spiritual intention or ritual. The obverse, however, is a different matter, for inner ritual *is* sufficient for an enlightened soul. This in no way diminishes the importance of a harmonic outer ritual since this not only forms a personal bond, but also a social bond that unites, through common experience, all those within a belief community.

In addition to ritual, every religion has a corpus of myth. Sometimes these myths form a coherent narrative and relate to the core of the religion. Indeed, they sometimes represent the only oral or written tradition that is available. In other religions, they are somewhat peripheral to the core beliefs but are, nonetheless, important to an understanding of the religion.

The word 'myth' is often taken to mean a fictional story about the far distant past. By this means, myths are dismissed as irrelevant. Yet they are far too potent a force to be disposed of so easily. A myth is a traditional story that embodies religious ideas or mystical concepts. Told and retold, myths are refined and densely packed vehicles that convey huge amounts of emotional information and connect to us all on a very deep level of our being. The question of the historical veracity of their content is neither relevant nor important.

What *is* important about myths is the truth that is to be found embedded within them. The stories relate, often in highly symbolic form, many aspects of religious and spiritual teaching and behaviour. Historical factuality would simply be an added bonus in the eyes of some, strengthening their significance. A formidable element of belief is involved in this, with myth and reality merging – something that can be confusing for outsiders. It would be wrong, however, to assume that adherents of a given religion cannot or will not tell the difference between fact and fiction. It does happen, but not of necessity. In fact, it is a mark of true religion that an adherent *can* tell the difference and is encouraged to do so.

The third dimension is doctrine, which is the attempt to both systematize and clarify what has been revealed by experience. This is done through the medium of ritual and by the use of myth. In creating doctrine, there is a conscious attempt to provide an intellectual aspect to what is revealed. Although the aim is to produce a coherent body of teachings, creating systems and producing clarity do not always go hand in hand. Indeed, too rigid a system can inhibit the exploration of the often difficult and seemingly conflicting symbolism and ideas of the religion.

To confuse matters further, the differences between myth and doctrine are often very slight. They are often two ways of approaching the same truth with myth being intuitive and doctrine being intellectual. This is reflected in the nature of the material involved and of those who approach it. The intuitive soul accepts and even delights in the wildness of the 'raw' mythology in which they can lose themselves, whereas the intellectual soul strives to create an ordered coherence that they can control.

Indeed, a great deal can be revealed about a religion and its adherents from the degree to which doctrine is considered important. Many scholars consider religions at the intuitive end of the scale to be 'primitive'. Rigidity and intellectualism are obviously thought to be signs of sophistication, maturity, and even progress. It is, perhaps, an attempt to paint religion with the limited colours available to analytical thought. Whatever the case may be, the greater the importance of doctrine within a religion, the more we find that reliance is placed on the need to conform unquestioningly to and stay within a system that was originally intended to make exploration easier.

Adherence to doctrine is one of the many elements of the behaviour of an individual with which religion is concerned. Behaviour is an important outward sign of the degree to which individuals have been shaped by their religious experience. It is normal for a code of ethics to be central to or incorporated within the teachings of a religion. Such a code will usually refer to the religious motivation of conduct and to the practical direction of the lives of people. Some are very simple, broad guidelines encapsulated in a single phrase. Others are minutely detailed sets of rules that leave no aspect of behaviour unregulated.

In addition to the rules, there are often sanctions to urge adherents to due observance of the rules. These can be both immediate and long term; this worldly and otherworldly. It is generally the case that the more complex an ethical code, the greater and more complex the number of sanctions. These levels of 'sophistication' also reflect the degree to which adherents are allowed to exercise their freedom of will.

There is, of course, a great deal of difference between the ethical teachings of a religion and the actual behaviour of those who claim to follow that faith. In many cases, a religion will set an ethical standard to which it expects adherents to aspire rather than make perfect attainment. Because of this, some argue that the teachings and the observance of those teachings should be considered separately. In terms of defining religion, this may be valid. When it comes to actual religions, it is a different matter. Religions have had and still do play a major – if not absolute – part in moulding the ethics of the societies in which they exist. For this reason, when applied to an actual religion, the argument for separation should be treated with caution.

The ethical dimension of religion is indicative of the fact that a religion is not merely a system of belief. It also has a cohesive power, binding people together into a community of those who live their lives in accordance with that belief. What is more, it is a social organization with structures, functions, networks of relationships, and communal patterns of behaviour that have social significance both for those who hold to that system and for those who do not.

The social shape of a religion is inevitably formed by its religious and ethical ideas and practices. It is also true that the ethical ideals and practices of a religion are shaped by or adapted to the existing social conditions and attitudes in which the belief system first came into being. It will also be shaped by the social climate of other peoples if it spreads beyond the society of its origin. How far such ideals can be adapted to new social climes before the religion loses its original identity depends, of course, on how essential such ideals are considered to be to the identity of the religion. This is determined not only by the people in whom it finds expression, but also, and largely, by the degree to which a specific religion is the product of its time and place of genesis. Some religions have a more widespread appeal than others, although it is always dangerous to assume this is simply because of the religion itself. There are many non-religious factors involved in the spread and acceptance of a religion.

For all that, it must be remembered that the wellspring of all religion is experience. Rather, religious experience is the wellspring. Without such experience, there would be no religion, nor any of the dimensions discussed above, for it is that experience from which everything else derives and to which everything relates.

The nature of religious experience is extremely varied and wide-ranging – from the prosaic to the sublime. At the prosaic end of the scale, where most people find themselves, religious experience is derived from any kind of conscious activity concerned with religious concepts or phenomena – prayer, reading a sacred text, even cleaning a place of worship. This may be humble, but it is not to be despised for it is in the everyday world that most people live. At the other end of the scale, are direct experiences of the transcendent and the divine, of the mysteries. These experiences cannot be taught or truly shared except with others who have also experienced them. It is in the hope of this type of experience that many come to religion and stay faithful to it. It is in this hope that many continue their daily acts of prosaic experience.

Any discussion of, or attempt to describe, religious experience presents us with special difficulties. The very nature of such an experience puts it largely beyond words and wholly beyond analysis. This is not to say that many have not tried and, to some extent, succeeded. Ultimately, however, the only way to understand fully such communion with the divine is to experience it for oneself.

The context of such an experience must always be kept in mind when considering the content and form of any description. Much of the language and symbolism used will be specific to the person giving the account and will be highly coloured by their prior social status and religious beliefs as well as their own attitude to such things. Often, the way the experience is described and the doctrine that is believed have a strong influence on each other.

This does not mean that those who equate divinity with the world about them, or who believe the divine is simply beyond us at this stage, are incapable of such sublime experience. It is, indeed, the very transcendence of the universe that is most commonly cited as the 'primitive' spur to the religious impulse. This is a clear example of how belief and an understanding of the world can influence the nature of the experience and its interpretation.

Most people will content themselves with gaining some sense of the divine through ritual. Doubtless, they will also maintain a hope of some direct communion with the divine. Such experience, of course, means a great deal more than mere awareness. This is where the great step is made – the step from faith to knowledge, the step from belief to certainty. Of course, knowledge, certainty, and experience of the mystery are not necessary for religiousness. Faith is sufficient – and in many ways is more difficult to live with as it comes always with doubt. Faith requires a sustained effort on the part of the faithful, not least because faith is always tested by the everyday world in which we live.

Knowledge is not an easy burden to bear, either, but the changes that come with it provide a certainty and an energy that sustain the one who knows. However, it can be isolating, as there are far fewer people with whom to share the vision of the world that knowledge brings. It also places a burden of responsibility on the one who knows for the knowledge brings with it a certainty that knowledge in itself is not enough. The knowledge must be shared and must be acted upon.

The six dimensions discussed above can be brought together into two distinct groups. The first is 'belief', which is comprised of the doctrinal, mythological, and ethical dimensions. The second is 'practice', which is comprised of the ritual, social, and experiential dimensions. The distinction between these two groups – as with the dimensions themselves – is far from hard and fast. After all, if you are genuinely religious, you practice what you believe and you believe what you practice.

Beyond this core, which is essential to all religions, there are a number of other distinct dimensions that are important to specific religions. Foremost amongst these is the charismatic dimension. A number of religions are based upon the revelation vouchsafed to and through a particular individual. However, revelation to an individual is insufficient in itself to warrant a distinct dimension. Many people have messages revealed to them from an apparently divine source. Very few have the personality to persuade others that their message is genuinely divinely inspired. Fewer still have the power to convince large numbers of people. Less than a handful have had their message passed down from generation to generation.

This, of course, applies to those religions that are derived from the life and works of an individual and refers to the attraction, inspiration, authority, and example of that person. But it goes further. Any religion based on or around an individual has the potential to inspire individuality in others, as well as encouraging cults of personality. Moreover, where the religion outlasts the lifetime of the individual who inspired it, there will inevitably be prominent adherents, saints and mystics, martyrs and teachers, who also exert a charismatic influence.

Although not essential to a definition of religion, all religions have a historical dimension. Whereas the mythological dimension is concerned with the symbolic importance of past events – real or imagined – the historical dimension is concerned with the path of a religion through time and how it has influenced and been influenced by social forces distinct from itself.

There is a close connection here with the social dimension. Religions tend to be universalist (in theory, at least, and with many notable exceptions). They are supposed to look beyond the boundaries of tribe, nation, race, gender, class, and society to offer a message of general significance for humanity. In such cases, it is the awareness of belonging to a living movement with sacred origins in the past, as well as sharing in its history, that provides a powerful element of universal appeal, uniting all the diverse members.

Finally, there is the artistic dimension. Religion is supremely creative. Its very essence is one of synthesis and this dynamic has inspired all forms of creative expression. Nor is this confined to what we would now consider 'art' – an activity that has lost a great deal of meaning by being divorced from functional life. Artistic expression is just as likely to be found in the most utilitarian of sacred objects. This ranges from buildings and earthworks to sacred texts; from music, dance, and drama to gardening, flower-arranging, and embroidery; from the grandest ceremony to the commonest and most private act. All of these may be creative manifestations, executed with care as acts of veneration and acts of communion.

Whatever one may think of these – and one should not become too tied to actual examples – it is evident that one dimension is considered the most important. That is the dimension of experience. Without it, none of the others would have substance. It is the spark of life that lies at the heart of it all, the bright sun around which the rest must revolve.

This living heart is essential to an understanding of religion. Smart calls religion an organism. For many that would seem to be a metaphor. That may be so, but it is an apt usage that resonates with a stronger truth than mere allegory. Each religion has its own dynamic and has to be understood in terms of the interrelation of its different dimensions. However, there is more to it than that. Religion and religions have life, for they are an intimate part of human existence, born out of our quest to understand the metaphysical mysteries of that existence. They would not exist without the agency of mind to create them and give them complex and evolving form, shaping what is familiar in order to express the unknown.

This is not to suggest that religions are in any way a mere invention of human beings, any more than it is a conflation of religion with the divine. Religion is a creation of human beings, not an invention – and there is a subtle difference. Invention is merely the rearranging of already ordered things. Creation is identifying and highlighting the patterns of order in the universe or, at a more sublime level, producing that order out of chaos. Religion is a creation because it is a response to our apprehension of the divine (in whatever form we understand that most primal of forces), an identification of the order that gave form to and that underlies the universe.

In this, we can find the missing element of Smart's definition, which is that religion is our means of coping with the apprehension, knowledge, and understanding of our metaphysical existence. It is the means by which we hope to increase that knowledge and understanding. It is an organic system through which we can come to live in accord with what we learn. It is a system through which we can come to commune with the divine.

WHAT IS THE DRUID WAY?

Just as there are many definitions of what religion consists in, there are many definitions of what constitutes a Druid and the Druid Way.[60] However, one thing is certain – Druids today are not what Druids were. To begin with, many present-day Druids are not of Celtic origin, nor do many of them have command of a Celtic language[61] (although it has to be said that others are highly fluent experts). Nor are Druids any longer considered the intellectual class of society. That is partly a matter of expression, for the idea of an intellectual class does not sit easily in the modern mind where the notion of intellect has been debased.

Indeed, not only has the intellectual come to be identified with the detached and rarefied atmosphere of a system of educational privileges, many efforts have been made to divorce it from and denigrate the use of intuitive faculties. Yet intellect is the faculty of knowing, perceiving, and thinking. This does not exclude the use of intuition or creativity any more than it excludes manual skills. People come to know the world through all their senses and abilities, as well as through their interaction with the world, and not by divorcing themselves from it. All people have intellectual potential, which they all fulfil in different ways. In some, it is developed to a greater degree than in others. A person can know trees by reading about them in the classroom and thinking about them. They can know trees by climbing them. They can know trees by planting their seeds and watching them grow, and by taking timber and crafting furniture. Who knows the world better, a gardener or a philosopher? It is, of course, a false question. Neither knows it better. They each know it differently – if, indeed, the gardener and the philosopher are different people.

This means that the Druid Way, as it is perceived and practised today, is an intellectual activity. Nevertheless, it is an intellectual activity in the way that ancestral Celts would have understood, because Druids, past and present, engage with the world in all manner of ways. All that the Druid does is from an intellectual base for all that Druids do is driven by the way in which they perceive the world and their relation to it. To be Druid is an expression of the whole being.

This also means that the Druid Way is an organism – one that functions at ever-increasing levels of sophistication within society to achieve a number of outer and inner goals. These goals, and the methods by which they are achieved, are what tie modern Druids closely to their ancestral Celtic counterparts for the goals are one and the same, even if the emphasis differs to suit current needs. The all-encompassing goal is balance.

Underlying these bald statements are basic beliefs about the world that were held in times past by Druids. These were derived, as we have seen, from the way that ancestral Celts saw and understood the world. For them it was second nature. That is how the world was. For Druids today, it is something they have to reclaim. Our psychologies are different from those of our distant ancestors. We have been brought up in a post-Freudian society that is largely material and reductionist, one that has a belief in the absoluteness of humanity.

In the first instance, there was a belief in the unity of all things. This is a brave statement to make, as it has not come down to us in such straightforward form. However, from the behaviour and attitudes of the Celts, we can tell that this was their belief. They understood and accepted that the universe was a system of distinct manifestations that were facets of a unifying principle that was beyond description. Being a highly practical people, they also accepted that such concerns were beyond them. Their veneration of many gods and goddesses was an expression of the impossibility of encompassing all things with the human mind. The gods and goddesses, the spirits, were all living symbols of various aspects, or qualities, that the divine might be presumed to have when manifested at a human level of comprehension.

As we have seen, this was much more sophisticated than an animistic pantheism. Ancestral Celts did not worship trees, rivers, lakes, and wells; they simply recognized that these were special points of connection between themselves and the divine. They saw spirit in all things and knew that all things are distinct manifestations of the divine. Immanence and transcendence. Panentheism.

Accepting this essential unity of being means accepting that there is no such thing as lifeless matter. It also means accepting that spirit and matter are not separable opposites, but distinct aspects of a single reality. Druids engage with all levels of being (not just the material) in their own environment, and they do this in ways that suit their understanding of the natural world – with which ancestral Druids had far closer ties than we do at present.

As an adjunct to the principle of unity, there is also an understanding that there are different states within that unity. There have been many ways of describing this, but these days it is usually expressed in terms of density. Different densities have often been referred to by the symbolic use of the elements. Although these have been given different interpretations by different cultures, not least the Celtic, where they figure as the Land, the Sea, and the Sky, there is still a shared idea in the symbolism of different levels, planes, or worlds, which interpenetrate and are interdependent, but nonetheless have distinctive basic forms.

Inherent in the notion of different states is to be found the idea of progressive development. In essence, this is the belief that there is movement from the densest, most rudimentary, forms of life toward the worlds of spirit and those that lie beyond that horizon. In one sense, this is an acceptance of evolution, but it extends well beyond the evolution of biological form.[62]

The idea of progression is far from straightforward. Biological evolution tends toward an increasing complexity of form and specialization of function. From this model, however, we cannot assume that complex forms or systems are necessarily superior to, or more desirable than, less complex forms. Complexity can lead to too great a degree of specialization, which is vulnerable to slight changes in environment. Many complex forms have become extinct whilst simpler forms have survived.

There is a lesson here for society – too great a level of social complexity can be considered a disadvantage in the evolution of social structures. This is especially so when coupled with the notion that progress simply means accumulation of material goods. Such societies are certainly more prone to catastrophic collapse. They also have a tendency to swallow less complex social structures as they expand. However, less complex societies and cultures, as well as those that are not obsessed with material wealth, have a strength not often recognized.

Biological evolution is, however, only part of the story. The life within the form also evolves and, as it evolves, increases its capacity to evolve. Yet no matter how evolved the life within the form has become, it is only there because it has passed through all the necessary prior stages – learning from each stage the lessons that enable progress.

Exposure to a materialistic society makes it extremely difficult to view progress as anything other than linear. This is one of the greatest differences between the metaphysic on which modern Western society is based and the Celtic metaphysic. It is also one of the greatest differences in thinking between Druids today and the world in which they find themselves. They exist in close communion with the natural world and are constantly aware of the distinct and ever changing seasons. The seasons and the change of the seasons have an effect on the world about us and on physical and spiritual being. This goes beyond simple operations such as change in temperature, number of daylight hours, and the emotional connotations that are built up as people move through life. The cycle of change is seen as being intimately related to a cycle of change in our inner life, from which it is possible to glimpse the many layers of the many cycles that involve the self and the other, the material and the spiritual, the tangible and the intangible.

The orthodox way of viewing our lives, for example, is as straight lines. We are born, we move inexorably through the years, we die. It is a bleak picture. True, the lines will run parallel, cross, and tangle, but ultimately each isolated line simply comes to an end. This way of looking at things, however, does not accord with a Druid's experience, any more than it accords with the thinking of most other societies in most other times. A Druid views life in a way that accords with the observable workings of the universe.

This way of looking at the universe is symbolized by the circle. Although the circle is perhaps the simplest symbol of all in visual terms, it is infinitely complex in its representation and interpretation. The most important thing to remember when contemplating any circle, however, is that it is not a static symbol. The circle always moves – either turning about its own centre so that the circumference rotates, or pulling the observer into and beyond the space contained within the circumference.

Druids use the circle as a symbol of the cyclical nature of life, to make clear the connection of humanity with the rest of nature. The cycles of night and day, of the moon, of the seasons, all resonate one with another. More telling is the fact that the cycle of life accords closely with the seasonal cycle of the year. What we know of the Earth and the sun, of the planets and the stars simply confirms all this. Indeed, the cyclical nature of existence is widely observed and recognized as a fundamental spiritual truth by many, if not most, religions.

Of course, the situation is much more complex than the mere turning of a circle. Nothing ever repeats itself exactly. In looking at the circle, we are looking at one manifestation, one cycle that turns within many others. Although each circle turns about a centre, that centre is not still for it, too, turns about another centre that turns about another centre, ad infinitum.

All these cycles move at slightly different angles so that although there is a constant return to the familiar, there is always something slightly new to contemplate. In this way, the circles become helices that turn ever on or spirals that move from or to a particular point. It is a dizzying prospect that is so vast and so complex that Druids believe we can never hope to understand even the tiniest part of it.

Because it is not possible to comprehend the true nature and purpose of creation in this plane of existence does not mean that Druids do not work toward that end. The path of their lives and the turning of the day and the month and the year as symbolized by the circle are outward events, manifestations through distinct agents of the cycles of life. However, they are seen as effects, not causes. They are the rim of the wheel, which has no meaning in itself. For that, it must be related to what lies at the hub, round which the rim ever turns.

It is this acceptance of the cyclical nature of the universe that forms the basis of a belief by Druids in reincarnation. Ancestral Celtic thought on reincarnation has not come down to us in any clear-cut form. Most of what we know has been passed on to us by people for whom the idea was alien. What they made of the idea of a series of lives is evident in the incredulous tone with which they report this belief. From what can be gleaned from Celtic sources, however, there is little doubt that reincarnation was an accepted part of Celtic thought. And so it is today.

After death, one is reborn in the Otherworld to live a life of rest and recuperation before being born again in this. Such a round of new births is not without point. A single lifetime is simply not long enough to learn all that needs to be learned on the Druid's journey to unity. Nor is reincarnation confined to human beings. All life is cyclical. That we do not understand some forms of life does not mean they are exempt from the basic patterns of existence. We move round the great cycles together, our own paths intertwining with the paths of others. Humans, animals, plants, minerals, single souls and groups, nations, species, planets and stars, whole galaxies. They all turn, live, die, and return in glory. It is unclear from ancestral practice or present-day belief whether this represents a long journey of a single identity, or whether returning souls must start afresh, although the idea of allowing loans to be carried over to the next world suggests that individuals would be able to identify others.

In completing cycles, of whatever type and duration, Druids believe they are contributing to an act of balance. Linear thinkers have trouble understanding a universe that is both cyclical and in balance. They do not understand how something that is constantly changing can be in equilibrium. However, keeping balance involves completing all the cycles; it involves constant change, constant readjustment, and constant learning about new conditions. The world changes and if we do not learn to change with it, we contribute to our own destruction.

One of the exemplars of balance is justice, which encompasses much more than social and legal structures. It also encompasses much more than the material world. Justice, an impartial sense of balance and fair play (rather than the retributive twist it has been given by some), is deeply embedded in the soul – part of the matrix that gives the soul form. This innate sense of equity – a reflection of the balance to which the universe tends – cries out against injustice and seeks to find ways to reinstate equilibrium. It is, however, extremely difficult in this day and age not to feel helpless in the face of all that takes place.

Druids emphasize, nevertheless, that everything we do has a consequence. That means that it is possible to make a contribution, no matter how small, to correcting the injustices of the world. Sometimes the effect is obvious and immediate. Sometimes it is a matter of faith, as the effects are difficult to see or unlikely to be manifest in the near future. Indeed, so long-term are some of these effects that they are unlikely to be manifest in this lifetime. That is the essence of Druidic service – individual Druids work to an end from which they cannot benefit.

These effects are not just external. They cannot be. Druids believe that we are all an integral part of the universe. What we do affects ourselves just as much as it affects other beings. That we must all accept the consequences of our actions is a given of their moral code. Some people equate this with the Buddhist and Hindu notion of karma, but that is inaccurate. Druidic justice is based on wisdom and an understanding of the workings of the world – on honour and responsibility. It is based on the primacy of truth and the need for reparation rather than retribution. It is centred in the here and now. Honour demands that all thought and action be carried out in right fashion. Responsibility demands that any injustice be put right by the person responsible. It is considered to be highly immoral to put these things off, to discount honour, and to avoid responsibility.

The Celtic view of the world was supremely complex and subtle. It was also extremely practical. Whilst they may have happily supported an intellectual class, they were a farming people, who were concerned with winning a living from the land. Furthermore, they knew that a successful living was only to be had by respecting the many levels of being that permeated their own. This view of the world and this practical approach was the basis of all Druidic thought. It is from this that present-day Druids derive their sense of identity and their strength of purpose. Recognizing that their fundamental role is unchanged from that of their ancestors, but that changes in society and the world have occasioned a change of emphasis, they now work to learn how to restore the balances that their ancestors once worked to maintain.

Today Druids will follow what they consider a threefold path. They have adopted the eighteenth-century notion of the three aspects of the Druid as Bard, Vate, and Druid. Although we know that ancestral Druids did not organize themselves in this fashion, the misreading of historical evidence has provided modern Druids with an extremely useful tool with which to approach their working in the world. Although originally established as a hierarchical system of grades, it is now largely used to provide a structure for the education of Druids, carefully moving them into new areas of knowledge and new perspectives from which to view the world. This threefold structure can be portrayed as a threefold knot, for each of the areas flows from and is interlinked with the others.

The first path, that of the Bard, is the one in which Druids work to know and preserve the history of the Druid Way and its peoples; know and protect the places of the Way; express the Way in all its forms through arts, crafts, and all the actions of their lives; keep alive the traditions of the Way; seek out and preserve the ancient wisdom; uphold the freedom to right expression; learn and understand and keep the sacred word; open doors with the power of the word; be a force for good in the world.

The second path, which is the path of the Vate, is the one in which Druids work to know, understand, and respect the trees and their ways; know, understand, and respect animals and their ways; know compassion and, in accordance with their skills, heal the hurts of the world; converse with their ancestors; explore and come to know the Summerlands; understand the mysteries of death and rebirth; cultivate intuition; open the doors of time and there travel freely; know ways of understanding what is to be.

The third path, the path of the Druid, is the one in which Druids work to achieve authority in ritual and ceremony; understand, make, and keep right law; offer good counsel and advice; investigate and understand the universe; develop intellect; seek balance; get wisdom; teach; generate and regenerate.

These are by way of being vows that bind Druids to the work they undertake. At first sight, they may seem increasingly abstruse, if not downright obscure. As they stand, they are merely a key to understanding both the Druid and the Way they follow. Their importance merits a more detailed examination.

It is a function of Druids to preserve the history of Druids, their thought, and the peoples amongst whom Druids live. Preservation is not a simple matter. It cannot be done properly without also knowing and understanding what is being preserved. History should never be reduced to just an academic exercise. There is much more to it than that.

Knowing one's history, be it personal or communal, keeping it accurate, and understanding it, is essential to the maintenance of identity. A person who loses access to their memories suffers not just a loss of identity, but also becomes rootless. Without the relationships they have built up over the years with the world about them and with other people, they face many problems. The same is true of a people who lose access to their history. If that goes, so, too, does their identity and their social cohesion. It is one of the reasons why the cultivation of memory was so important to Druids.

Loss of identity is traumatic. There are far too many examples of how peoples have suffered when others have denied them their past for this to be questioned. Nor can identity simply be restored by regaining the facts. The ways in which a history is handed down and the ways in which it is understood are also important. Understanding a history is a restoration of the emotional facet of identity – the dynamic that vitalizes the facts.

Identity does not reside merely within a person or people, any more than it is merely about a memory of events and relationships. Nor should it be confused with individuality – a misleading notion about cutting one's self off in order to stand out. Identity is rooted in and operates through both time and place. Temporally, identity spans all time. Not only does it evolve and stand at its present juncture based on what has been, but it also exists in the moment where all its potentialities are ready to be triggered, moving toward possibilities that may or may not come to be. Spatially, part of the context in which identity is based is the physical environment of a person or people.

It is, therefore, incumbent upon a Druid to know and understand the places that are of importance both to the identity of Druids and the people amongst whom they live. Moreover, just as history should be passed on, so, too, should place. It cannot be frozen, but it can be cherished and passed on in a healthier condition than when it came in to present care.

The idea that we cannot own the land, the flora and the fauna, but that we hold it in trust for the common good of present and future generations is not a new one. It was central to the thinking of ancestral Celts and it helped shape the structure of their society. This sensibility of place does have an obverse side, however, in that there is a very real sense in which Druids believe we belong to the land. This sense of place lies partly in emotional attachment. As with history or memory, emotion gives vitality to what would otherwise be a recognition of biogeographical facts. But beyond that lies the belief that, in common with all things, we are born of the earth. Many people profess this in a vague whole-earth sense, but for Druids we are all born of specific mothers as well and this finds resonance in attachment to a specific place.

In this day and age, when most people in Western society are born and live in an urban environment, often leading itinerant lives, it can be difficult to understand the relevance of place to our way of life. We have to remember, however, that we have millions of years of evolution behind us as a pastoral species. This is built into our being at all levels. We are, genetically, physically, emotionally, and spiritually, inhabitants of a wilderness and pastoral landscape. Urbanization is a recent cultural innovation that has slowly gathered pace in the last five thousand years. It is only in the last two hundred years, however, that urban existence (with its increasing levels of itinerancy) has become a norm.

Loss of sense of place is not an inevitable consequence of urban living. To retain that awareness simply involves delving a little deeper. Anyone who is prepared to investigate an urban environment will soon find that the houses, shops, and factories are a thin veneer over a landscape as fascinating as any rural scene. Sadly, people are all too often unable to see beyond the built environment – important as that is. Perhaps if they were able to appreciate the landscape beneath, then the structures they place upon it would be more sensitive – constituting a better place in which to live.

Of course, there will always be those whose roots seem to be in some place other than the one in which they were born or presently live. Not all attachments are evident or easy to discover. Some people may feel rootless all their lives, as it is the travelling that they find important. Others may discover the place and though they may never get the chance to move and settle there, simply knowing it exists can be a source of great strength in their lives.

This awakening to a sense of place may be serendipitous, or it may come as the result of a spiritual and geographical search. To all who know it, however, there is always a sense of being at or returning to one's home – a place where one belongs, where there is always a seat at the hearth, where one's inner being is perfectly reflected in the landscape without.

There are wider implications in all this because knowing and understanding place carries with it a deeper understanding of the natural world as a whole – of how people stand in relation to it, of how the actions of humanity are slowly but surely destroying the strands of the web of life that support it. Druids believe that we cannot know this and do nothing about it. If people hold the land to be precious and sacred, if they accept their unity with the land, then they must surely work to protect and to heal it.

To talk about preserving, knowing, understanding, and becoming emotionally involved with the temporal and physical dimensions of Celtic sensibilities is all very well, but it is important to recognize that this is no game, no hobby, no weekend pastime, and no mere academic interest. The Druid Way is a living tradition that requires more than just knowledge or occasional flirtations with an ideal in order to express its existence. Indeed, one of the important things about the Celtic metaphysic was that those who held it refused to indulge in a sterile analytical, empirical, materialistic approach to life. Druids, for example, may have been the intellectual class of their society, but much of their learning, their wisdom, the genealogies they guarded, and the laws they made and kept were expressed in poetry and song. The Celts were – and still are – renowned for their artistry and their exuberance. Life was not a spectator sport. It was for living.

The Druid Way, then and now, is a constant celebration of life in all things. This celebration is most obvious in distinctive forms such as artwork, craftwork, music, and the like. Yet it runs much more deeply than that. For a Druid, there is life in all things because all things are one. This means that *all* the actions of a Druid's life are a celebration. This may seem extreme to some, but it derives directly from that recognition of the ultimate unity of all things. Nor is it enough to say that it is so. Druids are conscious of all they do and all they think, and of how their actions and thoughts affect everything else, including, as we have already implied, the natural environment. Druids are aware that they must act with responsibility in all that they do and think, in all that they are.

Celebration can be, and often is, expressed in spontaneous eruptions of emotion. Dancing, singing, and many of the shared joys of laughter and conversation are examples. It is, however, equally possible to celebrate life in a measured and calm way over a prolonged period. After all, organic gardening is a perfectly valid way to celebrate one's sense of union with the natural world.

There are also, of course, many other ways to celebrate. Those that are chosen, along with many other aspects of the Druid Way, are a matter of tradition. Tradition, however, is a term that is often misused in order to give a stamp of authority to a thing or activity that does not rightly deserve it. Something is not right because it is traditional – it is traditional because it continues to be right. Both continuity and rightness are the keys because in its essence a tradition is a handing on, an entrustment, a teaching, not of facts or events, but of a way of doing things – a right way of doing right things. It is clear, from a moment's thought, that this relates to the spirit rather than the letter. If people were to stick rigidly to a practice simply because that is how it has always been done, then there would never be any innovation, never be any chance to consider whether it was still appropriate – or desirable. Without change, things stagnate and become irrelevant. Sometimes they become poisonous cankers.

We cannot, therefore, just repeat what has gone on in the past simply because it has gone on in the past. To hand on a way of doing things from generation to generation requires that what is being passed on is worthy, right, and relevant. In other words, it must live and grow, adapt to the times. And when it is time for it to depart, it must be allowed to go with grace.

Until that time, what is passed on must also retain its identity, otherwise it mutates into something else and the tradition dies prematurely. To achieve this, a profound understanding of the Druid Way by adherents is considered essential. Not only does this ensure continuity at a deep level, it provides those who practise within the tradition the courage to initiate change where it is relevant and necessary. That is how the Druids of today are different from their ancestors whilst continuing a recognizable tradition. Certain aspects of Druidic practice have changed to remain in concord with present circumstances. However, the essence and the dynamic are the same – a tradition kept alive and handed down through the centuries.

This tradition derives from the teachings of the Druids and the metaphysic of the Celtic peoples. They considered the universe to be a spiritual entity in which all forms of life are sacred, each being, each aspect, each feature invested with a spark of the sacred. In accepting this and in accepting the fact that human life, though divine, is not special, the Celts did not try to master the universe or impose their will on others – spiritually, philosophically, or materially. What they sought was an inner illumination that would light the way to an ever-growing spiritual awareness in the outer world.

Much of the guidance for this path is to be found in the teachings of Druids past and present. There is, of course, no accepted canon. There is not even an agreed corpus of literature, although certain texts (ancient and modern) will be found on the bookshelves of most Druids. Here, once again, it is the truth that is sought. It is the task of each Druid to seek out the truth, to assimilate what is learned, and to test it in practice. That which stands the test of time tends to be preserved.

In order to do this properly, Druids have to give voice to their thoughts, just as they have to listen and respond to the voice of others. Giving voice is not restricted to speech, for Druids can and do express themselves in many ways. The dialogue that ensues works at many levels, but always with the same enlightening aim. This means that there is no special licence for Druids to do and say whatever they please. They believe they have a right to express themselves freely, but they also believe that with the right to free expression there goes an integral and reciprocal responsibility to express only what is right and true.

Much that passes for right expression in the world is badly tainted. In their desire to shine brighter than others, in their desire to be different, in their desire to impress, people neglect truth. It takes second place to ego. Some fall under the spell of others and speak with a voice that is not their own. Much of this sort of thing has become the norm in our media-rich world. It is easy to feel insignificant, especially where an adherence to truth is concerned. However, all this derives from a morbid desire to cut one's self off from the rest of life, as if it were somehow possible to survive without the sustenance that others provide.

The Celtic understanding of the world included a strong sense of identity with the tribe, the people. Nor was this anthropocentric, for the tribe was rooted deeply in the soil of the place it inhabited, and its being was often symbolized by the adoption of an animal totem. Being part of a tribe does not mean subsuming one's person in some slavish allegiance. Personal identity derives not from the self, but from everything around us. We are a node, a nexus, a unique point through which all about us flows. That unique point is what identifies us as distinct entities, but it cannot exist in isolation. If we cut ourselves off from all that makes us what we are, we become nothing. This is a notion that many find difficult to comprehend. We have been brought up in a society that venerates the individual. The great and glittering prize of recognition – not to mention fame – is a hypnotic poison.

Fame for fame's sake, and cults of the celebrity, are some of the more obvious symptoms of a spiritually empty life. The pursuit of fame is one of the drugs that keeps our dying society alive just a little longer.

Within Celtic society and within current Druidic practice, the idea is to be straight and true. If what one did made one's name known, it was incidental to all else. The voice of the Druid is considered a conduit for the truth. Further, the voice in the outer world is mirrored by the voice within the inner world. Every word, every form of expression has power. We all know this in its crudest form. Words *can* hurt, music *can* inspire, and pictures *can* be thought provoking. But the words used in this world to hurt someone else do nothing but hurt the one who spoke them in the inner worlds. Words used to heal strengthen the healer.

All expressions, be they made concrete or simply held in the potential of one's thoughts, are reflected in this fashion. As the Druid works and matures, all expressions work within as much as without. Within, that expression takes different forms, is vastly more refined, yet it still reflects in the outer world. But there, on the inner planes within the spiritual dimension, are sacred words, forms of expression that contain great power. These are words that reach deeply into the mysterious heart of the universe where they resonate and ignite the great light of truth. It is a long work of many lifetimes, the heart of the Bard's mystery, learning and understanding – knowing the word, knowing the voice or other form that will carry the word.

As with other aspects of the Druid Way, the learning must be put to use, must serve, if it is to be truly part of the Way. That is why it is a Way. Not just a road to be travelled, but also a method of travelling. It is a method to be shared, a Way on which to bring others. It is here that the power of the word is best put to service, opening the Way to others.

None of this is worth anything without an absolute commitment to the central tenet of the Druid Way – truth. For some, truth is a harsh light to face, but life cannot be lived properly without it. Be this personal or communal, the truth is the only real measure of how we live our lives, of how right and good our part in the world has been.

Truth can be taught by many teachers. Of all that Druids do and Druids are, it is their connection with trees that is best known and least understood by those who are not Druid. Even in this ecology conscious age, many still do not understand or value trees quite as they should. The ecologist and the biologist well understand their vital place in the life of the land, but only those who have depended upon trees to provide them with food and shelter know of their life and wisdom. Druids contend that if we would but slow down and learn to listen, we could learn much from trees, just as we could learn a great deal from the rest of the natural world. It is not an easy task. Trees live at a different pace. One or two great and ancient yews have been alive for thousands of years, first shooting up from the earth in the Late Neolithic, long before there were Druids, long before there were even stone circles.

It is not just trees from which Druids learn. They observe and listen to all the life with which we share this planet. Through this, they come to appreciate our place in the web and understand the world. This understanding is one not just of seeing what is, but also of feeling what is. The better we know the world, the more we enter into it, and the more we develop a fellow feeling for all other forms of life. Such compassion, they believe, is essential if we are to see the balance that must be restored, the healing that must be done.

Much of the deeper healing and the restoration of a balanced metaphysic can be derived from a wisdom that has been available to us since human beings first became self-aware. By far the greatest proportion of that wisdom is a legacy from our ancestors. To understand it fully, to get the best of it, Druids learn how to converse with those who have gone before. The most obvious ways of doing this is through conversation with their elders, the reading of books and documents, and the study of folkways. However, there are other ways to understanding.

To converse with the ancestors is to be aware of the cycles of life and death and the mysteries that attend those cycles: awareness and acceptance. To accept that we will all die, that the ones we love will be taken from us, is to be set free of the fear that many feel. Many who profess a belief in some form of afterlife seem unable to accept the fact that death is a reality of life. It is one of the most difficult things we must all face.

Acceptance and the abeyance of fear do not mean that we do not and should not mourn loss. When the emotional ties that bind us to others are severed in any way, it is always painful. True mourning is part of the healing process that restores emotional balance. However, those who have gone have a journey to make, as do those of us who remain, and those journeys cannot be conducted properly if we are held back by ties in a world to which we do not belong. We can accept our own pain, but we should also celebrate the life that has passed and be happy that those we have lost are in a far better place.

By removing the obsession with a particular point on a particular cycle of our lives, we loosen the grip that time has been allowed to place upon us. This, in turn, weakens the importance that is given to a linear view of events. In doing this, we allow our intuitive faculties to emerge from the diminished shadows of analytical intellect and take their rightful place as a method of apprehending the world.

Once we come to acknowledge our existence as cyclical, once we are free of the notion of time as linear, and once we give free rein to our intuitive faculties, we can open the doors of time. Time becomes something that we can explore. The past, the future, and the present all become open to us in ways that are otherwise hard to imagine.

Travelling freely in time does not automatically endow us with infallible hindsight or foresight. There are many futures, just as there are many pasts. The present in which we live is where they all meet. The key lesson to learn is that our visions of the past and of the future are what guide our present actions. Moreover, it is our present actions that are the most important, for it is those that validate the past as we see it and will bring about the future that is consequent upon them.

Druids see this as vital. The future is not a foregone conclusion, a fixed point to which we are bound. That would make a nonsense of the idea of free will. It would also make a nonsense of the idea that we are responsible for our actions. The future is, in fact, an ever-changing entity that is rooted in the past and given form by the present.

All that has just been described, the paths of the Bard and the Vate, provides the foundation for the path of the Druid. Another turn of the circle comes. The first turn is that in which all is absorbed, often portrayed as a journey into the labyrinth. The second is that in which what is absorbed is fixed into form – the facing of the mysteries in the heart of the maze. Finally, there is the return from the centre to face outward, radiating into the world all that has been learned.

Before giving out, however, Druids must be certain of their own authority. This is wide reaching in many respects, for not only must the Druid know that they are ready for this role, they must also radiate that authority to others. It is a peculiarly difficult stage for many Druids to reach, not because they are lacking in knowledge and understanding, but because attaining a high level of knowledge and understanding makes one realize how little one really knows. This is just one more turn of the circle, the teacher realizing they are but the humblest of pupils.

Very often, the role of Druid is one that circumstance thrusts upon the person. Just as the novice finds a teacher when the time is right, the teacher finds a novice when it becomes expedient. Indeed, any person who seeks the role of teacher is unlikely to be ready for the task. When it does come, it is the beginning for the teacher as well as for the pupil.

One area where authority is important, especially in the sense of strength, is in conducting ritual and ceremonial. These are the areas where all the worlds touch, inner and outer, public and private. Many forces come into play and are focused on a particular place at a particular time. Although the main concern is with right working with the souls and spirits of those involved, other important issues are involved. Not least of these is the fact that ceremonial occasions are those where the Druid Way is most likely to be exposed to the public eye. What people see of the Way at these moments is of great importance.

This is not a matter of image, at least, not in the sense beloved of politicians – all surface and no substance. Nor is it a matter of ego. Yet what people see of the Way, and the conduct of those who profess to follow it, are of great importance. The Druid Way is a serious and vital undertaking. Those who make it look ridiculous, those who cannot control themselves or others, those who have neither the strength nor the dignity to conduct themselves well, bring ridicule on the Way and its followers. This in turn damages the prospects of those whose search has led them in the direction of the Way. They may well be put off by what they see and possibly lost in this lifetime to a proper understanding of the world.

Control is a contentious issue. The Druid Way is not about having power over others. It is, however, about taking responsibility both as an individual and collectively. It is also about exercising discipline. Learning and practice go hand in hand throughout one's life, but the more adept one becomes, the greater the emphasis that must be placed on living what one has learned.

By the time one has walked the Druid path, the transmutation of the spirit is such that one has become a new person whose every thought and action is guided by the metaphysic of the Druid Way. This requires great discipline, especially in the face of so much alluring opposition from the prevailing worldview. As a Druid, one has to govern one's life in accordance with a law derived from one's own view of the world. No one else's will do. A Druid has to govern the life of others as well, giving advice to and counselling those who are in the early stages of following the Way. The Druid is no longer the novice, sheltered from the world by guides and teachers, but has in turn become a guide, a teacher, and taken on the task of bringing others into service.

Even from this partial elucidation, it is clear that the Druid Way has distinct dimensions. Where religion is seen as having six essential dimensions, the Druid Way consists in nine.

The first of these is what might be termed the tribal dimension. It encompasses the languages, history, traditions, myths, wisdom, and the geography of the people who follow the Druid Way, both past and present. In essence, it is everything that has to do with the identity of the tribe, as well as its place in and relation to both time and space.

Then there is the dimension of craft. The term is used in its broadest sense, running from what we now call the arts (decorative and performing) through to handicrafts, domestic arts, agriculture, gardening, and, of course, all other manifest forms of magic.[63] All of these are outward, physical manifestations of the metaphysical stance that informs every nuance of what Druids do.

The next dimension is that of healing, the restoring of balance. Fundamental to this is an understanding of the world and all that is in it, on both material and spiritual levels; of the ways in which the world and all who live there come to be damaged; and of the many ways in which each Druid can best use their own skills to aid in their renewal. Although Druids will treat the symptoms as and when the need arises, their major work is in re-balancing the very basics of being – healing the battered soul of the world.

There is also a metaphysical dimension, which is concerned primarily with the mysteries of and reasons for being, of life and death and rebirth, of the cycles in all our lives. It is also that aspect of the Way concerned with the understanding and wisdom that can be distilled from contact with our ancestors and with the Otherworld. It is exploration in this dimension that lays open the ways in which Druids see the world, the foundation of all they are and do.

Complementing the metaphysical dimension, which draws a great deal (although not exclusively) on the past, is the dimension of seeing. Many assume that seers are simply concerned with the future, but that is only part of their role. They also look into the present, which is no less obscure to us than the future might be. When the developed forces of the intuition are allowed to range across the wheel of time, nothing is irrelevant to the place and the time that is the now.

With all that goes on around them, there are times when Druids need to stand back and make formal and measured communion. It is the dimension of ritual that defines this. This dimension does more than enfold the major rituals and ceremonies – the rites of passage and the eightfold cycle that celebrates the turning of the year – it encompasses also the many private rituals and ceremonies, exercises, prayers, meditations, teachings, and disciplines involved in becoming and being Druid.

Druids are intimately involved with the world about them and a further dimension to the Druid Way is that is concerned with natural philosophy. This is the search for an understanding of the ways and workings of the world of which we are all a part; a search for an understanding of the universe by actually studying the universe itself.

The eighth dimension is that of teaching. Although this refers to the strict sense of teaching the Way to others, guiding them to and through the forest of the spirit, it does have a wider application. Druids engage in a constant dialogue with the world. They listen, they respond. It is part of the giving back. Often, that teaching is accomplished by example, by living in a way that might inspire others to follow suit.

Finally, there is the dimension of service, the very heart of the Druid Way. The goal of a Druid is not to better the self. All Druids do that as a matter of course, but as a means to an end rather than as an end in itself. To be Druid is to work to make the world a better place for all. To be Druid is to celebrate and venerate existence. To be Druid is to become an adept so that one can better serve.

None of these dimensions exists as a separate entity. They are presented here as distinct facets of the Druid Way for the purpose of this discussion; this is a description from a specific perspective. And even in this context, they must be seen as overlapping, intertwining aspects that complement one another. In reality, they are a unity. All is in each and each is in all. This approach has been taken as a device for comparing these dimensions with those of religion outlined earlier. And in so doing, it is easy to see that there are correspondences, both direct and indirect. All of the dimensions of religion are to be found within the dimensions of the Druid Way even though none of the correspondences is exact.

To take two examples, neither healing nor natural philosophy seems to have a mainstream function within religion as defined above. That may explain why some religions have so assiduously turned their backs on the material world and considered it a loathsome burden from which we must escape. Their concern has been almost exclusively with the next life of human beings, and in achieving that, they have been prepared to sanction the neglect or destruction of the rest of creation. However, to do this is to deny the unmistakable connection of humanity with the natural world, not to mention its place or purpose within it.

Religion also lacks a dimension of service in the Druidic sense. True, there are aspects of service within the social and ethical dimensions of religion, but these are tied in with the doctrinal aspects, which state that right social and ethical behaviour are not only prerequisites of right religious behaviour, but also the way to get your reward in the afterlife. For the Druid, however, service does not accrete to or derive from other aspects of the Druid Way. It is not there because of doctrinal demands or to gain reward. Rather, service is the reason for the Way's existence. Service *is* the Druid Way. The Druid Way *is* service.

Conversely, the Druid Way has no apparent dimension of religious experience – which sits at the heart of religion. That is because the Druid Way is not a system that has evolved from such experience merely to codify it. This is not to deny an element of mystical and religious experience to the Druid Way. It is there in abundance. It is simply that the Druid Way has evolved from a broader base of experience.

To be Druid is to make a commitment to the whole world both spiritually and materially. This derives from the understanding that all is one and that the actions of people interrelate with and affect the rest of the world at all levels of being. It also derives from a belief that we are endowed with free will and its concomitant responsibilities. The Druid Way is, therefore, derived not from a set of special experiences, but from all experience interpreted through the medium of the Celtic metaphysic, which sees the whole world as imbued with spirit.

We have now moved a step closer to resolving the original question. From the above we can see that there is an extremely close relationship between the Druid Way and religion. In many respects, they are identical. There is not enough yet, however, to answer the question unequivocally. To do that, there is one further point that must be touched on as it will help to clarify the position and resolve the issue.

In 1913, the Swedish scholar Nathan Söderblom noted a distinction that is embraced by most of the world's religions – in practice, if not in doctrine. He wrote: 'Holiness is the great word of religion; it is even more essential than the notion of God. *Real* religion may exist without a definitive concept of divinity, but there is no real religion without a distinction between holy and profane.'[64] [Italics mine.]

Two words here need our consideration for they both have a number of meanings that are relevant: 'holy' and 'profane'. 'Holy' means 'sacred, pertaining to deity, held in religious awe, saintly, free from sin, pious, connected with religion'. 'Profane' means 'showing contempt for sacred things or persons, blasphemous; not concerned with sacred matters, secular; not initiated, ignorant of sacred things; wicked'. In the context of the discussion that has gone before, and juxtaposed as they are, 'holy' is used to mean 'sacred' and 'profane' is used to mean 'secular'.

Given that a Druid accepts both the unity of all things and a spiritual dimension to existence, the above distinction means that the Druid Way is not a *real* religion. It cannot be. To be sacred is to be endowed with spirit. To the Druid, all things are endowed with spirit. For them, there is no profane aspect to the universe.

The thoughts and actions of human beings are another matter for they are, in the main, inventions – re-arrangements of already ordered things. Those re-arrangements can work in concord with the world, or they can be in discord. Our freedom of will allows this. By becoming a Druid, a person enters into a particular relationship with the world, one that works to bring harmony, one that accepts the sacred in all things, one that exists to create rather than invent.

So, just where does that leave us – apart from with a large number of new questions? Is the Druid Way a religion? In the end, it all hinges on whether we accept the distinction made by Nathan Söderblom, who was writing from the perspective of the Abrahamic tradition. Paganism makes no such distinction. Moreover, there is no reason why it should accept or be bound by definitions made from the perspective of other religious traditions. If the distinction between sacred and secular is one that is not accepted, then the Druid Way is a religion. If it is believed possible to divide the world between the sacred and the profane, then the Druid Way is not a religion. That is, it is not a *real* religion. Of course, if the Druid Way as described above is not a religion, then the question has to be asked – what is it?

This is a major area of debate amongst Druids. A large number do not think of the Druid Way as a religion, preferring terms such as 'spiritual tradition', 'spiritual path', or 'mystery tradition'. This reluctance to identify with other religions is understandable and is common to many pagans. The religious beliefs of ancestral Celts were not constituted into a formal religion as we now think of it and the Druid Way is much the same. Some Druids even refrain from using 'spiritual' or 'mystery' and think in terms of the Druid Way as a philosophy. For the most part, however, this is more a matter of terminology than one of substance.

That may not be the definitive answer to the question that was expected, but that does not invalidate the exercise. Indeed, it is not every question that has an answer. However necessary philosophical proof may be in some areas, it cannot ever be sufficient to define religion or prove the existence of deity. After all, one of the basic tenets of all religion is acceptance – the need to accept the validity of our experiences and accept that others can and do share those experiences in some form or other. It means we have to take some things on trust.

Accepting things on trust is not, of course, the same as acquiescing. Accepting that there are bad things in the world does not mean we must not seek to eliminate them. Accepting the divine does not mean that we should not enquire after it in order to achieve a deeper understanding. Indeed, as far as a Druid is concerned, the only things that go unquestioned are the importance of service and the central role of truth in our existence.

7

TEACHINGS

Teachings

All religions have doctrine – a set of teachings from which are derived ethical principles and other such propositions about the particular religion or the world in general. In some cases, these are transcriptions of the words of deity as revealed through the medium of a messenger or prophet. In others, they are the respected writings of renowned figures and sages within a given tradition. So it is, for example, that Christians have the Bible; Muslims have the Qur'an; and Taoists can read the writings of Chuang Chou or Lao Tzu.

Although the Druid Way certainly has teachings and a profoundly ethical stance, the source of its doctrine is not to be found in any corpus of specifically doctrinal writings. Anything that may have been taught in times past would not been written down. Nor were there, as far as we are aware, any other forms of specifically religious text. The reason is simple. Celtic religion was not separate from the rest of Celtic life. It *was* Celtic life. There was no charismatic person to whom Celtic pagan religion had been revealed. There were no prophets or preachers in the biblical sense. The pagan religion of the Celts had always been there, a fundamental aspect of life.

That being the case, it is reasonable to ask from where modern Druids derive their teachings and their ethical stance. The answer is that they have been reconstructed (and, indeed, are still being reconstructed) from sources held in common with ancestral Celts, as well as from writings that were made from the beginnings of the historical period onwards.

There are five main sources, supplemented by the historical and archaeological record. The first of these are the myths, wonder tales, poetry, and folklore of the Celtic people, which are sometimes collectively known as the Matter of Ireland and the Matter of Britain. Insofar as these paint an authentic picture of ancestral thought and practice,[65] they contain genuine fragments of the spiritual, religious, and ethical teachings of the forebears of modern Druids. In many cases, these fragments are embedded in the stories and can be gleaned from the actions and reactions of the characters. Were it not for this inadvertent teaching, much might have been lost.

The second source is the natural world. A precise definition of this is given below, but as a source of teaching, it is available now just as readily as it was in the past. Pagans throughout the world (and throughout time) hold much in common in how they see the world and their relationship with it. It is why Druids are now encouraged to become familiar with their natural heritage. This extends well beyond the confines of scientific natural history, for it is about working magically (in the sense already discussed) with the world, especially that part with which they are immediately connected.

The third source is the Celtic metaphysic. This has already been discussed. Its value as a source of teachings is twofold. In itself, it is the exemplar for right thought and behaviour. However, it also provides a key to understanding other sources. It is all very well studying the natural world or reading about Cúchulainn or Gwydion, but if these are not viewed from the correct perspective, it is not possible to tease out fully the motivations and meaning that are embedded within.

The fourth source is the collection of non-fictional writings that have come down to us, principally the law texts from both Ireland and Wales.[66] Although it is true that much of this material is to be found in texts that are less than a thousand years old, they derive from material that was originally at least twice that age. The Irish laws in particular, which are the oldest surviving purely Celtic system and one in which Druids are still mentioned, preserve in large part the pagan attitude to ethical matters.

The final source is the language of the Celts. Even today, when Celtic languages have been subject to alteration from outside pressures, word use, syntax, grammar, and vocabulary all provide clues as to how the Celts thought about the world and dealt with ethical matters. We have already looked briefly at how concepts of ownership are reflected in vocabulary. Technical terms and the way in which words are used also offer an insight into the way in which texts should be considered.

These five sources, in combination, provide a fertile ground from which the doctrine of modern Druids is gleaned. Yet it is clear that this is not doctrine as most religions would understand it, especially in ethical matters. There are no hard and fast rules about behaviour or ritual, for example, but this is because such rules are, largely, both unnecessary and inappropriate.

When people become Druid, it is usually out of a realization that they have already been Druid for some time. They have already developed a view of the world that is closely akin to the Celtic metaphysic and are living their lives in accord with it; they have a heightened awareness of the natural world; they have an openness to the spiritual aspect of life. All they lack is a formal framework through which this can be expressed.

Of the people who have a worldview similar to that of the Celts, not everyone is attracted by the pagan Celtic path – they may feel happier with other traditions; not all those who follow a Celtic path go as far as to call themselves Druid. The important point is that they have already chosen to live by certain codes of behaviour. They further choose to express this in a particular way. No one can be forced to adopt the Celt metaphysic; that would be to violate its basic precepts. It is why Druids do not evangelize (to borrow a term from another religion); and it is why Druids are reluctant to undertake formal teaching of the Way to anyone under the age of eighteen. They consider such things to be unethical.

For all that some of the doctrine of Druids may seem vague to others, their inner convictions are strong. Certainly, some of the teachings from which they are derived are clear and unequivocal. This is particularly so with the central and supreme concept of truth. From this, all else is derived – the convictions, for example, that one should live with honour and responsibility, that all life is sacred, that a Druid should serve, seek balance, and be respectful. There are, of course, other teachings, but they all stem from these. As with all religions, there are those who claim to be Druid but do not live by the precepts set out below. We should not, however, accept what a person claims to be. Rather, we should judge people on the way they conduct their lives, for no one can be Druid if they do not adhere to the truth.

TRUTH

As with many such abstract concepts, truth does not lend itself easily to anything like a comprehensive definition. And, as anyone who has studied philosophy knows, the more complex any attempt at a definition for truth, the less comprehensible it becomes and the farther it strays from reality or usefulness. Abstract as the concept of truth may be, it must be defined simply, and be in accord with the world, if it is to be of use. If it is not anchored in the reality of being and experience, if it cannot guide people and reflect what they are and know, then it fails at all levels.

Truth is sensitive to time and place. It is relative, dependent upon the metaphysic from within which it is being expressed. This is not to say that there are no universal aspects, but truth as we experience it is not absolute. This makes it both subjective and objective at one and the same time – a notion many of us have been taught to reject by the metaphysical orthodoxy of modern Western culture.

Several philosophical theories concerning truth have emerged in recent times. Correspondence theory, for example, which is widely held by some to represent a 'common-sense' view, asserts that a statement is true if it corresponds to a fact. This, of course, rests largely on our understanding of what constitutes a fact and ignores the circularity inherent in the theory — that most facts exist solely as statements. After all, even a simple statement like 'the sky is blue' is fraught with problems. If the sky is blue, then the statement is true. The whole thing, however, is self-referential. The blueness of a thing called sky rests far more in our perception and description of it than it does in any independent and objective factors.

Coherence theory was proposed in order to avoid this problem by internalizing it, making it self-referential. It asserts that statements are only partly true or false, to greater or lesser degree, as truth is essentially a system of wholeness in which the internal coherence of sets of propositions is the key factor. In other words, in a given set of statements, the more the statements relate to one another and logically support one another, the more they can be said to be true. Of course, as any student of logic will tell you, it is entirely possible to have a coherent and mutually supportive set of statements that bear no relation to anything we might consider to be the truth, let alone the real world.

There is also Pragmatic theory, which is an application of Utilitarianism. This asserts that the truth of a statement should be measured by the consequences of its declaration. The more fruitful the consequences, the truer the statement must have been. Such a theory operates in a moral vacuum and is devoid of justice and ethical considerations. It is increasingly the basis by which modern politics is conducted.

There are a number of other theories, but they tend to be variations on or combinations of the above. None of them is satisfactory, not least because they fail to relate to the everyday experience of people or connect with the lives they lead. They also, however, have a much more important failing. In these theories, and in accordance with what most of us think, truth as a concept is all too often connected solely with language.

In our literature-rich society, it has become far too easy to fall into the trap of assuming written and spoken words to be the sole arbiters of our fate and the fount of all things. All the theories mentioned above, and the many variations thereof, are essentially about language. Truth, however, cannot be limited to language. Indeed, language is just a small part of the realm of truth, for truth is to be found throughout the much wider world of our being. It applies to our actions, behaviour, thoughts, and to all the ways in which we live our lives and to all the places in which we live them.

In fact, it takes little enough thought to realize that language is particularly ill suited as a medium by which to express truth. Not only is it all too easy to use language to create plausible falsehoods, but it is also a medium that is capable of only limited expression of human experience. If we confine discussion and understanding of truth solely to language, then we restrict ourselves to a system that poorly reflects the world.

Language is essentially a medium that is linear. It is also two-valued (a word is used or it is not used; it is used correctly or it is used incorrectly). Furthermore, it is a medium over which the majority of people exercise limited command. Yet language is used to convey information about the world, which is multi-valued, non-linear, and saturated with information. Too much emphasis on language leads to people trying to make sense of reality through a means of expression that is inadequate in so many ways. It is akin to a single monochrome pencil sketch, made by someone who is not skilled at drawing, being used to represent the visual, aural, and emotional content of a full-colour motion picture. It can be done, but it is very far from adequate.

Unfortunately, for all the claims that we are becoming less literate, the emphasis on language has become inevitable in our culture. It has made itself so. Too great an emphasis on acquiring the skills of alphabet literacy at too early an age actually biases our thought processes, developing one side of the brain to the detriment of the other. This is not an irreversible process, but it is one that is little understood, and buried deeply away from casual enquiry. Much of the contemporary Western metaphysic is rooted in this bias.

That is why those who seek a new way of looking at the world often find it necessary to break away from the printed word, from kinetic visual media (itself based on the printed word and the linear narrative forms derived from language), even from other people. Walking barefoot and alone in the forest (literally and metaphorically) without the need to codify the experience for the benefit of others opens up a whole new perspective on the universe, one not distorted by words or the need to organize experience in a way that can be conveyed to others. The mystic apprehends truth, but the mystical experience is notoriously difficult to convey to others.

This should not be taken as an attack upon literacy. The alphabet and its analogues, along with reading and writing, are all marvellous, magical gifts. Literacy, however, should be seen in perspective and treated with greater respect for what it is as well as what it can and, more importantly, cannot do.

If we consider truth in a much wider context, it then becomes necessary to reconsider certain definitions. Truth itself has to apply to and derive from *all* things, and take on many extra dimensions that expand it from a narrow notion of the verity of language to one that applies to the rightness or fitness of all things, in whatever form they exist or are made manifest. This applies to spoken and written statements, certainly, but it also includes actions, constructs, thoughts, emotions, places, and ideas. Notions of falsehood must then take their shape from this.

Suggesting that truth is, in its widest context, something to do with the rightness or fitness of a thing is not simply plucking an idea out of thin air. It is based on the metaphysic of our Celtic ancestors, who held that all things are connected, part of a whole. To them, this was the natural order of things. Although they recognized the distinction between such things as agriculture, politics, social culture, spirit, art, craft, this world, the Otherworld, language, action, thought, ideas – or any other such concept – they did not separate them. Farming, for example, was just as much a matter of spirit and politics as it was of soil fertility, crop rotation, and good husbandry. Each aspect was a facet of the whole, each investing and illuminating the others with a complementary energy. It still is, no matter that we do not behave as if it were. Nor did our Celtic ancestors separate their actions, their being, and the rest of the universe although, again, they well understood the distinctions between them. Indeed, in understanding the distinctions they more clearly understood the fundamental connections.

At a superficial level, this may seem like Coherence theory writ large. It is not. There is an immense difference between truth residing in the coherence of sets of statements, which may all be falsehoods, and recognition that truth is a measure of the degree to which something is rightly integrated with the underlying unity of all things. If we take that unity to be implicit, then truth and reality are necessarily isomorphic. Indeed, in some Celtic languages, truth and reality are denoted by the same word. Yet it is not just a matter of identifying different aspects of the universe by referring to them with a single word. The fact is, these are not different aspects. We are dealing with one thing seen from different perspectives.

Many of the problems we face today, a Druid would contend, arise from our continual and frenzied seizing upon distinctions as we try to separate them out from unity.[67] But the distinctiveness of a thing does not lie in the thing itself. It lies in the way we choose to look at the world. A particular way of looking will highlight specific things. What we look at, however, is always the same. Underlying whatever we see, underlying that which distinguishes one thing from another, is the larger unity of which everything is an integral part. The facet of a jewel does not exist without the jewel. There is no thing in the universe that is separate. That, after all, would be a contradiction of terms.

Each facet of a jewel relies on the existence of all others for its own being and shape. Likewise, underlying all the diverse facets of the universe, and weaving them inextricably together, are the patterns and relationships that constitute what some call the natural order and others call the laws of nature. Understanding and working in concord with those patterns and relationships to achieve some particular right end is what Druids do. This is also, as we have seen, sometimes known as magic. It may now seem that I have strayed into something of a diversion, but that is not the case. Magic and truth not only have a great deal in common, but are also strongly connected. For both magic and truth are about understanding and working with those patterns and relationships that underlie and bind the many facets of the universe into a whole. Indeed, truth and magic might often be one and the same thing.

If we were to look for a distinction, what we would find would be two aspects of the underlying principle of the universe. Magic is the right working with that principle. Truth is the right measure of that principle. That is, magic is when we understand the rightness or fitness of a word, of an action, of behaviour, of the way we live, and then use that understanding to achieve some right desired end. Truth is the degree to which the word, the action, the behaviour, the way we live is in accord with the underlying patterns of the universe. The distinction is subtle; it is between the inherent property of a thing and its potential to bring about some other thing.

Of course, it is all well and good talking about the universe and the natural order that lies beneath it, but it is important to know just what is meant by the phrase 'natural order'. More specifically, we need to be clear about what is meant by the word 'nature', especially when it is used in conjunction with the activities of humankind, for it is the human realm that concerns us most in this particular discussion. It is also worth bearing in mind that 'universe' and 'world' are interchangeable, both terms meaning the totality of things.

We certainly cannot use the term 'nature' to mean 'the world as it would be if untainted by outside influence' because the world is, by definition, everything. There can be no outside influence. Nor can we satisfactorily put it in opposition to something we might call human activity because no matter how harsh that activity might be, it is the product of a species that is part of nature.

What we need is a borderline that exists somewhere within the field of human activity. Though part of nature, we are no longer wholly bound by the natural order. What is more, it is apparent even from a casual study of the world, that some, if not many, of the things people do are actually causing the breakdown of the natural order. We can and have caused breakdowns in the natural order without forethought and without intention. The first cities turned the fertile areas around them to desert. Equally, many people have, by design, left no material footprint behind them to spoil what they temporarily inhabited.

It would be best, therefore, to draw the borderline we seek between those things we do by instinct and those that we do by choice. The reason for this is simple. We cannot alter, from one day to the next, what we do by instinct. Those are things that arise from an evolved behaviour, from an unconscious following of what has been bequeathed us by the natural order. We are not, however, creatures of instinct alone.

Many of our instinctive behaviours have been traded over the millennia for learned behaviours. Through these, we have been endowed with free will. Our learned behaviours are something over which we *do* have control – we can choose the degree to which we exercise them, we can choose between them, we can choose not to use them at all. But as well as choosing, as well as having a much wider scope than mere instinct would allow, we also have a consciousness of the world and of what we do in it – which means we are fully aware of the consequences of what we do or choose not to do. That combination of control and awareness means that the consequences of our actions are our responsibility and ours alone.

What we do by conscious and informed choice, be that in concord with nature and the natural order or not, results in what will be referred to hereafter as the World.[68] It is that which is distinct from nature and the natural order. It is that over which we have control. It is that alone for which we have to answer.

Most of the planet today might be called the World, as the direct and indirect marks of humanity are to be seen and felt almost everywhere. Ever since the first tools were fashioned around the first campfire, the Land, Sea, and even the Sky, have all been moulded to and by the uses of humanity. This is a process that has continued for several million years.

As recently as two thousand years ago, however, the World had barely had an impact on the planet, most of which was still wilderness. Having knowledge of wilderness as something in its own right, and easily distinguished from and untouched by the areas altered and cultivated by the hands of humans, was far easier than it is today. It was more or less possible to use the word 'natural' in the sense of 'untouched by humanity' and compare that with the World as made or altered by humans. It was in that climate that the Celtic metaphysic and the teachings of the Druids first found expression.

There was another important difference in the past. Not only was the World of humanity much smaller and more easily defined than it is today, but also the interface between the World and the rest of the universe was a soft, amorphous thing decided upon by humanity and the universe in equal measure. This was partly because human beings were not in a position to wreak mass havoc upon the universe, but it was also because they would have had no desire to do so. They had learned from, understood, and worked with the universe to whatever degree they were able. In so doing, they had come to know what the universe was. They respected it, understood the wisdom inherent in it, and knew its importance as a unified entity. Without its support, they knew, we all perish.

Today, now that the World has expanded to engulf the planet, the interface between World and universe has become sharply defined. That sharpness takes no account of the universe. It is a brutal and arbitrary thing, its position decided upon solely by human beings — most of whom would not even know the voice of the universe if they heard it, let alone understood what it has to say.

The interface between the World and the universe is far more complex, however, than most people realize. This interface is not a barrier, but the sum of those things that distinguish what is the World from what is not the World. It is, in itself, a living organism that requires careful oversight and sensitive management. It is a conversation between interpenetrating entities in which each must listen carefully and take into account the needs of the other if one is not to be destroyed.

We have grown away from the instinctive behaviour that originally governed this conversation. We have grown away from an understanding of our place as part of the whole and thus of our fundamental level of concord with the rest of creation. Deprived of the instinct to work in concert with the universe, we no longer manage our place in the universe. We have turned our backs on it; we pretend it does not exist. Moreover, where we cannot ignore it, we pretend it is of no importance. Not only is this a gross insult to the universe, it is self-destructive in the extreme. What we have turned our backs on is the larger part of our own being. And in so doing we have increased the level of our ignorance of all things.

It is an ever-increasing problem. Management of our place, knowing the relationship, understanding the interface, requires of us all a profound understanding not only of the workings of the World, but also of the universe – and not just an analytic understanding of the material parts of existence. That is as partial an approach as denying our connection to the natural order.

All this is not to argue that the World is necessarily a bad thing. Many would argue that it is, but that it need not be so. What we are as creatures makes our position in the universe inevitable. The form and effects of that position, however, are *not* inevitable. We could have all the genuine benefits of the World — shared equally with all — without the current drawbacks and the dangers. That can only be achieved, however, through a radical change in the way we view the World.

Ancestral Druids understood this. They were lovers of wisdom, judges of rightness, seekers out of truth, and were constantly measuring and assessing the World. This is a task faced by Druids today as well — in a world more complicated than our ancestors could have imagined. Which means that those who follow the Druid Way must know and understand the universe and the patterns and relationships on which it is based. It also means they must know and understand the workings of the World. They cannot turn their backs on it and follow their own fantasies.

To know and to understand what is about us and within us and that of which we are a part, Druids have to shed many notions about themselves and the World — notions bequeathed by centuries of an ever-evolving Western metaphysic that is based on a notion of the supremacy of analytical materialism. It is a metaphysic that embraces what we have made of the World, considering it to be inevitable. It is a metaphysic that shuns the universe, imagining it to be a hostile place.

The universe is not hostile, however, any more than it is cold or savage. The World is neither predetermined nor necessarily a place of conflict. These ideas, so beloved of the Darwinists and their predecessors, have long since been shown to be false. Savagery is an attribute solely of those who can choose their behaviour. Only humanity has that choice. The same is so with good and evil. These are only part of the natural order in that they are inherent in the free will possessed of human beings. They are not imposed upon us by outside forces but are behaviours that we choose – which makes them an integral part of the World. They are manifestations of our rational existence and of our intentions – which makes them our responsibility and ours alone.

The universe, by its very nature, cannot be savage any more than it can be good or evil, competitive or co-operative. It is true that the universe is a movement toward unity and that many of its facets do work in concord toward complex, climax forms, but this is inherent in the laws of nature. It is what the universe is, not what it has chosen or chooses to be, not what it has had imposed upon it from without.

SERVICE

Of course, the solution to our problems does not lie simply in gaining knowledge of the universe, in discovering the underlying patterns, and divining the truth. Knowing and understanding simply provide the raw material with which to work. Whereas the universe *is*, the World is distinguishable from it by the fact that it needs consciously chosen actions to keep it maintained. Druids believe, therefore, that they must use the knowledge and the understanding they have to bring about change and to restore balance. There are many paths to knowledge and understanding. There are just as many ways of working with that gift and making change. After all, knowing and understanding plants, soil, weather patterns, and the like give a person the ability to garden. Having the knowledge, however, does not make a thing so.

Knowledge has to be applied – and it has to be applied in right fashion. Indeed, knowledge and understanding are quite meaningless unless they *are* applied. This can be interpreted in two ways. On the one hand, it could be argued that there can be no such thing as purely abstract knowledge. All knowing is simply a facet of practice, just as all practice is a facet of knowing. Yet, on the other hand, even if it could be proved that there was such a thing as purely abstract knowledge, one is forced to ask what its purpose might be, what meaning it could possibly have.

There are also layers and directions to the practical application of the knowledge. Just as there are gardens that give joy and maintain life in great abundance, so there are also gardens that poison and destroy – gardens maintained by the use of genetically engineered plants, fed with chemical mixes, and regularly doused with toxins. For all that knowing and understanding the universe enables Druids to work with its principles, for all that they actually go out and work for change, it is their values that determine in what *way* they should work as well as the sort of changes to which they should aspire.

Broadly speaking, the values in question are concerned with the restoration and maintenance of order. This is not some reactionary stance. A true understanding of the universe will show that the one constant is change. Nothing is ever still; nothing remains fixed – no matter how things may appear to us in each of our short spans of cognizance. Restoring and maintaining order means understanding the ever-evolving principles that form the universe and ensuring that everything we do adheres to and maintains these principles. Not in some ill-defined esoteric sense, however, because, for all that their work is largely spiritual, Druids are rooted firmly in material existence and in the World. Their heads may be in the clouds, but their feet are set deep within the earth.

The role of a Druid is to come to know what is truth and consequently to work to ensure that the World is moved forward increasingly in accordance with it. Truth is the ultimate standard to which the Druid aspires. The World is their work. That work, at whatever level it is done, is service. Truth and service, therefore, are inextricably linked – one the active mode of the other. Moreover, if they are so linked, if everything a Druid does is directed toward ascertaining and proclaiming the truth, then the Druid Way *is* service.

For ancestral Druids, service was ultimately concerned with maintaining an existing balance – materially, socially, and spiritually. Celtic society was highly developed in all areas. Whilst it was not perfect, it was more highly attuned and far more just than most societies and cultures today. The work of Druids was about defining boundaries, listening to the voice of the universe, and guiding others. In this work, they used the knowledge, understanding, and wisdom gained from their many years of rigorous training.

Today, service has a different emphasis. It is about restoring the balance that once existed but has now been all but destroyed by centuries of abuse – it is about showing that there are boundaries, showing that the universe has a voice that must be heard, showing that there are better paths to tread. And although the tasks of Druids today may differ from those of ancestral Druids in emphasis and perspective, the measure is the same. Truth.

Druids acknowledge that absolute truth is well beyond our comprehension. We might glimpse its form in and through particular instances of truth because they are examples of the absolute at work. These examples reveal a pattern that exists just beyond our normal perceptual level – a pattern that is the essence of mystical experience. It is tantalizingly out of everyday reach, yet the glimpses are sufficient for Druids to work with it and understand it at an intuitive level.

Seeking out the truth, be it reaching for the absolute or working with particular instances, enables the Druid to right action. Right action has two essential elements. To begin with, it must be in accord with natural law. The means to an end must be in harmony with the end, otherwise the enterprise fails before it begins. The other essential element of right action is that the end must not be personal. Right action might benefit those who undertake it, but that must not be the goal – otherwise it is not right action. If you grow vegetables organically, you should do it because it is in concord with the universe and beneficial to wildlife. You still get tasty and wholesome vegetables. The difference is that the means by which you achieve that end are in harmony with natural law and increase the degree to which unity is achieved. Insofar as Druids have a concept of good and evil, it is to be found in this: good is that which most accords with truth; evil is that which least accords with truth.[69]

This is a difficult concept to grasp in a society given over to a superficial adulation of the individual and in which personal responsibility is effectively abrogated. For the Druid, service is selfless. If not, it is not service. Druids are selfless. If not, they are not Druids. What they are and what they do is detached, sacrificial (an action which makes sacred), and non-violent. Through the detached vision of service, the Druid is enabled to see truth (of all kinds) much more clearly.

The tribal life of ancestral Celtic peoples made the task easier. Service was part of everyday life for everyone. When the welfare of the group is as important as – if not more so because it supports – the welfare of the individual, working and providing for others is quite natural. Right action is normal, everyday practice. This is especially so in a culture with a metaphysic that regards the universe as cyclic rather than linear. In a cyclic system, 'means' and 'ends' become intimately connected – the nature (the how, the why, *and* the what) of one residing in the nature of the other. Our own linear, dualistic thinking has no place within it for such open fluidity. 'Means' and 'ends' are no longer considered to be related in any but a mechanistic and linear form – they are stripped of any meaning beyond 'cause' and 'effect'.

As the absolute is closed to us, Druids work through the beacons of relative truth. Dealing with relative manifestations can bring its own problems if one is not forever aware of their relative nature. To understand and work with truth, Druids believe that it is necessary also to serve and to know one's self. Knowing one's self, knowing and acknowledging all our faults and foibles, allows us to compensate for them and judge to what extent they make truth both relative and subjective. Knowing the flaws means it is possible to compensate for them and get closer to a true picture. Service allows a better understanding of those flaws, and therefore a better understanding of the truth. It is a continuous cycle of enlightenment.

These are all grand-sounding sentiments. Questing for and knowing the truth; understanding the universe; service. Druids realize, of course, that they can never hope to achieve these things fully in a single lifetime, just as they can never hope to change the World overnight. What they can and do undertake are steps toward the ultimate goals they set themselves – steps that they can manage, steps that make a small but definable difference to the World.

The part that Druids play, the service they undertake, cannot be engaged in fully until they have some idea of the present state of the World. To come to that understanding, they measure the World against a standard. As we have seen, the standard by which they measure the universe is truth. The World is part of the universe and must, therefore, submit to that same measure.

Placing the truth against the World – that is, measuring the conscious creations of humanity against what we know of the underlying principles of the universe – reveals to us that the World is not an unqualified success. However, Druids believe that they (and, indeed, all of us) are capable of changing things for the better. Finding their own, personal way is one of the quests Druids undertake as they learn the basic teachings of their tradition. Moreover, as with the quest for truth, it is not just a cerebral exercise, but also a striving to achieve right action.

The personal circumstances of a Druid must, of course, be one of the prime factors in deciding how each Druid can best be of service. They can only start from where they are. They can only work in the World as it is. Whatever a person's circumstances may be, and however those circumstances might dictate the way in which they work to restore balance and heal the planet, the overall aim is to bring about a lasting spiritual impression with minimal hint of a material impression; to make the work easier for future generations and leave no footprint in their passing.

Such work is hard and at times a burden that is heavy to bear. Nevertheless, Druids are part of a tradition that has immeasurably ancient roots and will flourish for millennia yet to come. They believe that as they work, ripples will flow across the surface and currents will run in the deeps of their lives and their relationships with others and the planet — connecting with truth and, through service, spreading its influence throughout the World.

Honour and responsibility

Although pagans in general and Druids in particular have no single definitive moral code handed to them by a deity or a prophet, they do have a highly developed sense of ethics. Because the rules are not available in a handy little book, they have to work all the time to ensure that what they think, say, and do are both ethical and relevant. Their adherence to the central importance of truth, combined with their belief in freedom of will, leads them to practise a form of Situation Ethics.[70] That is, their ethical stance is based on certain precepts, but is also dependent upon the circumstances of a given situation. This does not mean they have no basic standards, as we have already seen. It does mean that they are acutely aware of the importance of environment in the widest sense of the word.

Social structures, ethical considerations, and the judicial system were very different two thousand and more years ago – especially in the Celtic world. Yet the basis on which Druids approached ethical questions is still workable and relevant today, even in a world dominated by a different metaphysic from theirs, a metaphysic from which are derived strict and complicated legal and ethical systems that are backed up with the threat of retributive punishment for those who transgress.

The trouble with a system like that, a Druid would contend, is that it exists outwith the person. There is no sense of inherency, no sense of engagement. In particular, responsibility is perceived as lying elsewhere. Society is so complicated and disjointed, so highly competitive and adversarial, that it is easy to feel that laws and ethical systems are lacking in relevance to everyday life. Law-makers, enforcers (a term that says a great deal in itself), judges, and moralists are rarely part of the community they are meant to serve.

Whilst recognizing that this may be the case, the Druid does not accept it as necessary or inevitable. Those whose outlook on life is derived from the Celtic metaphysic will have two watchwords to guide their behaviour – honour and responsibility. These are much-devalued concepts. The terms are used loosely these days and have other meanings that are not directly relevant. We are not talking about medals and prizes or positions of authority bestowed as a reward, any more than we are talking of a system of respect based on the idea that the older people are, or the higher up in a hierarchy, the more worthy of honour they are. These are all 'honours' bestowed from without and by others who hold similar positions. Honour, as expressed by ancestral Celts, and as adopted by modern Druids, comes from within. It is about thinking and acting correctly, with honesty, respect, and courage. It is about being guided by truth. Moreover, it is about behaving like this for no other reason than that it is the right thing to do.

Honour has nothing to do with reward. Some honourable acts may be rewarded, but that is incidental. After all, most, if not all, of our lives are concerned with the everyday. We do not expect a medal for doing the weekly shopping (even if it can seem like an Olympic achievement). Honour is living a life that is true, from the humblest of everyday activities through to the most profound of experiences. The more a person's actions, speech, and thoughts accord with the truth, the greater is their honour.

Of course, we have already seen that truth cannot be rigidly codified. So it is that honour, if it is to flourish, requires an intelligent and free response to life in general and to all specific situations. Freedom of will is crucial. If someone has no genuine choice, then no matter how well that person may seem to behave, it has not been done honourably. It is the same with responsibility. Where one acts from freedom of will, one has to be prepared to accept responsibility for what one has done. No one and nothing else can be blamed. The two – honour and responsibility – are inextricably linked, part of a cycle. To take responsibility (in any sense of the word) is to behave honourably. To behave honourably is to take responsibility for one's place in the world.

This is exemplified by the tale of the boy Sétanta, as we have already seen. Our own lives rarely carry such mythical resonance, but for Druids the episode is instructive. Not only does it epitomize the concept of honour and responsibility, but it is also a fine example of a judgement based on truth, taking the situation into account. Moreover, it demonstrates the importance of service and of respect as factors in Celtic life. The episode is also important for another reason. Although it concerns an event in the life of one of the great mythical heroes of the Celts, there are no high deeds involved. Everything is centred firmly in the domestic arrangements of a household, in the everyday economy of Celtic life. Sétanta may have become a great warrior and accomplished wonderful things, but his lessons were learned at the hearth.

RESPECT

Respect is extremely important to Druids. In ancestral times, it was the basis of the notion of hospitality and the responsibilities of both the host and the guest. These were strictly regulated by law and by custom. A host was expected to provide food and shelter for a guest with good grace – even for a stranger who knocked at the door. Equally, a guest was expected to act with respect and not outstay the welcome.

Respect, of course, extends well beyond the behaviour of hosts and their guests, just as there are many other ways of being a host (or a guest) than the traditional one of welcoming someone into one's house. For example, many Druids live unconventionally and their metaphysical stance often places them at the edge of or completely 'outside' of the society in which they live. This can make life difficult, but Druids do not consider themselves beyond or superior to the society in which they live. They are respectful of the ways of others, even if they do not always like them.

This does not mean that Druids are acquiescent. Where there are points of conflict, they work to resolve these issues. If there are aspects of society they feel to be wrong, they work to change them. However, they will do so in a way that is in accord with their principles. It is why Druids do not preach their religion to others, but why they will teach it if asked (by someone who is old enough to make an informed decision). They believe everyone has the right to choose their own spiritual path and to follow it without prejudice.

Respect for the self is also very much part of the Celtic ethos and is embraced by Druids. Good health was held in high esteem and one was meant to care for one's self physically, mentally, and spiritually. Those who allowed themselves to become overweight or who deliberately neglected their health in other ways could be fined. For people who became ill, were injured, or faced other health problems, physicians, hospitals, and sick maintenance were provided by law in all tribal localities. The Druid community today is health conscious and cares for those who are misfortunate enough to be ill.

Respect is not confined to the human realm. It also applies to the rest of the world. Druids believe that the non-sentient environment is endowed with spirit. This does not mean that the world should not be touched. All life has an effect on the world and the non-sentient world certainly has an effect on all life. What it does mean is that Druids recognize an essential unity of life. Believing that all things are connected, they identify with the rest of the world. That means they take care, as a matter of respect, to live there as lightly as they can.

For some this means embracing vegetarianism or becoming vegan. Those that do not, take care about the sources of their food, eschewing anything produced by factory farming and artificial genetic modification. They are generally extremely well informed on these issues and are often actively involved in campaigns to protect animals from cruelty, forests from destruction, the Land from wholesale devastation, the displacement of indigenous peoples by large corporations... tree-huggers one and all.

UNITY AND IDENTITY

Respect for the natural world is inevitable when all life is considered one and all life is considered sacred. Yet this goes beyond mere fellow feeling: Celtic poems, often ascribed to Bards, display a much deeper affinity with the rest of creation. Whereas most people might consider or express their connection with the natural world by analogy, Druids believe they are identical.[71]

This stems from the way in which ancient Celts and modern Druids think and how they view the world. The ways in which we think are fundamental to the ways in which we act. How we think stems from the metaphysical stance that each of us has come to adopt. Our metaphysical stance or worldview, therefore, sets the ways in which we respond to the world. Moreover, central to our worldview is the view we hold of our self, for it is the self that holds that view. This does not refer to our personality – although that is of importance – but to the distinction we learn to make between what is our self and what is not our self.

Who we are as people is not determined by genetics, although that plays its part. Who we are is the result of all the environments in which we circulate. Genetics sets up the parameters within which we are and can be influenced. However, without influence we remain as day-old babies and would soon perish. In all the environments in which we circulate, the single largest influential factor is other people and we evolve as persons by interacting with them. We all do this in different ways and to different degrees but it is people who make people.

Druids contend that this is often to the neglect of other elements of the many environments in which we exist. We should also interact with the wind and the rain, the sun and the stars, with city streets and sheep filled meadows. We are not normally taught how, but without that interaction and that dialogue, we do not fulfil our potential to develop as persons.

This, however, presents us with an enigma. Each of us is, in part, an evolving complex of relationships. We behave differently in different situations and in the presence of different persons, and we learn from them. This is partly social training (an automatic response), but it is also different facets of our being that are waking and manifesting. Yet even with no people around, we constantly interact with our environment. And that, too, constitutes a series of relationships. The complex of relationships involves the non-human world – animals, trees, rocks, buildings, in fact, the totality of experience. And if this is so, where does each person stop and the rest of the world begin?

This is not a spurious question. It is fundamental to the way in which we treat the planet. For Druids believe that if we answer that, as persons, we stop at the epidermis and that that is where the rest of the world begins, then we have alienated ourselves from everything else that exists and cannot, thereafter, truly claim to know anything about the world with any certainty. The world becomes other, unknowable, and untouchable – intellectually, spiritually, politically, and in any other way you care to name. If someone takes that view, they cannot even logically talk about 'them' because they can only know their self. Thus isolated, their vision of their self becomes synchronous and synonymous with their body. That becomes their central concern. They have become truly selfish.

This will cause distress because it is an untenable position, no matter how much someone may pretend otherwise. It is untenable because there has to be interaction with the rest of the world just to survive (food, water, air, people, and all the rest). The rest of the world is essential to their being, no matter how it may be denied. Their distress will be manifest in ever-stronger denial of the world, in aggression, and in attempts (subconscious or otherwise) to destroy the world that is so embarrassing to them and their beliefs. This is an extreme position, but it is far from unknown.

There is another position that is adopted by pagans in general and Druids in particular. That position is that we interact with the world. Not only that, we interact with a world that is real and what we are is due (if only in part) to that interaction. Therefore, as persons, we do not stop at the epidermis, but extend beyond that to include all that we experience at any given time. This will include other people, animals, plants, objects, machines, ideas, sensations, and so on. This is not to say, however, that we are *only* these interactions for there must be an essential self or soul that is interacting.

If during normal, everyday life, our being enfolds all that we interact with and experience, then we are inseparable from the world. We go through life expanding and contracting in a vital dance in which the essential self lives its own life without ever being separated from creation. We are all part of one another, part of every creature, part of all that is.

If this is so, then if we harm any part of the world, we harm ourselves. We cannot avoid changing the world as we pass through. That is a function of living. We can recognize, however, that we are a part of it and a part of other people as much as it and they are part of us. We should make our passage through the world a gentle one – if only to minimize harm to our self – recognizing that we are each of us composed of others. Do this and we become, not selfish, but self-interested, and that is synonymous with becoming interested in others and, through the many overlapping fields of being, the whole of the planet.

There are many other teachings, although most are derived in some way from the basic precepts discussed above. By its very nature, the Way of the Druid is organic and those who follow it explore at great length, read widely, and think deeply. The sources on which they base their teachings and from which they draw their ethical position are often enigmatic. This means that nothing ever becomes rigid for each new contribution to the debate moves things forward in a way that keeps the teachings alive and relevant, firmly rooted in the real world.

8

DEITY

DEITY

Whereas there is undoubtedly common ground in most areas of the Druid Way, irrespective of the particular tradition a given Druid might follow, in the case of deity it is a different matter. The difference lies not in what is known about Celtic deities – what little there is to be known is well documented – but in a Druid's approach to deity. Rather than worship a remote figure (or pantheon), a Druid will usually develop a personal relationship, often quite intimate, with a particular deity. This relationship will grow out of an honouring and working with that deity, rather than out of worship. Nor does this relationship exclude work with other deities. It is simply that a Druid will work most, and therefore become most closely linked, with a particular aspect of the divine that best suits that Druid's own work in the world. The relationship is not always the most obvious, or the one that a Druid would initially choose. Indeed, it often takes a number of years for the relationship to develop and for the purpose behind it to become apparent.

Before we can discuss this further, however, it would be as well to be clear about the nature and structure of Celtic deity, and the basic beliefs of modern Druids. Ancestral Celts were, and many modern Druids, are polytheistic. Of those Druids today who eschew polytheism, most still honour different expressions of a single, overarching divinity – those expressions sometimes manifesting as, or being described by, the names of ancestral Celtic deities. Of all areas of debate within the Druid community, it is this that is engaged in most often, and it is this that best discloses just how broad a community it is. Irrespective of how Celtic deities are interpreted, however, what they represent still plays an important role in the lives of Druids.

It would be impossible to deal comprehensively with all Celtic deities in the confines of a single book, let alone this chapter. There are, after all, somewhere in the region of 375 names of Celtic deities extant, with indications of others whose names have not come down to us. Most of these names, it must be admitted, occur once or are confined to relatively small localities. These local deities were probably connected with specific tribes, and are often referred to as *teutates*, which means 'deity of the tribe'. Some twenty names occur with greater frequency and are to be found (sometimes in cognate form) across the entire region once inhabited by the Celts. These names are also often found in place names.

It has been suggested that the main Celtic pantheon actually consisted of thirty-three deities. Thirty-three was a highly significant number to the Celts, and other cultures with Indo-European roots have pantheons of thirty-three. It seems unlikely that we will ever know for certain. With the spread of Christianity, the Celtic peoples nucleated into distinct nations subject to different influences, and this, combined with the Celts abiding sense of place, resulted in the pantheon taking on local aspects and the deities gaining variant names and attributes.

Several things are certain, however, even through the filter of Christian redaction. The first is that Celts did not always depict their deities pictorially or as statues. Indeed, early Celts were known to find the idea absurd. It was only after contact with the classical world that they began to produce formal imagery. The second point is that the Celtic pantheon is very much like an extended family or tribe, with all the concerns and conflicts that are experienced by mortal humans. The third is that Celts considered their deities to be ancestors rather than creators. The difference is subtle, but important, as it explains a great deal about the way in which Druids today relate to their deities.

When Celts did eventually come to depict their deities, on the whole, they were shown in human form and were already well organized as a pantheon. The principal deity of this group, now as then, is the mother goddess Danu (sometimes given as Anu). Her children are known in Irish mythology as the Tuatha Dé Danaan and her name is closely associated, if not directly connected, with the river Danube, along with many other similar river names throughout Europe. The Welsh equivalent of Danu is Don, whose children also form a central pantheon. The similarity of name, together with the fact that both are considered to represent the 'waters of heaven',[72] suggest an origin common to all Celts, if not all Indo-European peoples. The river's edge, lakes, pools, sweet water springs, and wells are all places where wisdom, knowledge, and poetry were revealed, suggesting the importance of fresh water to the Celts as a symbolic source of all goodness.

The children of Danu are locked in conflict with the children of Domnu (in the case of Irish mythology) and the children of Ll?r (in Welsh mythology), who have connections with the deeps of the sea. The waters of heaven and the deeps of the sea are, of course, extremities on a cycle so their natures are completely different. This is bound to lead to what seems like conflict, which takes place on the Land. That the conflict is never fully resolved but goes through cycles shows an understanding on the part of the Celts that both aspects are essential to the world we all share.

This conflict is often portrayed as a battle between light and dark with the implication that they are forces of good and evil. This, however, is a later Christian gloss. We have seen already that ancestral Celts and modern Druids do not see the world in quite this way. Certainly, modern Druids are as likely to be found working with or attracted to the children of the deeps of the sea, as they are the children of the waters of heaven.

Of all the examples and variations of the Celtic pantheon that must have existed, only two have survived in anything more than fragments. The Welsh version can be pieced together from various sources, especially the fourth branch of the *Mabinogi*.[73] The Irish version, more popular though less comprehensive in terms of characterization, offers more concrete glimpses of the structure of the pantheon and its evolution. It also offers a clearer view of Celtic attitudes toward deity as the gods and goddesses have not been conflated by the Romans with Graeco-Roman deities.[74]

The story of the Irish Tuatha Dé Danaan is to be found in the *Lebor Gabála Érenn* (Book of the Taking of Ireland).[75] Although members of the Tuatha Dé Danaan clearly pre-date the text, it is there that they are first endowed with a literary characterization that makes them accessible. They are one of several peoples who arrive on Irish shores in successive waves from the Otherworld to displace their predecessors. Their arrival out of the West and just before Beltane was heralded by a three-day eclipse of the sun.[76]

The Tuatha Dé Danaan brought four great treasures, one from each of the great cities they had previously inhabited. From Falias they brought the Lia Fáil, the stone of destiny that cries out when stood upon by a lawful king. From Findias came the sword of Nuada, a fearsome weapon since all wounds inflicted by the blade were fatal. The third treasure, from Gorias, is the spear Gáe Assail. This is used with devastating effect by Lug Lámfhota.

Finally, from Murias, is the cauldron of the Dagda, which provided food (and possibly much more) for all of the Dagda's faithful followers.

These treasures have been mentioned as they are of enormous significance to Druids and are often referred to in ritual, if not actually represented by physical objects. They will certainly be well known as symbols and objects to anyone who is familiar with Arthurian literature, which suggests that they also had a place in British mythology from an early period.

The leading figures of the Tuatha Dé Danaan include the Dagda, who was the Druid of the tribe and is sometimes also known as the Good God (in the sense that he was highly skilled rather than an exemplar of rectitude); Manannán mac Lir, a god associated with dominion of the Irish Sea; Dian Cécht, a healer who could restore to good health all but those who had been decapitated; Lug Lámfhota, a great warrior, who was also a master of all arts and all crafts; Brigid, a goddess of fire and inspiration; the triune goddess of conflict, Badb, Macha, and Mórrígan; and Ogma, a warrior of great eloquence to whom is ascribed the invention of ogham.[77] These deities, and many others, have their equivalents in British mythology and no doubt existed in continental Europe as well.

The mother of these deities and, ultimately, the ancestor of all Celts and all Druids, has remained a shadowy figure who plays little or no active part in the mythological cycle as it has come down to us. To have brought forth and nurtured an entire pantheon is surely accomplishment enough. She remains, however, firmly at the heart of Druid ritual in her role as progenitor and protector. She is revered and loved as a mother and as the spiritual hearth where Druids draw comfort, wisdom, and strength.

Other deities are accorded roles that are more specific and are worked with by Druids in specific ways, at specific times, and in specific places. Many of these deities are anonymous spirits of place, but there are others who have universal roles and with whom most, if not all, Druids will work at some time or other.

With Danu in her role as hearth mother and perhaps also concerned with the cerebral and spiritual aspects of life, it is the Dagda who fills much of the rest of the world with his presence and takes a step closer to the practical realities of life. The Dagda and his equivalents, such as Bran and possibly Cernunnos, have very similar attributes. This principal male deity is a formidable character who can destroy with his great club and restore to life any creature, and who can provide for all who follow him from his ever-full cauldron and his ever-laden apple trees. He also has a strong affinity with the animal kingdom and is sometimes known as the Lord of the Beasts. This is a potent force, the exemplar of Celtic society, for the Dagda is an accomplished Druid, a great warrior, and a highly skilled artisan, upright and benevolent. Yet the Dagda also has a comical side. He dresses in a rough tunic that is too short to cover his buttocks, behaves in an amiably oafish way, and is extremely fond of porridge.

Like his counterpart Bran, whose buried head protected Britain from invasion, the Dagda's principle role is as a guardian of the Land. He is, after all, a king. Such a role requires great skill and great dedication. It involves adopting the power of death and of life along with a duty of care for all who live within the boundaries of the world for which he is responsible. It also requires a sense of humour, otherwise the burden of care and trust could drive even the strongest into despair and destruction.

Guardianship of the Land requires consent of the Land for it will accept none but those who are suited to the role. Consent can only be given by the Land itself, usually by a representative goddess of sovereignty. There are many examples of specific and local goddesses of sovereignty who bear the name of the region or the country over which they hold sway. In each case, their story follows a basic pattern, but there are often considerable variations, some of which have resulted from later Christian misunderstanding of sovereignty's role.

In non-specific terms, sovereignty manifests as the *cailleach*. The modern meaning of this word – 'old woman' – has also acquired the pejorative meaning of 'hag', which, although it has some relevance, has devalued the importance of sovereignty. Originally, the word meant 'veiled one', which is much more relevant to the original form of the goddess. A 'veiled one' might be an old woman, but it can also be a bride, a widow, or one pledged to a cause or calling. The veil sets them apart, by their own choice, and allows them the right to stay separated or to return to society as and when they please.

The veil is also a glamour, an illusion dispelled only by fortitude and wisdom combined. It is the semblance of a barrier that must be crossed in order to see the face of sovereignty and thus gain her consent. In allegorical tales concerning the *cailleach*, the glamour is a less subtle symbol. When she first appears to the hero, it is as an ugly old woman asking to be loved (emotionally and physically) or imposing an appropriate task. This is, of course, the final test of the worth of the hero, the countenance of the *cailleach* perhaps representing the burden of guardianship. When love is freely given (or the task successfully undertaken), the veil dissolves to reveal a beautiful young woman.

Long-lived sovereignty will take many champions in this way, renewing each cycle of her existence and ensuring that the Land is well protected. The relationship between sovereignty and her champion is sealed with a sacred or ritual marriage. Neglect of the relationship is and was a serious matter, the discord being reflected in the state of the Land. Ancestral Celts had an economy and a culture dependent on agriculture and the wellbeing of the Land was essential. A king who neglected his duties could be removed quite legally by the people.

Sovereignty is of great importance to Druids. To function properly as a Druid it is necessary to respect and work in service of the Land. Yet by committing themselves to such a relationship with the goddess, they gain personal and spiritual sovereignty. This is the gift that the goddess offers in return for the work that Druids do in her name. The gaining of freedom through responsibility and obligation is not unique to pagan religion or, indeed, any religion. Nevertheless, it does form an important part of the Celtic metaphysic. One of the ways in which Druids affirm their spiritual path and pay honour to their ancestors is by achieving freedom through a sacred bond with the goddess of the Land.

Along with the Dagda and the *cailleach*, there are two other quintessential deities that are important to Druids. They balance the maturity of the Good God and the Veiled One with their youth. One is Lug, a warrior skilled in all the crafts and arts; the other is the highly enigmatic figure of the Mabon.

Standing behind the cognate figures of Lleu Llaw Gyffes, Lug Lámfhota, and the Gaulish Lugus is the ancient and bright figure of Lug. Possibly pre-Celtic, this deity was worshipped widely. The word *lug* means 'light' and Lug is often simplistically regarded as a solar deity, a representation of the sun. He is solar, in part, but he is a much more complex and subtle deity than that. As a hero of Celtic tales, he is a warrior of great renown, famed for his use of the spear (hence his name meaning 'long arm' in Irish and 'steady hand' in Welsh).[78] Yet, as the texts make clear, he is a young man of many accomplishments – in agriculture, metalworking, woodworking, harping, magic, medicine, and as a cup bearer. He is also credited with the invention of the game *fidchell.*[79]

Once again, we see a quintessentially Celtic character, this time in youthful form with all the confidence and vigour of early life. Yet this overlay of Celtic culture does not altogether obscure the more fundamental and perhaps much older nature of this deity. The illumination he offers as a deity of light is both physical and spiritual, and like the light, he is swift and has the power to heal.

The importance of Lug to the Celts is indisputable and clear. His name can be found embedded in place names from the north of Britain right through Europe to Silesia. Furthermore, in Goidelic (one of the two branches of the Celtic language), his name is attached to one of the great annual festivals, Lughnasad, a feast in celebration of harvesting the cereal crops, themselves associated with the sun.

Lug, however, is not the only youthful deity of importance to ancestral Celts and modern Druids. In various traditions, there are tales of a Divine Youth, one whose conception and birth or early life occur outside of time, and who is imprisoned and rescued or, alternatively, who is fostered by a sisterhood of nine and trained for his role as a great hero. We only have fragments now of what appears to have been a great cycle of stories that may have drawn parallels between the life of the hero and the cycle of the year.

In British mythology, the child is known simply as the Mabon (which means 'child'). He is the son of Modron ('the mother') and is clearly a form of the deity Maponus ('divine child') found throughout Europe. Tradition now associates his birth with the winter solstice largely because, as an archetype found in many cultures, this is when the divine child enters the world. A new son is born as a new sun is born, ensuring a further year of fertility and prosperity. As the child grows, he becomes the champion of the goddess, his mother.

All these tales may have a familiar ring even to those who are not acquainted with the rich world of Celtic mythology. This is because the tales have never stopped developing, any more than the religion to which they belong. As always, the old deities were superseded, but instead of fading away, the Celtic deities went underground and have become increasingly confused with folk heroes and with the inhabitants of Faerie. In Britain, the tales continued to develop into the corpus now known as the Matter of Britain. The tales of Arthur and his companions bear strong resemblances to the older tales of deities and their adventures.

It is appropriate, at this point, to mention faeries, as they are often confused with deity in both general and specific ways. Reasons for this confusion are not hard to find, for like deities, faeries are Otherworldly, and they share many attributes with deities. It is not this confusion, however, that makes them worth mentioning. Rather, it is the important place they have had in the lives and affairs of Celtic peoples, as well as the role they now play in the lives of Druids.

Any mention today of faeries or of a faerie tradition will invariably conjure certain images in the popular imagination. Faeries, however, are not diminutive figures with gauzy wings who sit around in flowers all day, any more than they are elves (a similar, but different race). Faeries are a race of beings who have lived alongside humans in north west Europe for thousands of years. They are very much like human beings in appearance and stature, with many of the same concerns and habits. Their preferred colours, by which they are often identified, are green and silver. Ancestral Celts held them in great respect and avoided contact with them when they could as, for all the similarities between faeries and human beings, faeries live their lives by different rules. They are not deliberately malevolent, but certain of their ways are harmful to people and if affronted they can retaliate with absolute vengeance.

Faeries can move between their world and ours at will. But the fact that the realm of faeries is said to be underground (or sometimes under water) should not be taken literally. They do not live in caves any more than they are denizens of the Christian hell. The world of faerie is very similar to our own; it is simply that the entrances or gateways to this world are often to be found in hillsides or where there is water.

A great deal of ancestral Celtic folklore was concerned with faerie and they were taken seriously. Interest in faerie has grown again in recent times, although most popular depictions are based on Victorian conceptions and most books on the subject are, frankly, drivel. Many modern Druids accept the reality of faeries. A few even try to work with them. Most, however, whilst paying due regard to a people with whom they share the planet, advise caution when in their presence.

Although the deities of the Celtic pantheon are important to Druids, their beliefs and practices do not revolve around deity alone. That is why the Way of the Druid is not about blind worship. Druids work with their deities, identifying what they represent and seeking to understand how the deities can empower them to carry forward their Druidic service. There is no disrespect in this. Druids look upon their deities as mentors – great teachers and protectors – each of whom has a different lesson to teach. These deities are shown every respect, but it is clear from the myths that they have a great dislike for sycophancy.

A relationship with a deity is not, for Druids, an end in itself. They work with their deities in order to come to a better understanding of the world. This understanding is also a means to an end, for Druids use it to do what they can to bring about balance and harmony in the world. The ways in which Druids achieve communion with their deities and some of the ways they work in the world are discussed later. For now, it is enough to know that they are devout people whose attachment to their deities is both genuine and intense.

9

COSMOLOGY

COSMOLOGY

Unlike many cosmologies that are well stratified and described, the one that Druids have inherited from ancestral Celts is, in large part, a reflection of the real world – complex and organic. In essence, however, Celtic cosmology is comprised of two parts. The first of these is this world, the one we currently inhabit, which is comprised of three main elements. The second is the Otherworld, which consists of myriad realms.

THIS WORLD

The Land, as we have seen, was of great importance to Celts both physically and spiritually. It was, however, only one constituent of the Celt's cosmology. With the Land came the Sea and the Sky. These three elements make up the whole of the world. Fire is also present, both literally (as the sun, for example, or as flames on the hearth) and figuratively (as the heat of the soul, the spark of life, inspiration, and the like). Fire is the spirit that inspires the rest of the world, giving it breath, giving it life. With fire, the house we inhabit becomes a home.

For Druids, everything they are and do is informed by this cosmology. Together, these constituents represent the material and spiritual framework that shapes thought and action, belief and knowledge. The natural world, to Druids, is a spiritual force in its own right. It is the Land, the Sea, and the Sky inspired. It is where we reside but, more importantly, it is an existence of which we are an integral part. Everything we are is derived from this combination and if we abuse it, either materially or spiritually, we abuse ourselves.

There are a number of levels to this cosmology that are not easily separated for in reality they are aspects of unity. We can talk of the Land, the Sea, and the Sky as if they were clear-cut and discrete entities, but they each make the others – physically, spiritually, and symbolically. This is as true today as it has always been, although our largely urban and over-complicated social existence, a Druid would contend, tends to obscure this reality.

THE LAND

Whilst most people, if they gave it any thought, would concede that all we have materially is derived from the world, they would probably stop short of acknowledging the world, and, in particular, the Land, as having a part in shaping our spiritual existence. This is because most people no longer believe that we live in the world. Rather, they believe that we live on it.

Our connection with the Land has been severed. This is not specifically the fault of urban living as many urbanites have as much (if not more) contact with the Land as rural dwellers. In pagan eyes, the connection was severed when the prevailing metaphysic became one that objectified the world. Druids believe this to be materially and spiritually destructive. They believe it essential to know the world. They believe it essential to know the Land – and not just as we learn about it in geography lessons or by studying geology and geomorphology. An emotional connection must also be made.

In order to make such a connection, it is necessary to reduce our expectations. We think constantly on too large a scale because we have become used to seeing and hearing of things happening at a great distance. It is good to know what is happening in the world, but it is difficult to connect emotionally with the whole planet. It is good to know what is happening in the world, but it should not be at the expense of the intimate detail in our lives, of what is happening, in some cases, quite literally in our own back yard.

This is not intended to paint Druids as isolationists or as nationalists. Celts originally had no nation as such. Their bond was a common culture based on their particular view of the world. Their loyalty was to the tribe. And whilst they were undoubtedly territorial, their connection with the place in which they lived did not lead them to assume it made them superior in any way to their neighbours. This is largely because they knew they did not and could not own the Land – a view shared by Druids today. Indeed, if anything, the opposite is true, for we all belong to the Land. It is considered our mother. With care, it feeds us and provides all else that we need, both materially and spiritually.

Druids spend a lot of their time outdoors exploring the places in which they live, be they rural or urban. They tend to know their history, both formal and informal, and are usually involved in their local communities. In bringing the Land alive in this way, they assimilate themselves with it and help stimulate a similar interest in others (usually without ever mentioning the fact that they are Druid). They go further, however, for they recognize that as they become involved with the Land, it helps to shape them and their view of the world. Thus they also create an inner landscape that is contiguous, and eventually merges, with the outer landscape.

The inner landscape of the Druid is usually centred on an inner Grove.[80] This stems from the communion with the landscape of the outer world, and has its roots firmly fixed there. Druids believe that we are, in part at least, a product of the Land and that even if we do not awaken it within us at deeper levels, we always carry it with us at an elemental level. When Druids seek out their inner Grove, they are exploring the extension of the outer landscape that is nascent within us. It is usually envisaged as a landscape with which the Druid is familiar and comfortable and contains a specific place where the Druid can form a connection between the outside world and the meditative and ritual work they do within.

This is territory (literal and metaphorical) that is steeped in mystery. For Druids, it lies at the heart of their relationship with the Land. Here they encounter the very essence of sovereignty. Understanding the nature of sovereignty is crucial. Sovereignty is the right to rule. It is the right to control. However, this right is not absolute. It is, as we have seen, a gift bestowed on those who have earned the right and it comes with many responsibilities.

Often portrayed in terms of kingship (by a people who could elect their kings in full knowledge of the need for candidates to be approved of by the goddess of the Land), sovereignty is service – service to the Land and to the people. Yet sovereignty also has a personal dimension. The degree to which we can exercise an autonomous existence depends on how well we treat the Goddess and all that she represents. If we follow her precepts, say Druids, our inner and outer landscapes will be green and flowing with clear, sweet water. If we turn our back on the Goddess and abuse her gifts, our landscapes will become a deadly waste and we in turn will wither and die – first in spirit and then in body.

THE SEA

The Sea (by which is meant all water) has a symbolic and spiritual quality of a different order. The Land, we have seen, represents solidity, security, and a sense of belonging – albeit with attendant responsibilities. It is, a Druid might say, where the hearth is. The Sea, for all that ancestral Celts used it as a major means of communication and transportation, has always been seen as something other. It is not our natural habitat, being too vast and fluid. Yet it is not so other that it is wholly beyond our comprehension. For just as it symbolizes the largest and most mysterious of our spiritual concerns, it also symbolizes the smallest and most intimate.

In the case of the largest concern – the cycle of life, death, and rebirth – this is the Sea as personified by the Western Ocean across which Druids believe we all travel when our souls move from this world to the Other. This aspect of the Sea, along with associated *imrama* (sea voyages of exploration to other worlds, both material and spiritual) is dealt with later in the chapter.

Ancestral Celts knew (perhaps by instinct or by the very rightness of the idea), just as we know (by science), that the ocean is but one part of a cycle. Vast as the ocean may be, it is water and it manifests also in very small amounts that have a direct effect on our lives. From the ocean, water rises as vapour through the power of the sun. The vapour forms into clouds, which are the fruit of the cycle. They eventually let fall rain or snow. Each drop of rain or flake of snow is a seed that will grow, finally, to become an ocean.

In each drop, each seed, is to be found the basis for the cycle that Druids use to symbolize and celebrate the self. This is not self-aggrandizement. Rather, it is an acknowledgement in daily life of the existence of humans as beings integral to the world. This is an important teaching of the Druid Way. We lead humble existences, no matter that some may inflate the importance of their own being. We must all eat, drink, excrete, earn a living, keep house, and do all the other day-to-day things that keep body and soul together. And in this, if it is done in accord with truth, is the very basis of spiritual life.

By living simply and acknowledging the true nature of our being, by living faithfully to that, Druids believe that each humble act of life becomes a prayer, part of the conversation between the self and the world. This, of course, can be accentuated with words, as long as they are words said with feeling and with understanding. They must, after all, engage a person with the world and draw them into an ever-closer communion. Mindless repetition of a formula will have the opposite effect.

The point of striking up this conversation with the world in general and with the particular thing we are doing is to make us pay attention to our actions and to the reasons behind them. This, in turn, helps us to strip away what is superfluous as well as giving us time to see the simpler ways there are of doing things.

Within this simplicity and the focus on the relationship of the self with the world is to be found, also, the vastness of all existence and the great mystery of life, death, and rebirth. These are also symbolized by the water, the great Sea, which is created by and from those small drops, those seeds, as they flow together in rivulets, streams, and rivers toward the shore where, finally, they feed the ocean.

This cycle is also an apt symbol of how Druids see our lives. In material form, we think of ourselves as individuals. Yet, for the most part, we are far too integrated with the rest of the world for this to have any absolute meaning. After all, how long does a raindrop remain a raindrop? Even as it falls from the clouds it will collide with others, merge, and reform, just as our personalities are formed and developed by contact with others. Once the raindrop reaches the ground, it enters into a complex of cycles that help sustain all life (and sometimes destroy it). This experience ineradicably alters the water and all about it and may engage it in many different relationships before it reaches a free-flowing stream and can start on its journey to the sea where identity is lost in the whole. Yet that is not the end. Vapour rises, clouds form, and new raindrops fall to follow a new journey.

THE SKY

It is clear from this that the Sea is inextricably linked with the Land, and that both require the Sky. In many religions, the Sky is seen as the abode of deity. Whilst there were undoubtedly Celtic deities with a strong connection with the Sky, it is by no means an exclusive relationship. They inhabit Land and Sea as well. Indeed, the Celts did not look to the Sky for worship, but for the cycles that regulated the world in which they lived.

Like all people before the invention of mechanical timepieces, ancestral Celts regulated their lives (when necessary) by observing and working with the rhythms created by the movements of the sun and the moon. If we ignore them unduly, we become distressed or disorientated. Jet lag is a classic example. Even altering our clocks by an hour to conform to changes of 'summer time' and 'winter time' can be discomfiting, and it is certainly a change to which animals pay no heed.

Although artificial timekeeping and the advent of modern calendars are considered a boon to our modern society, this form of regulation does not fully accord with the way in which our selves relate to the world or attune to our environment. Nor is this simply on the physical level. Pagans also attune aspects of their spirituality to the rhythms of the natural world, believing that a basic level of spiritual harmony can be achieved in this way. They also believe that body and spirit should be in harmony with each other and thus try to allow natural rhythms to guide their everyday lives as far as is possible in a society governed by an artificial standard.

Day and night is the simplest rhythm, breaking life into units that we find easy to cope with. 'Take it a day at a time' is probably advice that goes back many millennia. Following the practice of ancestral Celts, Druids think of each new day as starting just after the sun has set. The setting sun is an obvious, natural marker. It means that all major tasks are undertaken after rest and recuperation and sets a pattern whereby dark and light are not considered opposites or separate entities, but aspects of the same cycle.

Two other major units of time that are important are those governed by the moon. The month, which, as far as we know, was measured from full moon to full moon, was one. The other was the fortnight or fourteen nights (fourteen nights from a given time being half a month). This lunar reckoning was the major calendar for the Celts, and is redolent with symbolism. It was also tied in with the solar cycle, adjustments being made each year (with a kind of leap year), and with a recognition of the coincidence of the lunar and solar cycles every nineteen years.

For all their internal and cyclic variations, these cycles provide a strict underlying order, originating as they do in the realm that is least accessible to the meddling ambitions and hands of people. The order cannot be altered. The basic rules of life are derived from this natural order – which is why Druids consider many of their teachings to be derived from the world. Yet this realm, the Sky, is also the least rigid for it is the realm of air and the wind.

The air, as represented by the Sky, has important symbolic qualities for the Druid. As living, breathing creatures, our distinct material existence is defined by air. Our very first autonomous act is to inhale; our last is to exhale. The movement of air keeps the fire of life present within us. As we take in air, it follows a journey much like the spiritual journey of the Druid. Inward, first, it traverses the labyrinth until it reaches the very heart of our being. There, in the darkness, it is transformed before being exhaled in new form to contribute to the world.

This is by no means all that is important about, or is symbolized by, the tripartite arrangement of this world. These and many more ideas are studied, as are the relationships between the three, component parts of the three, and the inspiring fire that animates them all. Moreover, as with many other aspects of the Way of the Druid, these are not to be seen as delimiting superstitions. They are tools used to aid in a better understanding of the world, an understanding that does not rely solely on the narrow perspective of analytical empiricism.

THE OTHERWORLD
THE JOURNEY OF THE SOUL

For a Druid, the final voyage of this life is across the ocean in the west, following the setting sun at the end of the day. However, it is not a voyage of shadows fading into eternal darkness. The soul is immortal. Death is not an end, merely a changing of place. For just as one day's end is the next day's beginning, so the end of one life is the beginning of another. Beyond the dark, beyond the well-earned sleep, there is light and a new sunrise. Reborn in the Otherworld, we begin the reciprocal to this life and balance out our time here with a life in which the spirit is predominant and readily accepted. There we work toward an understanding of and balance with the material. So, when the full cycle is complete, we are ready to return to this world to start on a new phase of our journey.

This cycle is much like the turning of the day, which has two phases – daylight and night-time. However, no attempt should be made to say which of the worlds is represented by night and which by day. Although the Otherworld is often considered a land of summer stars, when compared with the shadow world in which we live, it is also one of bright daylight. As with much else, it is a matter of perspective. And although the denizens of each world may find the other worlds perplexing, there is no doubt that the two worlds are inextricably linked – the common medium being ourselves and all other living beings that make the journey between the two.

Belief in the immortality of the soul was exceedingly strong amongst ancestral Celts. It made them fierce warriors, for they had little fear of death. They were not reckless, however, because they also knew they had responsibilities to the living in this world. The notion of personal responsibility and the immortality of the soul combined in the practice of some Celts of accepting the repayment of debts (monetary and in kind) being held over to the next life. Inherent in this is the belief that we travel together. That is, we are reborn amongst the same people. Our relationships may be different, but our responsibilities remain.

Some have taken this to be an indication that both ancestral Celts and modern Druids believe in a form of karma. As we have seen, this is not so. To begin with, although debts could be held over for repayment in the next life, this was not a widespread practice. It was a personal agreement that could be made between individuals. It had nothing to do with accumulating the brownie points necessary to improve one's lot the next time round. Such an idea is alien to the Celtic metaphysic.

Responsibility for one's actions lies with the self in the here and now and is an inherent quality of those actions. You do something and you take responsibility for it because it is right to do so, not because there is a reward of some description, be that heaven, a better life, or nirvana. Nor is anything done, or refrained from, because of the threat of punishment, whether damnation and torture in hell, or returning as a 'lesser' life form.

Some have cited Celtic tales in which people lead many lives as different animals as evidence of karmic metempsychosis. Most of these tales, as it happens, are about shapeshifting. Those that do indicate that souls are reborn as animals through a number of cycles are exceptions rather than the norm – which is why they feature in these wonder tales. Besides, even if they were the norm, they cannot be taken as an indication that punishment for being bad is to return as a 'lesser' life form. Celts did not consider animals to be lesser life forms. They have spirit and are our equals. Many of them are teachers; all of them are guides.

That there is a way to move on from the cycle of rebirth is also beyond doubt. The Celtic metaphysic is based on truth and a search for the balance between the material and the spiritual. In our case, that means increasing our understanding and the integration of our spiritual natures into our material being. Having achieved that balance, we are well placed to become teachers (as humans or in animal form) in these worlds before looking to master other aspects of being in places and times beyond our current comprehension. This is not an obsessive concern of Druids. Whilst they may speculate on the nature of this progression, they also accept that it is a state of affairs well beyond our current level of comprehension. Druids are anchored in the here and now and are more concerned with how they might best serve today than with what might happen in the future.

An understanding of the balance between the material and spiritual can be seen in the ancestral Celtic custom of burying personal belongings along with the bodies of those that owned them. This is often taken to be a primitive expression of the belief that you can take it with you. In a sense this is true, but not in the crude way that most commentators imply. All things are imbued with spirit, even lumps of rock. Personal items such as jewellery, weapons, professional tools, games, and the like, all become endowed with the spirit of their owner through prolonged use and close personal contact. They are an integral part of who that person is. This was particularly so in a society in which personal material possessions were few in number and long lasting. Such items cannot be passed on to anyone with whom they have not already been shared. The pattern of the spirit of their original owner is too deeply embedded in their being for them to be transferred to anyone else. This is especially true of any item that is used in ritual. That is why Druids ask for their ceremonial equipment to be buried or cremated with them.

Not only can others not use these objects, but they are also considered integral to the person who owned them. They derive their spirit from a given person, but that person also has their spirit shaped by the personal objects they possess. The same is true for relationships. We are shaped in large part by those people, animals, and landscapes with which we have close and prolonged contact. This works for our spirit and for our spiritual understanding as well. To move to the Otherworld (or back to this) without that wider spiritual endowment is to be reborn incomplete, is to be held back on our new journey.

Reverence for our ancestors (and the ability to communicate with them) becomes a great deal easier to understand in the light of this spiritual endowment. If we travel on a number of cycles between this world and the Other, then we *are* our ancestors, even though not, perhaps, the previous generation or two (although our journeys can be sometimes pitiably short in the worlds). We are now in the strange position in our media rich world of being able to look at photographs and film of people who may once have been us.

The search for past life experiences is not one that is much encouraged within Druid tradition, although there are individuals who take an interest. To spend time on lives we have already lived and can do nothing about is considered a waste of this life. As is an undue emphasis on a notion of karma, on living in the shadow of how we might influence the next life. We are here today to live today. This is not the first step to hedonism. It does not mean that a person should not live in right fashion. Living rightly in the now cannot be divorced from an understanding of the past or a care for the future. Indeed, living in the now by the tenets of the Celtic metaphysic demands, somewhat paradoxically, that our concerns and responsibilities take into account all the worlds at all times.

OTHER WORLDS

Of all the diverse worlds that Druids talk of, it is the Otherworld that is of most concern to them. This is the place to which souls migrate when our bodies die, the place where they enjoy new lives, and from whence they come that we may be reborn once more in this world. The Otherworld is not a land of the dead. It is not heaven or hell. It is not a supernatural realm at all. These concepts are alien to the Celtic metaphysic. Such definitions have come about as the result of attempting to understand the Celtic view of the world by comparing it with, and using the terminology of, the metaphysic of other peoples and of other times. Both worlds are natural. Both worlds are worlds of the living. They are contiguous one with another and, in places, they overlap.

The cycle that takes us from world to world by means of a series of rebirths is the normal way to make the journey. However, it is not the only way, as many ancient tales will attest. The denizens of one world can visit other worlds and then, with care and luck, return to their own. Such an undertaking is not without extreme hazard, not least because it is all too easy to mistake the Otherworld for Faerie.

These three particular worlds fit together much as the three circles in this diagram:

There is an area common to all three and each overlaps with the other. It is, therefore, possible to move from one to the other without having to 'die'. However, the diagram should not be taken too literally. Whereas some religious traditions have well-defined ideas of where one world ends and another begins, the Celtic notion is, in keeping with the Celtic metaphysic, extremely fluid. Each world flows into the other and there are times when the gateways and crossing points are easier to find and use than others. Nor should it be taken to mean that there are just the three worlds. There are many, and there is an ancient tradition of voyaging across the western sea in search of these other lands.

The *imram* was a quest in which whatever was sought was attained not just through physical prowess and endurance, but also through wisdom and a testing of the soul. Such was the power of these tales that they were adopted into the Christian tradition both as *imrama* and in much altered form as the Grail quest. Other worlds could also be reached through gateways on land, not all of them obvious. There are many tales of people crossing from one world to another without realizing until it is too late.

Many wonderful lands and islands are mentioned in these tales, each a world in its own right with its own inhabitants. They range from the truly bizarre to those places that might easily be mistaken for this world. Of all those visited, only one is the world to which souls from this world migrate to be reborn. For all that, no matter how unusual they may seem, none of these worlds is supernatural. The Otherworld, Faerie, and all the other realms are simply places and conditions beyond our full understanding. This does not mean they are fantasies or non-existent.

We no longer live in a world that is so accepting of such experience. Rather, we live in a world in which scientific materialism has come to dominate thinking and institutions. Talk of or belief in or, worse still, a statement of knowledge about a place like the Otherworld, is rarely taken seriously. Yet the personal experience of those who are open to the whole of reality (rather than the small portion that concerns materialists) is that the Otherworld and Faerie are real places and that their denizens are as interested in us as we are in them.

The Otherworld is a mirror of this world. Moreover, this world is seen by each of us through our own eyes and interpreted by each of us in ways unique to us. The mirror of this vision we each have of the world is, therefore, unique to us as well. Our experience of the Otherworld (and of

Faerie) will have much in common with that of anyone else who has been there, but it will also have much that is different. Again, this fact is often used to denigrate the experience as make-believe. If these are real places, say detractors, why do we not all experience them in the same way? Well, how much of this world have you seen? How much of those pieces of the world that you have seen are the same now as when you saw them last? Moreover, is your experience identical with those you were with?

If you have not journeyed to other worlds in general or the Otherworld in particular, you will find it difficult to imagine what it might be like. The easiest way to think of it is to call to mind the places and times in which you were happiest and most at peace. These are not the superficial or fleeting moments of fun that we all experience. The feeling is much deeper. The closest parallel is those times when you have felt at one with the world about you, when the peace within you was such that you could sink wholly into the universe and stand proud of it at one and the same time. Those are times when you stand close to or within the boundaries of the Otherworld. That is what it is like there. That is also why we cannot stay there without our bodies dying and our souls translating. We are not built to withstand constant bliss.

The Otherworld is a place of balance, countering the world that we currently inhabit. There are, for example, no cities to be found there, as we would recognize the term. Cities are manifestations of the materialistic way in which we live. Civilization (literally 'living in cities') has brought with it as necessary concomitants the likes of war, famine, ecological destruction, crime, poverty, disease, and an erosion of the spiritual side of human existence. Our lives in the Otherworld are lived in spirit and when there, our life's task is to come to understand the material side of our existence so that we may better cope with it when we are incarnate in this world. The mirror of this is true when we are here, for now our life's work is to understand better our spiritual side so that when we move to the Otherworld we can concentrate on understanding our material being. And in both worlds, we are meant to strive for order and for balance.

Our journeys back and forth between the worlds come in two forms. When our material form dies, as all material forms do, the soul moves to a place on the shore. All souls gather here and are then ferried across the western ocean by the likes of Barinthus and Bíle, deities whose honoured task it is to conduct souls between the worlds. We have little choice in this, as it is the natural order of things.

Many people fear death, yet there is no need. The material body dies, and that process can be uncertain. Fear of pain, of loss of control, and of loss of dignity is understandable. We all face this. These are inevitable aspects of the decay of the material body. Yet death itself, the moving on of the soul, is merely the start of a new journey. It is the sunset, with the promise of a new day inherent in the demise of the old.

It is why Druids celebrate a death as the beginning of a new life. They certainly mourn for the loss of a loved one. It is painful for any of us to see someone we love suffer; it is painful coping with the wound caused by their amputation from our lives. Yet Druids never lose sight of the fact that mourning and grief are for our benefit, part of the healing process. Those who have started their journey to the Otherworld do not need our tears. In fact, obsessive mourning, an unwillingness to let go, is unhealthy and unnatural. It does great harm because we cease to live our own lives properly. And it does the departed harm, as they cannot move on as they must to a world where they deserve and need to be.

When Druids lose loved ones in this world, they remember them, give thanks for having had the chance to share time with them, and celebrate their existence. And one of the best ways of doing that, they believe, is to move on. The lives of the departed can be celebrated each Samhain and, ultimately, all souls will be reunited.

There is, of course, another way in which it is possible to travel to the Otherworld. This, however, is not recommended to anyone unless they are extremely experienced and know precisely what they are doing. Even then, it is not something any Druid would willingly endorse. The whole enterprise is fraught with danger. That our souls make the journey on the demise of our material beings is one thing. To attempt it in corporeal form is quite another. This is the prerogative of great heroes imbued with prodigious amounts of strength, courage, *and* wisdom – and often even that is not enough, for the other worlds have rules and denizens very much unlike our own. Arthur made the journey with a number of heroic companions. Of all those who went (three shiploads) only seven returned and even then it is not entirely certain that they gained the prize they sought.

The Otherworld is not our natural realm when we are incarnate in this world. Moreover, Faerie is not our natural realm whether we are incarnate in this world or the Other. To travel, or even to attempt to travel, to these places puts us in great danger. Caution and experience can assist us, but even then, they are not absolute guarantees of our safety.

Working with our ancestors should not be confused with travelling to the Otherworld. When Druids consult with their ancestors, it is done with their consent at times when, and in places where, the worlds are coexistent. Samhain is, of course, the best known of the times for this, although this festival of remembrance has become corrupted into Hallowe'en. Druids consult with their ancestors at other times and places, however, as do other people – this is why so many need to know where their loved ones are buried or their ashes are scattered. Many people talk to their dear ones at their grave. It does not mean they believe that person is there, but it is a ritual that enables them to open themselves up and continue the conversations they had when both were still in this world.

This aspect of connection with the Otherworld is harmless and, in some degree, to be encouraged, as long as it does not become obsessive. Keeping open the dialogue we had helps to keep alive the memory of those people as well as allowing us to tap into their wisdom. 'What would Granny have done?' is a more potent question than many imagine – especially if everyone knew Granny well. Her wisdom continues to live in her offspring and she is quite capable of adding to that from her new existence. She has not incarnated in the Otherworld as anyone's Granny, but her soul continues and is well aware of its responsibilities and obligations to the family and to the tribe, even when the concept of tribe has become lost within the other social constructs of our time.

The great voyage that all of us will make (and which Druids believe we have already made on many occasions) is of great importance to us. So, too, is our connection with our ancestors. But our hunger for an understanding of what is to come and of the places to which we will eventually travel does not, and is not allowed to, divert the Druid from their real work, or from the place in which that work is to be done – the here and the now. Sunsets may be spectacular and linger in our memory, but they only last for a tiny fraction of the day. Moreover, if we spend all our time waiting in anticipation of them, the rest of the day is wasted. Treasure each moment. When the sun does finally touch the western horizon, your joy of it will be all the greater for knowing that it is the glory that crowns a day well spent.

10

TREES

TREES

Trees have always been an integral part of humanity's existence. So deeply embedded is this relationship between humanity and trees that they are to be found at the heart of many religions and spiritual mysteries as sources of wisdom and structures for understanding. The cosmic tree stands at the centre of the world, which it supports and nurtures. All the great and momentous occasions of our lives occur through the medium of the tree. We are born from it, it feeds and shelters us, gives us wisdom, and we make sacrifice to it.

Few peoples held trees in such high regard as the Celts and their Druids. This was not a blind and primitive worship, but a genuine veneration based on an understanding of the importance of trees to material and spiritual human existence. The evidence of the close relationship between Celtic peoples and trees is clear in the landscape, with woodlands that have been carefully managed for up to three thousand years, and extensive networks of hedgerows. Certain trees – alder, apple, ash, birch, elm, hawthorn, hazel, pine, oak, rowan, thorn, willow, and yew – are mentioned persistently in Celtic tradition.

Indeed, so important were trees to Celtic peoples that there were laws to protect them and govern how they might be used. In Ireland they were divided into four classes: 'Nobles of the Wood', 'Commoners of the Wood', 'Lower Divisions of the Wood', and 'Bushes of the Wood'.[81] Misuse of timber and living wood was punished with fines according to the class of the tree involved.

Many of the methods of woodland management that are still in use today (although much in decline) were used by ancestral Celts to ensure that their precious resource was renewed. Pollarding, coppicing, planting, drainage, hedging, and so on, along with foraging (by people and animals) were all used to good advantage. The qualities of different timbers were well known and there were even woodworkers who specialized in operating with a single timber. Yet this mundane use of woodland never obscured the emotional and spiritual relationship that ancestral Celts had with the trees that surrounded them.

Although most people no longer consciously acknowledge this bond, it still exists and there are times when it makes itself known. The Great Storm that tore across southern England in October of 1987 uprooted 15 million trees in a few short hours. The wind wrought great damage on houses and other human constructs, and there was even loss of human life, but it was the destruction of large numbers of trees that left many people in a state of shock. Even now, the landscape is so altered that it can be disorientating.

Mythologically, the Celts believed we were descended from trees, springing like fruit from the branches. In particular, they believed we were descended from the sacred oak (Bíle). How widespread or absolute a creation myth this was is uncertain, but a sacred tree, regarded as a 'tree of life', was to be found in the heartland of many Celtic tribes. There is no suggestion in extant sources that Celts had an equivalent of the highly formalized Germanic conception of the world tree. The importance of the tree to the Celts, however, is well attested in classical and Celtic sources and it is likely that a tree did stand at the centre of sacred cosmology in the same way that it stood at the centre of tribal life.

The central role of the tree in human life is also to be found in popular evolutionary terminology – in the expression that we 'came down from the trees'. Our earliest ancestors dwelt within the forests and up within the protective branches away from larger predators. There we were provided with shelter and food, nurtured, allowed the opportunity to become aware of the universe. Even when we became creatures of the plains, we never wandered far from the trees with which our evolution has been so intimately entwined. Indeed, until very recent times, trees have continued to be a major source of materials and food, a major source of understanding.

Even today, we are heavily dependent on trees, although, as with much else, they have become commodified – shattered and torn from the earth faster than they are replaced, processed through factories with no regard for the properties that lie in the timber after the tree is felled, reduced to a form (chippings or dust) that requires toxic chemicals to bond them and lasts a fraction of the time of well-seasoned timber. They are used without respect for their spirits and without realizing that they are far more important to humanity alive than they are dead. What use a roof over our heads and a daily newspaper if the soils have been washed way, the rain has stopped falling, and the air is foul with carbon dioxide?

The importance of the tree to ancestral Celts and to Druids past and present is enormous, but we should not confine this to individual trees, significant as each one and each species most certainly is. Woodland and the deep forest – the tribes and nations of trees with which humanity shares the land – have also informed the metaphysic of the Celts, providing a model by which to understand the world and human life within it.

This is readily apparent in Celtic art. The first recognizable appearance of the tree motif in illuminated manuscripts is late, some time in the mid-eighth century AD. Yet there it appears fully formed as if it had long been in the collective mind. It may also be that it had appeared much earlier, but in a more abstract form. Or that, like Celtic deities, trees were not depicted at all until the influence of the classical world began to alter artistic conceptions. Whatever the case, it was not until the early Christian period that forms that are more naturalistic began to appear in decorative work. Moreover, those representations that do appear are not of any particular tree. The symbolic quality of the tree is so strong that it cannot be tied down to any specific species. Indeed, the tree form that appears in this period resembles mistletoe in its structure far more than it resembles any other type of flora.

This is unlikely to be accidental. Mistletoe was said to be sacred to the Celts, particularly that which grew from the oak tree – a rare occurrence, as mistletoe much prefers the 'sweeter' woods of apple, lime, and pear. Pliny's description of white-robed Druids using golden sickles to cut mistletoe from an oak are considered fanciful, although this has as much to do with dubious translations of his text as it does with actual Druidic practice.[82] There may be more than an element of truth in what he wrote because we know of the reverence with which the plant was treated. The many forked branches of the plant and the white fruit containing sticky liquid are clearly male symbols befitting the sacred tree, which was consort to the Goddess. This constitutes just a small part of the hugely complex web of symbolism that is woven from the presence of the tree and the life of the forest.

The form of a tree presents itself readily for contemplation of the self and our relationship with the rest of the world. Roots deep in the soil speak of the past that nurtures us and of the environment in which we live. Whilst the environment is complex and vast, we can each make our own contribution, we can each put something back, as does the tree each year when it sheds its leaves and its fruit or seed. If soil, environment, and roots are healthy, then the tree will be well nurtured and will grow true.

The trunk is the soul, the self, the great centre, which must stand steadfast in the world. Into this are fed the nutrients that come from the soil. Yet that is only part of the story, for the trunk puts out branches that spread toward the sky and the sun. There, too, is nourishment, but of a lighter form. The land in which the tree grows, and the water that nourishes it, represent the material world, whilst the sky and the sun are the worlds of mind and spirit. Nourishment from the material flows through the trunk to build the branches and leaves, and nourishment flows from the spirit to build strong roots into Mother Earth. This is an extremely important lesson. Druids believe that the material welfare of humanity, indeed of all life, and the spiritual welfare of humanity, are of equal importance. We are a meeting place of matter and spirit and as such should deny neither.

The branches of the tree are the means by which it touches the rest of the world, growing ever outward, forming leaf and dying back with the seasons, fruiting and giving forth to the world that which has been formed by the meeting of matter and spirit. The canopy of the forest forms a vast network (as do the roots), connecting the individual with the community. And whilst we are all familiar with lone trees, the majority thrive in the company of others, for it is in company that the individual finds strength and identity.

That the tree does this all at a slow pace is also a great lesson for us all. We cannot hope, of course, to emulate the great yews, but we can learn to slow down. Many people lead frenetic lives in order to support a host of things they do not actually need (or have time for), whilst others are denied the necessities of a dignified life. We can, however, learn, by example, what is important in our lives and what is dross; how to flow with the seasons of the world in order to be simpler and wealthier.

The forest, too, remains a rich symbol that is worth much contemplation. Much of Arthurian quest and adventure takes place within the forest, which is populated with all nature of beings and spirits. In these days of psychoanalysis, we might be tempted to see the forest as a metaphor for our psyche. It is, however, far more complex than that. Much modern theory about our inner lives seems to be based around the idea that we go in fear of the dark depths within us. Our ancestors, however, did not fear the forest – wolves and bears notwithstanding. They respected it, knew its vagaries and dangers, but did not fear it or see it as something to be conquered. They lived with it and learned from it.

The forest is also, therefore, the great symbol of the Druid Way. Finding their way into and through the forest (or Forest, as some describe it, in order to distinguish between the symbol and the reality), coming to know its glades and groves, its springs and flowers, the high places and shady dells, the tangled thickets and dark places, learning the paths between these things, and the ways of all who inhabit this forest – all this is the life journey of the Druid.

In particular, Druids will learn what they can about specific species of tree, their traditions and place in mythology, and the symbolic qualities that can act to teach lessons relevant to today's world. It is in this way that they 'read' the natural world, drawing spiritual inspiration and understanding whilst caring for its material aspects. There would not be room here to go into detail about particular trees. Whole books can be and have been written on this. However, some brief examples can be given.

BIRCH

The hardiness of the birch – one of the first species of tree to colonize the land as the ice retreated – is often belied by its graceful appearance. Where there is no competition from other species, it will form extensive woodland. The trees, which have a life span comparable to humans, make an excellent habitat for a rich variety of bird life. The epithet 'silver' is thought to have been popularized by Tennyson.

The timber is extremely versatile. It is strong enough for all forms of construction, furniture making, fences, gates, and the like. The bark can be used in the tanning of leather, and is fibrous enough to make rope where there is no better source of material. It makes excellent fuel, the spray being used for smoking hams and herrings. A very pleasant wine can be made from the birch. It is also renowned as the source of materials for the construction of besoms. On these grounds alone, it is a valuable tree and this is reflected in its status under Irish law, where its all-round use to the community meant it was classed as a 'Commoner of the Wood'.

Quite aside from its functional role, the birch was much treasured by Celtic folk, who loved it for its early spring greenery and the dappled golden summer light in its shade during warm weather. They considered its qualities to be feminine and in many places it is still known as the Lady of the Woods.

It is also much associated with love, which is perhaps why it was also used for maypoles. The name of one of Arthur's early companions, Bedwyr, may mean 'birch hero'. This association with love is appropriate as Bedwyr filled the role later occupied by Lancelot. As a tree that buds and comes into leaf early, the birch is connected with new starts and the first life of the year. The first letter of the ogham represents the birch and is used today as a symbol for someone new to the Druid Way (belonging to what some Orders call the Bardic Grade).

YEW

Although now strongly associated with Christian places of worship, to Celts in ancestral times, the yew was possibly the most important of all the trees. A whole Gaulish tribe, the Eburones, took their name from the tree and 'yew' is the root word of a number of place names. Of the three woods most commonly used for the making of wands, yew was certainly preferred over apple and oak. Quite possibly, the longevity of the tree, its propensity to become hollow as it grows, and the fact that cavernous groves can form from the outgrowth of one tree, made it singularly attractive to Druids as a tree in whose shade learning and meditation could take place.

The longevity of the tree is certainly what has led to its being connected with immortality and the cycle of life, death, and rebirth. The tree itself can appear dead yet start growing again after centuries of dormancy. That yews are now found in churchyards has more to do with the fact that Christian churches and burial sites were placed on earlier pagan sites than with any specific Christian connection. Folktales of the trees being protected in order to provide timber for longbows and of keeping livestock away from the berries are largely apocryphal. British yew is not much good for longbows and many churches allowed cattle and sheep to graze the burial grounds.

Judging the age of individual yews is notoriously difficult as tree ring evidence is lost after three hundred years, when the tree starts to become hollow. Yews also go through long periods of dormancy in which little or no growth is recorded. Estimates have to be made based on historical evidence and recent observation. The most conservative estimates make the oldest trees a mere two thousand years of age, but most experts agree that some yew trees may be at least five thousand years of age – predating Celtic culture itself by some one and a half thousand years.

The timber is especially prized for its density and hardness, as well as for the silky, pale golden finish of the sapwood and the dark mahogany-like lustre of the heartwood. The oldest known wooden artefact ever found in the world is a 250,000-year-old yew spear. The timber was and is used for domestic ware such as bowls and cups. In Ireland, the *saí ibrórachta* ('expert in yew-work') was a special category of craftsperson.

The connection of the yew with the life cycle meant that yew staves were used for divination (although we do not know the method). This mystical connection is enhanced by the five-pointed star to be found within the berries. The number five has many mystical and religious connections within Celtic mythology, and the five-pointed star (or pentagram) has suffered the fate of much symbolism connected with pre-Christian religion in that it is now condemned as a symbol of evil. These days the tree is the emblem of those Druids who practise the Vatic arts and is also used to designate the Ovate Grade that is used by some Orders. The yew is closely associated with Samhain and the ending of the Celtic year.

OAK

Of all trees, it is the oak that is most connected with Druids in the popular imagination. This is for good reason. As we have seen, the word 'Druid' derives in part from a connection with the oak, and some sources claim that the god Bíle was, specifically, an oak tree. It is extremely likely that the religion of the Celts developed in and around oak forests and that their veneration for the oak was, in part, due to the versatility of the tree. Indeed, so important was the oak to the people, that it is rare to find a Christian cathedral or older parish church without some depiction of the oak, its leaves, or acorns.

The oak is long lived, sometimes reaching 600 years of age. In this time, it provides a home for a large number of insect species, which, in their turn, attract many species of bird and small mammal. The shade of the tree encourages such flowers as bluebells, foxgloves, primroses, wood anemone, and wood sorrel. The acorns were used for the fattening of pigs, their meat being a staple for ancestral Celts.

The timber of the tree has long been used in building, specifically for the main structure or framework of houses. Oak is also well known for its use in shipbuilding, with tall and straight growths being used for the masts of sailing ships. It carves well and can be used for ornamental panelling and decorative work. Because of all this, it was considered the noblest of the 'Nobles of the Wood'.

Oak groves feature widely in accounts of Druids, as do place names based on the root word for oak. For this reason, some Orders use it as a symbol of the Druid Grade, and all Druids venerate the tree as a symbol of strength, constancy, and protection. It is also connected with fire and the sun and is the tree of the summer solstice.

HAZEL

These days, the hazel is best known for its glowing yellow catkins, universally called 'lamb's-tails'. Its other two major products – nuts and coppiced rods – are less in demand, although the trees are still kept, harvested, and coppiced on a large scale. Rods of hazel have been used for millennia. The timber can easily be split and its fibrous quality allows it to be twisted and bent without breaking. This is why it is used for coarse weaving and for making fences and wattle panels for houses. Forked wands are also much favoured by diviners – especially those seeking water.

Water also plays another part in the life of the hazel. The plant itself (usually only ever seen as a coppiced shrub) prefers to live near water, which immediately associates it with the Otherworld and with Faerie. The wood was sacred to poets, who drew inspiration from their ability to walk between the worlds, usually in places where the hazel grew. Because of this, it was forbidden to use the wood for fires.

More esteemed than the wood, were the fruits of the tree. The nuts are small, sweet, and often to be found in confectionery. We know from archaeological evidence that hazel nuts were an extremely important part of human diet. They are also a staple for squirrels, mice, and birds. Quite apart from being a source of nutrition, however, the nuts are considered to be a source of wisdom, particularly esoteric or magical wisdom. The nuts falling into the water of rivers or of springs and wells caused bubbles of inspiration or were eaten by salmon, which were considered to be creatures of great wisdom. Certain salmon were much sought after and feature in tales of the transformation of ordinary folk into great heroes.

APPLE

Whilst the other trees are of this world, the apple is very much of the Otherworld. The Isle of Avalon of Arthurian tradition is also known as the

Isle of Apples, with the fruit of the tree being able to heal all mortal ills and, in some cases, bestow immortality. Like the fruit of the yew, an apple cut through horizontally will display a five-pointed star. Mistletoe, also known as 'all-heal', grows most readily on apple wood.

The Otherworld, of course, is the place where all ills are healed, but it is also a source of wisdom, and the apple tree is closely associated with both Morgan (a great seeress and head of a sisterhood of nine) and Myrddin. Wands of apple wood may have been the fabled 'silver branches', which bore bells and were used as symbols of Druidic authority. Myrddin speaks of his orchard containing nineteen apple trees and it is conceivable that these represent nineteen years of Druidic learning. Poisoned apples appear on several occasions in the story of Myrddin. In a culture that considered guests sacrosanct, poisoning any food was bad enough; when the food was a sacred food, the crime was heinous.

In this world, the apple tree was prized as a fruit that could be stored throughout the year, cooked in a number of ways, and turned into a potent alcoholic brew. The cider could also be used to produce vinegar, popular as a disinfectant, general medicament, and hair conditioner. The timber could be used for making things, although the tree was much more prized for its produce and was only felled when the tree no longer bore fruit. When burned on an open fire, apple wood releases a delicious scent, reminding one of summer in the depths of winter.

Druids work with the properties of individual trees and of woodland in a number of ways. Trees produce materials that heal, they are replete with complex symbolism that can be used to stimulate and guide meditation and other teaching work, they are the whole spirit of the Druid Way made manifest in this world. Yet Druids are always aware that trees and forest are more than just symbols. They are living entities that have given to us without cease and without question. They have fed us and clothed us, sheltered us and provided us with all manner of things. They have given us life. Druids believe that the least they deserve in return is our respect and our protection. The Druid who does not in some way support reforestation schemes or work to protect threatened forests, trees, and hedgerows is a rare creature.

11

STRUCTURE OF THE DRUID WAY

STRUCTURE OF
THE DRUID WAY

HOW PEOPLE BECOME DRUID

There is no single organization that embraces all Druids or to which all Druids belong. Indeed, there is no single organization that even represents all Druids. Attempts have been made in the past to set up councils and forums through which items of mutual interest can be discussed and (sometimes) agreed upon, but the various groups and Orders have different perspectives and are sometimes fiercely independent. This is hardly surprising and simply echoes the way in which the loyalty of an ancestral Celt was to the tribe rather than to any wider Celtic identity.

It will come as no surprise, therefore, that there is no single hierarchy or overarching authority. There are no true Archdruids, elected by national assemblies and having responsibility for all Druids in a given region. There are no sets of rules or codes of conduct drawn up by a central authority to be imposed on all who wish to be called Druid. There are no doctrinal courts. Some of the larger Orders do have fairly rigid hierarchies, constitutions, and the like – although they almost all state that these are merely administrative. Many other groups, Groves, and networks deliberately avoid such structures, and where individuals have titles, they are explicitly neutral.

It follows that there is no officially agreed syllabus of teachings, no accepted single form of ritual, and no universally recognized form of initiation. Some, recognizing this as anarchy, dismiss it, believing anarchy to be synonymous with chaos. It is not chaos. True anarchy requires that all participants accept responsibility as individuals and collectively for the welfare of the commonwealth. Just as being Druid requires that all participants accept responsibility as individuals and collectively for the welfare of the communion.

Druids follow a common path with common goals. There are many variations and different approaches, but they are all in the Forest, and are all searching for Light. They often do this in groups, helping each other along and teaching others about what they have discovered. The majority do so without feeling the need to impose their authority on, or to accept it from, other people. Even so, you may come across the title Archdruid now and then, but it is generally self-bestowed and more often than not with tongue firmly in cheek. Those rare individuals who have tried to claim such authority in seriousness have no standing in the larger Druid community.

This situation exists because material and spiritual autonomy or sovereignty of the person is central to the Druid Way. For this reason, Druids do not preach to others with the intention of converting them. The very idea is anathema to the Celtic metaphysic and to the essence of what it is to be Druid. Druids *will* explain what they believe if they are asked. They will offer guidance to others, if asked. However, Druids believe that one of the spiritual lessons that has to be learned at a very early stage is that each person must do it for themselves, and that includes finding people who are willing to guide their early steps along the Way.

The notion of autonomy applies particularly to children and young people. Whilst Druids will bring up their own children in the spirit of their beliefs, they will not impose those beliefs on their offspring. In ancestral times, the Age of Choice (at which a person was deemed old enough to be responsible for their decisions and actions) was fourteen. Whilst some children these days may be mature enough to decide on a spiritual path at that age, Druids will rarely formally accept people under the age of eighteen into an Order or Grove. This does not mean that Druids will not teach about their beliefs to people who are younger, but they believe that everyone should make their own choice about their spiritual path, and only once they are knowledgeable and mature enough to take this step.

Given all this, it is legitimate to ask how people become Druid. It is certainly not something that comes in a flash of light. They have to be looking for it before they can find it; yet it is the nature of the quest that people who are searching for a spiritual path do not know precisely what they are looking for. The problem is compounded by the fact that the Druid Way is far from being the easiest spiritual path on which to find information. There are a number of books available, most of which are very basic introductions. More in-depth treatments of the subject are unlikely to be found on the shelves of high street bookshops.

Most Druids have actually been Druid for some time before they can put a name to what it is they are. Not all of those accept the name of Druid. Some prefer to think of this path as a generic Celtic pagan spirituality. Whatever the case, they generally start alone, finding themselves attracted to Celtic history, and beginning to lead lives that are closely in accord with the Celtic metaphysic. Many are happy to continue with that and feel no need to become involved with others. A significant number, however, eventually feel that it would be good to share this interest and growing awareness. There are many ways in which this can occur. Local groups and moots (open pagan meetings) may advertise, friends may know people, and very often chance encounters or happenings will open up contacts at the right time.

In whatever manner the path takes people, they will invariably encounter, or become involved with, some of the larger groups and Orders, or may be invited to join a Grove. For some, this is just a phase and they move on after a few years to explore the path in their own way. For others it is like coming home after a long time away and they immerse themselves in the new group of like-minded people.

DRUID ORDERS

Originally, Druids were just Druids and integral to Celtic Society. The Druid Orders are a 'modern' invention of the revivalists of the eighteenth century. They often owe their present-day existence to individuals or very small groups whose drive and personal vision have shaped them in specific ways. Some Orders are very small, much like extended families, and have grown out of the common experience and shared ideas of members in a relatively small location. Others have thousands of members and necessarily work to a different dynamic.

Most Druid Orders have a hierarchy of people responsible for the running of the organization. There will often be a Chief Druid in overall charge, with others in positions of responsibility within the Order. These positions vary, but revivalist Druid titles such as Pendragon and Scribe are often used. The senior members usually form a Council, which will discuss the running of the Order on a regular basis. Any large organization has to have people working in such a way if things are to run smoothly. The members belong either directly to the Order or to Groves within the Order (the latter especially if the Order covers a wide geographical area).

A number of Orders offer correspondence courses on Druidic teachings to which people can subscribe. Indeed, with some Orders, you may not be considered a member unless you are prepared to study the course. The quality and content of these courses varies and often reflects the particular interests and perspective of the hierarchy. Some are very much influenced by the eighteenth-century Revivalism whilst others eschew this material entirely and work from Celtic literary and folk sources as well as historical and archaeological material. Some Orders also organize lectures, workshops, and camps, where more focused forms of learning can take place. None of them offers anything approaching the intense level of learning required of Druids in ancestral times.

The organization of most Orders, and the construction of their courses, is tripartite – Bard, Vate (sometimes known as Ovate), and Druid. These are usually referred to as grades. This is another invention of the eighteenth-century Revivalists, based on a poor reading of classical sources. Those Orders and groups that use the grade system tend to be the ones that have the most rigid hierarchies.

Some Orders, and a great many Druids who work alone, reject the whole idea of grades, which tend to treat each aspect of the Druid as separate and linear. Most Druids, however, see the threefold division as a useful means of understanding what it is to be Druid. Although the Revivalists of the eighteenth century originally intended their Orders to be hierarchical, with elaborate initiations, rituals, and the like, today, the terms Bard, Ovate, and Druid have taken on a new meaning. By chance or guidance, this new meaning is very close to the way in which Druids originally learned. Rather than being considered grades, the three divisions are now more akin to branches or paths.

In learning to become Druid in the present day, people explore all three branches. Because of the nature of our existence, it is necessary to do this in a certain way, learning basics and building slowly and carefully on these foundations. Unfortunately, this is all too often wrongly interpreted as following a hierarchical structure. Bardic studies come first, however, not because they are at the bottom of a hierarchy, but because they are the ones best suited to unlocking the mind's potential to understand the world in a new way – essential if one is to understand and adopt the Celtic metaphysic. Through an emphasis on the arts (in the broadest sense of that term), people learn to see things as connected and as unified. They also learn to see things intuitively and to value that form of cognition as being as important as any other.

It is not until Druids have overcome what they see as the artificial barriers erected by Western society's metaphysic that they are ready to handle studying those areas that are associated with the Vate. Their studies so far have also prepared them for the move beyond familiar grounds by making available to them an expanded means of expression. Words alone cannot adequately describe the worlds they explore as an Vate. Yet they must describe them in some way, as this is how we all make sense of things for ourselves.

Having made the journey inwards to the very heart of the mystery, having faced themselves, having become familiar with the many other worlds and levels and layers of existence of which they are a part, and having become attuned with them (rather than forcing them into compliance), a Druid is then ready to guide others on to the Way. Any Druid will tell you that once they begin teaching others, they also go back to basics and start again on a new cycle of learning. In this way, they bring an entirely new perspective to their connection with, and understanding of, the world. They are able to refine what they know and understand, coming that bit closer to wisdom.

It is obvious that being Druid is no simple task. It involves changing one's whole self in order to gain the knowledge, the strength, and the wisdom to effect real change in the world. That is why so many Druids and would-be Druids opt, at some stage, to join an Order. These offer community, support, teaching, and advice. Yet, for all that, joining an Order can be a daunting experience. It is a big step, a real commitment to one's personal and spiritual development.

OTHER DRUID ORGANIZATIONS

In addition to the Orders, with their structured and formal (to lesser or greater degree) approach, there are a number of organizations that cater for Druids who shy away from hierarchical structures, or find working with large numbers of people out of tune with their current feelings. These networks, coalitions, and commonwealths cater for a large number of Druids. Some of them also belong to Orders or Groves, but feel the need to communicate more widely; others work alone, but feel the need to maintain some sort of contact with the larger Druid community without being restricted by the ethos of any particular group.

A number of these groups offer correspondence courses, or will put individuals in touch with those who are willing to teach. On the whole, however, they act as non-partisan forums. Usually through the medium of a newsletter or magazine, they provide a means of linking those of like mind so that they can share and discuss their experiences and ideas; encourage and help those who are new to the Druid Way; provide the strength and backing of a community without any strictures; and disseminate news of relevance and interest to the wider Druid community.

GROVES

A Grove is a working community of Druids. By their very nature, they are local, giving an opportunity to meet face-to-face. In this, they provide companionship, an opportunity for like-minded people to work and explore together, and a much more immediate sense of belonging. There are many such Groves and groups. Most not only celebrate the cycle of the year but also organize other activities such as camps, retreats, and initiations.

Groves can be part of the main structure of, or affiliated to, an Order, and many are. Equally, they can be independent groups of Druids who meet on a regular basis, but have no connection with any other grouping. If a Grove is part of an Order, members will need to belong to the Order before they can be invited to become part of the Grove. Some Orders have Grade Groves, which means that the Druid Grove can only be attended by those in the Druid Grade; Vate or Ovate Groves welcome both Ovates and Druids, whilst all grades can attend a Bardic Grove.

Size is immaterial. A Grove can be as small as two people (in which case, it rarely maintains the formality of a larger group), while there is no upper limit on numbers – although, as with any collection of people, group dynamics dictate against too large a gathering being successful. When a Grove reaches a certain size it may split into sister Groves, which function separately for formal rituals and teaching, but come together for informal celebrations. How the Groves are organized internally is very much up to the members (although some Orders insist on certain formalities). It is normal for the most experienced Druid or Druids to be responsible for any teaching that takes place.

CLOSED GROVES

As with groups in other spiritual and magical traditions, some independent Groves – known as open Groves – will advertise for new members, whilst others remain as closed Groves. Closed Groves have an air of mystery about them and can attract a lot of undue attention. There is, however, nothing different about them other than the fact that entry into the Grove is strictly controlled and by invitation only. Such Groves usually come about as a result of a group of people who are already friends deciding to work together spiritually. Most members use the forum of the Grove for formal occasions and ritual, and for group teaching, working on their own to explore particular interests in, and aspects of, the Druid Way.

Druids are alive to the fact that others are seeking a way into the Forest. They are sensitive to those who are true seekers and will often go out of their way to point them in a direction that is appropriate for them. This may sometimes come in the form of an invitation to attend a closed Grove. To begin with, the person is considered a guest. They have been invited to see whether they are compatible with the rest of the group and can join without upsetting the group dynamic (although it will, inevitably, change).

The process can seem both patronizing and elitist, as well as having overtones of secret societies and cults. As with joining any group, the exercise of caution and common sense is advised, especially if it is the group who has made the first approach to the individual. Demands for money, loyalty, changes in social or work life, and so on, are all indications that whatever else the group might be or call itself, it is not a Druid group. A closed Grove will exist simply so that members can preserve something that works for them, not least their close friendships.

HEDGE DRUIDS

A Hedge Druid is one who works substantially alone. There are probably more Hedge Druids than there are Druids in the Orders. This is not surprising. There is, after all, a streak of anarchism in the Druid Way that derives from the fundamental belief that each person is responsible for their own thoughts and actions – something that cannot be fully realized within a hierarchy. Furthermore, most people, on deciding to explore the idea of being Druid, begin alone.

Eventually, most Druids come to feel that it would be good to have contact with others of like mind, share what they have learned, broaden their perspective, and deepen their understanding. This normally means joining a Grove or an Order. However, whilst the Orders have done much to provide teaching, many people do not find other aspects of Orders of interest.

Joining an Order involves embracing the ethos, rules, and structures devised by other people. It is a big step – one that an increasing number of Druids are unwilling to take.

There are, of course, other reasons why people work alone. They may not know any other Druids, or their personal circumstances may make it difficult to meet with others. Some do not wish to practise openly for fear of persecution – a reality, even today. On a more positive note, many Druids simply feel that working alone is the best way for them to explore the Forest.

There is a long and venerable history of Hedge Druidry. The majority of Druids in ancestral times would have worked alone once they had completed their training. They would have been attached to something like a ditched enclosure, a sacred site, a tribal leader, or even a village – offering their wisdom and practical skills to all who were in need of them.

Hedge Druids fulfil an extremely important role within the tradition and are by no means any less Druid for not working within a Grove or an Order. They tend to focus on their own exploration and concentrate on their own practices without having to do what others ordain. They do not need to become involved with group politics. They can do things how they like and when they like, following their own path and adding to the great commonwealth of knowledge and understanding as they go. Their withdrawal, paradoxically, enables them to form an outward looking and intimate bond with the Land, practising for their beliefs, for the Goddess, and for truth, rather than for a human organization, be it Grove or Order.

Of course, there is a down side. It is always good for a person to be part of a community of like-minded souls. It is here that they can discuss things and pass on what that have learned, as well as gain emotional and spiritual strength from knowing they are not alone. Without the contact afforded by a Grove or an Order, this is not possible. Moreover, it takes a particular strength of will to carry on when there is a lack of connection with the wider Druid community – a particular problem at the festivals. It can be difficult finding the enthusiasm to perform a ritual alone, especially on a cold winter's night. That is why most Hedge Druids maintain contact with other Druids, usually people with whom they have become close friends. Absolute isolation would be contrary to the basic ideas of the Druid Way. However, retreating from the World in order to become closer to the world is a time-honoured tradition.

There are variations in the nature of the organized groups and Orders, depending on the traditions they follow, the countries in which they are based, and so on. However, the basic pattern is very much the same wherever you look. The older structures set up by the eighteenth-century Revivalists and patterned on Masonic groups are slowly fading as more and more Druids are going directly to Celtic source material for guidance and inspiration, and not just for spiritual exploration, but for social organization as well.

12

CEREMONIAL AND RITUAL PRACTICE

CEREMONIAL AND RITUAL PRACTICE

Everything that Druids are and do is informed by the rhythms of the Land, the Sea, and the Sky. These are the slow and steady beating of their spiritual heart. Their recognition of this is marked by an annual round of ceremonies. Some are fixed events, working with the dance of sun, moon, and stars. These are Imbolc, spring equinox (Alban Eiler), Beltane, summer solstice (Alban Hefin), Lughnasad, autumn equinox (Alban Elfed), Samhain, and winter solstice (Alban Arthan) – collectively referred to as the eightfold year or sometimes as the wheel of the year.[83] Others are more intimate rituals, determined not only by the major events of their lives, but also accompanying the daily and mundane activities that Druids undertake.

There is, of course, a great deal more to being Druid than performing rituals. Indeed, many Druids, although recognizing the importance of these events, do not make a great song and dance of them. Hedge Druids in particular often mark the important times with quiet periods of meditation and simple ritual rather than elaborate ceremony. Yet in whatever way these events are approached, the underlying spirit and the intent are the same, for celebration is both important and integral to the Druid Way.

The act of celebration through ritual is, of course, one of the major means by which Druids integrate the material and spiritual aspects of their lives. The most obvious and overt way is in their use of material objects and physical expression to create a space in which they can focus on the spiritual. For Druids (and for many other pagans), this space is not delineated by a formal structure, such as a church or temple. They much prefer to work outside and set up their working space by drawing a circle. Strictly speaking, they work within a sphere, but as the casting of a circle creates a sphere and they move in circles within it, it is easier to continue referring to it as a circle.

The circle and its centre are seen as dynamic symbols, made manifest through the actions and thoughts of all living beings and of the systems in which they exist. This circle is a microcosm of the world, and into it Druids welcome symbolic representations of the spirit of the world at large. There is more to the circle than this, however, for it is also a place in which Druids may work safely and without distraction. They retreat in order to connect more closely. They cut off the World in order that they might experience the world. In creating a safe and quiet place in which to work, they also provide themselves with a place from which they can travel and to which they can return – a spiritual hearth.

Beyond their work, rituals, and times of quiet and prayer, Druids are still Druid. All life takes place within the circle of their being. Although they might set aside a special place at certain times, it is vital to remember that for them the whole world is a temple and all things within it are sacred. That is why they feel they can cast a circle wherever they are, upon the ground or in their minds. That is why the Druids of old built no temples or places of worship. They had their places apart, the sacred groves and places of power, but they moved through the world and were part of everyday life, seen by the people as the roots of life, stabilizing the world; seen by the people as doorways, giving them access to the many other worlds about them where their ancestors lived and where they, one day, would travel.

The symbolism of the circle is enormously complex for such a simple figure, yet the circle is important to Druids for more than its symbolic value. The physical shape in the material world, even if it is drawn in the air or the mind, is a powerful presence. What is more, in keeping with all that Druids hold sacred, it is temporary. No matter what positive energies may radiate from the ritual performed within, the circle is always closed at the finish and the physical place of ritual is left as if no one had been there.

The circle is a shape in which thought, light, and other energies radiate evenly from the centre. It is also a shape in which all who form it are of equal standing. What is more, a circle is easy to draw. To make the physical presence of a circle, a single person simply needs to turn on the spot, marking the ground with a stick or staff; a group can hold hands and spread out evenly. Many experienced practitioners who work alone often envisage a circle in their mind –a far easier shape to imagine and hold there than any other.

The creation of this space is a first and simple step in using the material to bring thought and action to bear on the spiritual. However, the integration of these aspects goes much further. Druids do not simply use one to gain enhanced engagement with the other. Rather, they work within the space they have created to move onward, using the aspect of their being in which they are deeply seated (the material) to secure their integration with that aspect of their being to which they strongly aspire (the spiritual).

The shape of the ritual within the circle is also important to Druids. Although no rituals survive from ancestral times, those that are used have been developed over a number of centuries from what sources are available. Each ritual has evolved complex, multi-layered forms that entrain the whole being, opening the Druid up within protected space to the wider existence of which they (and all of us) are a part. The objects used, the words spoken, and the physical actions – all act as triggers. Their cumulative effect is profound as they become imbued with universal and personal symbolic significance, working as keys to unlock those aspects of the Druid's being that require constant release.

The more a given ritual is enacted, the more a Druid is able to concentrate on content and meaning rather than form. This creates a journey through the years from formal expression and the matrial into the underlying principles on which these are based. This is not to say that form is unimportant. Far from it. The formal shape of ritual is the hearth from which a Druid journeys and remains as a haven to which they return. Druids believe it important to journey away from the hearth if they are to discover its importance; they must journey away if they are, ultimately, to return.

The form also has importance because it is in the repetition and in the use of specific objects that Druids build up the associations and charge the symbols that unlock the mystery within themselves. There is a balance to be kept here as elsewhere. Too much emphasis on the material aspect and it becomes a habit, a chore, something to be cast aside. However, if the material is wholly cast aside in favour of a simple meditation, then the specific and special ritual or ceremony that is essential – be it to celebrating the turning of the year or the cycle of life – is lost. A further facet of this is that whilst meditation alone does not constitute a full and specific ritual, performing ritual on a regular basis *is* a long-term form of meditation. Moreover, as with all meditation, the more it is practised, the easier it becomes, and the more it is of benefit.

Meditation is not used by Druids to try to attain a state of disconnectedness. Rather, they focus on particular symbols and myth cycles, as well as deities and entities, in order to reach a deeper understanding of, and more profound connection with, the worlds they inhabit. The rituals that mark the turning of the year, the rites of passage, along with any other rituals Druids choose to perform (welcoming the day, honouring the quarters of the moon, and so on) are themselves hugely complex and living symbols that contain pointers to myth and deity. The process of enacting these on a regular basis is much the same in the long term (although on a much larger scale) as sitting down each day for a short, personal meditation. In terms of effect, however, there is a great difference. Much as each ritual itself unites the material and spiritual aspects of our lives, the cumulative effect of a lifetime of ritual is a calming and ordering of the environment in which the rituals take place.

This is not simply the physical environment. Rituals have a beneficial effect on the location in which they are conducted. The effect, however, is in time and it is in spirit as well. Continuity over a long period creates a sacred space within, from which the Druid can work. Not only does this enhance their own being, but it also works through them to enhance the worlds they inhabit. The place of ritual itself becomes a centre of harmony and a source of power. It is protected and calm. This is seen as having a beneficial effect on the surrounding flora and fauna as well as radiating beyond that into the contiguous spiritual and material planes in both space and time. It is also seen to work inwards into the environments of those involved in ritual, balancing their inner ecologies.

The meditative effect of ritual allows Druids to become aware of the connection between the material and spiritual aspects of being. It guides them to the realization that these are not separate, but are merely the same thing seen from different perspectives. That the spirit is withered in many of us is another matter altogether and part of the larger work of being Druid. Ritual is an important method by which the spirit is nurtured. Ritual also provides a disciplined approach through which an openness to the universe is guided by the wisdom inherent in its structure.

Such grand sounding intent would seem to imply that all ceremony is a matter of gravity and pomp – robes, paraphernalia, obscure rites, and archaic language. This is not the case, public examples notwithstanding. Ceremony can be enacted simply and alone or in small groups, and it is often more appropriate to do so. Large formal events have their place, but just as people cannot always live on a mystical high, so Druids cannot always approach their veneration of the worlds in a formal way. They learn, rather, to touch and appreciate all the worlds in an intimate fashion.

This more intimate approach is often accomplished through prayer. Prayer is problematic for many pagans. They see it as belonging largely to the Abrahamic tradition. However, prayer is much older than these faiths and we all indulge in it, quite often without realizing that we are. Prayer works in much the same way as more formal ritual except that it rarely takes place within specially created sacred space. Rather, it is the daily conversation we have with the sacred that is all about us.

That prayer is a conversation is important to remember. There are two sides to it and whilst we are all very good at our side, when it comes to listening to what the world has to tell us, many of us have closed ears. One of the things that Druids learn very early is how to open their ears to the other side of the conversation – and also that their 'ears' are not always those things on the side of their heads. Indeed, the conversation can be carried on in many ways, through many different media. Learning to pick up that other half of the conversation is why Druids pay such close attention to the natural world, for that, they believe, is their greatest teacher. Druids are not made by reading books (although books certainly help in the absence of Druid colleges and mentors). Druids are made by learning to see (rather than just look) and learning to listen (rather than just hear). They are made by engaging with the world and with the sacred.

Prayer is a method of training as well as a way of keeping up the conversation. It is, in fact, the way in which Druids attune themselves to the everyday. And the everyday is important, for it is in the everyday that Druids believe true magic is to be found – in such things as the growing of food, cooking, companionship, and all the other basic sights, sounds, and experiences of our lives. Therein lies the majesty and wonder of the universe, for whilst things such as the stars are a great glory, Druids recognize that we cannot touch them as yet; merely watch them from a distance.

It is clear, then, that one of the purposes and results of ritual is unity. Druids must bring all aspects of their being to bear on a single focus; they must concentrate all that they are into a single event. If done properly, this unification stays with them once the circle is closed. It becomes habitual in the sense that they live within it. This is important. Ritual, like mystical experience, is of necessity short-lived. The physical body could not stand the strain of constant ecstasy or of constant focus. This was recognized in the

Grail stories. Those who achieved the Grail died as a result. The physical bodies of even the strongest and most battle-hardened knights could not withstand the constant presence of mystical understanding. This is not to say that a person is not changed by enlightenment. However, life goes on – lived in a new way with different priorities. This is because an enlightened person perceives the world in a new and more comprehensive way, with the lessons learned from their brief glimpses of the infinite carried with them into their everyday lives.

Unity is not confined to people becoming more integrated within themselves. Druid ritual also acts to help each Druid unify the self with the rest of creation. One of the greatest problems facing humanity, Druids believe, is the erroneous idea that humanity is somehow separate from the rest of the world. Ritual is an excellent means by which to open participants to a new understanding, and create a new metaphysic, one that accepts the fact that people are just a small part of an enormous whole. It is one of the mysteries of such understanding that in recognizing that we are each infinitesimal on a universal scale, we also see that we do exist, we do have a place. Ritual plays its part in this understanding. It integrates each of us with the universe, but it also enables each of us to celebrate our own uniqueness.

Druids celebrate in a particular way. Moreover, individual Druids adapt the form of celebration to suit their own circumstances and understanding. Their rituals are very much part of who they are and develop with them. They allow Druids to express themselves in ways true to their own natures whilst also celebrating the ineffable. Druids should celebrate the ways in which they each react to the mysteries and to their own development. It is a dimension that is often overlooked in ritual. The intent may be serious and profound, Druids may be dealing with mysteries and intense emotional experiences, but they take joy in that. Indeed, they take joy in the very fact that they can celebrate and that they each have their own way of doing it.

Druid ritual, therefore, is a way for Druids to celebrate their own existence and provides them with a way to recognize that they each do have a part to play. It also provides a means for them to consider how they are playing that part and how they might better be serving the world. Once again, this occurs not just within the ritual. The symbols they use are not confined or confinable to the sacred space. By marking specific times of the year and specific events in their lives, they continue to open the doors that release their potential, that release their spirit, and that release their understanding.

The annual rituals make use of myth and of deity, but they do not make use of it all. Nor do they confine it. They act, rather, as a focus in order to revitalize the feeling of community and to make the participants think about specific things. Each ritual is like a beacon lit upon a hilltop. Druids will dance within the warmth, gather within the light, and celebrate while it is there. The flames never really die, however, as they live on in the memory, illuminating everyday thoughts and actions. Druids extend the celebration beyond ritual by allowing the lessons they have learned to be applied to the rest of their lives.

For the Druid, everyday actions and activities carry with them the sacred – even cleaning and shopping. In addition, there are many practical ways beyond the domestic in which Druids tend to express their joy. Many are involved with helping animals and in other forms of conservation work; many help their fellow human beings. After all, the different cycles of celebration undertaken by Druids are seen as aspects of a unified celebration of their very existence. Although each ceremony focuses on a different aspect of their life and its connection with the rest of existence, they are part of a larger pattern in which ritual is seen not as something special (although it undoubtedly is), but as essential to right living.

THE EIGHTFOLD YEAR (WHEEL OF THE YEAR)

Of all the rituals associated with Druids in the popular imagination, it is those (or some of those) that mark out the turning of the year that first come to mind. As they are celebrations of the shape of the year and their timing is determined by the movements of the sun and the moon, they are referred to here as Sky rituals. This is not an absolute demarcation, but a matter of emphasis. Although there are also distinct Land rituals and Sea rituals[84] (so representing the three elements of Celtic cosmology), all three elements are represented in each of the groups.

It is important from the outset to remember that what is being celebrated is a cycle. Linear thought and application belong to the modern scientific metaphysic that currently dominates most people's thinking. Yet purely linear features are rare beyond modern human thought and construction (and then mostly to be found within the mineral kingdom). The Celtic metaphysic, the view of the world shared by Druids, has it that everything unfolds and evolves in a cyclical fashion.

The most obvious examples are the diurnal cycle of light and dark, the lunar cycle, and the changing of the seasons. These particular cycles are caused by the movement of the earth and moon about each other and the journey of both about the sun. The rhythms created by this cosmic dance are a major influence on our lives and govern much of our behaviour. There are minor regional variations (affecting the length and form of the seasons), but the overall effect is the same and they have shaped us all at a fundamental level. It is no accident, therefore, that many different peoples have celebrated the significant stages in the cycles of the sun and the moon and formalized their celebration with ritual. Woven in with this reverence for what has helped to shape us are the many mythologies that help connect the abstract concepts with the everyday and reflect people's experience of these events.

When it comes to the cycles of sun, earth, and moon, there are eight festivals in all, one celebrated every six weeks or so. In terms of ancestral practice, there is a degree of controversy over the eightfold year. Four of the festivals are well attested and some have even survived to the present day – still being celebrated in some form or other in various Celtic countries and regions. These are the four lunar[85] festivals (called, as we have seen, Imbolc, Beltane, Lughnasad, and Samhain), sometimes also referred to as the fire festivals. They delineate the seasons and celebrate the agricultural cycle. The solar festivals mark the equinoxes and solstices.

The solar and lunar festivals are interwoven to reflect the complex and holistic nature of being. The lunar festivals were governed by the agricultural existence of our ancestors and had to reflect their daily life and experience. Celebration was woven in with practical concerns. The need to meet, exchange goods and news, perform ceremonies in the public eye, conclude deals and settle disputes, and ask the gods and goddesses for continued protection, was as much an occasion for song, dance, gossip, and a drink as it was for solemnity. Truth and joy are good companions. That all this was presided over by Druids is without question. Their position within Celtic society would have demanded it. They were not just there in their official capacity, however. Druids were and are just as likely as anyone else to want to celebrate the material, be it a good harvest or the treasured memory of loved ones.

The solar ceremonies acted as a counterbalance. For all that they were probably held in broad daylight, they celebrated the spiritual cycle of the year and of life. In all likelihood, they were quiet, formal occasions creating a mystical atmosphere in which people could reflect on and give thanks for their relationship with the spiritual domain. Perhaps, too, Druids had private ceremonies at these times, when they could reflect on their own being rather than ministering to others. Although the content of these ceremonies may have been lost to us, the intent is still apparent. Christmas (winter solstice) and Easter (spring equinox), for example, may have become heavily commercialized, but many people still recognize in some way that these are times of the spirit. In contrast, we still light fires at Samhain and have parties, albeit that many now call it Bonfire Night or Hallowe'en.

The solar festivals are absolute within the year, since those four days define the year (even if the Gregorian calendar moves a day or two back and forth about them). The lunar festivals are more problematical. We know the Celtic lunar calendar was sophisticated, but any system that tries to meld lunar and solar cycles will only coincide every nineteen years. The months drifted back and forth in relation to the fixed framework of the solar cycle. Festivals, therefore, could not be standardized to the first day of certain months, as their movement would mean that a ceremony to celebrate the harvest, for example, could be held weeks before the crops were even ripe. Most people today are too used to a solar calendar to appreciate this. The basic calculations, however, are simple. Lunar festivals fall approximately forty-five days after solar festivals. Given the complexities of modern life, most present-day Druids celebrate the eightfold year on the conventional dates (and very often on the weekend nearest those). Others perform quiet private rituals at the correct time and more open ceremonies at the nearest convenient date – believing that an understanding of the cycle and the keeping of it in spirit is much more important and effective than soulless pedantry.

The summer solstice is often cited as the most important of the eight annual rituals performed by Druids. This is reinforced in popular thought by scenes of people performing rites each year at such places as Stonehenge.[86] However, not all Druids agree with this emphasis. For many, the most important ceremony is at the winter solstice, whilst others mark their year from Samhain, the ancestral Celtic New Year. Whatever the case, what follows is a brief description of the focus of each of the eight rites. Individual groups will have their own specific emphases within this broad framework.

IMBOLC

Imbolc is the ceremony that celebrates the promise of spring. Although the days are still cold and wet, they are becoming perceptibly longer – final proof that the sacred child reborn at the winter solstice has survived and thrives. The essential feature of Imbolc, however, is the honouring of the Goddess, of Woman, of the Land – all imbued with the power and the responsibility of bringing forth life. This ultimate and essential act of creativity is celebrated in verse and song and is personified by the goddess Brigid. In common with many Celtic deities, she is triple-aspected. She is a goddess of healing and fertility, a goddess of smiths, and a goddess of poetry – all of which are associated with fire and flame, with the hearth, with creativity.

Brigid is a daughter of The Dagda and is often represented wearing a crown of light. A perpetual flame was kept in her honour in a sacred grove at what is now known as Kildare (which means 'church of the oaks'). This was a female enclave, not uncommon in ancestral times, and was a centre of learning for medicine, the Bardic arts and, quite possibly, the martial arts.

Although Imbolc is a time to celebrate the promise of spring, it is also a reminder that it is just that – a promise. Nothing is certain during the early steps of any journey. This is also, therefore, a time to be wary, a time to call on reserves of strength, a time to learn to pace oneself. Ancestral Celts knew this well. By this stage of the year, they had survived the winter on what they had stored away and although the sun was gathering strength, their own supplies would be low, and the new growth and early vegetables could still be blighted by late frosts.

At this time of renewed vigilance, Brigid's gifts are most appropriate. Life in its early stages is always precarious, be it for the lamb, the human child, the seedling, or the community. And so it is for the spirit. There comes that stage in the journey when the first reserves of enthusiasm for what is new have worn low and the length of the journey can be seen clearly. Brigid can heal and reinvigorate, Brigid can sing a charm, and Brigid can arm everyone at the forge for whatever battles they may face. So important was Brigid to the Celtic peoples that her cult was almost wholly subsumed into Christianity.

SPRING EQUINOX

The spring equinox is a fleeting moment of balance. Night and day, light and dark, inner and outer – all these things and so much more stand, at that brief moment, in equality. As this is a solar ceremony, this balance is symbolized by the moment when the waning powers of winter are evenly matched by the waxing powers of summer.

Balance is important to Druids in many ways. This ceremony celebrates that, whilst making it clear that balance is not a static state, but one which can only be achieved by accepting and living with the cyclical nature of existence. If balance were static, nothing would progress and nothing new could be learned. It is in the completion of each cycle and the venturing into the next, that wholeness is achieved.

At each equinox, Druids pause for an instant in the act of crossing a threshold. They stand poised, in acknowledgement of the moment, before stepping from one realm to another. In crossing the threshold at the spring equinox, which they must if they are to be a part of the cycle, they leave behind the enclosed and contemplative world of the Winter King, which is centred upon the hearth. From that, they move towards the open and active realm of the Summer King, which is centred upon the forest grove.

They pause on the threshold to reflect on the fact that their sojourn in one realm is, amongst other things, a preparation for work in the next. The hearth work, the closeness of relationships, and the inner journeys they make during the six winter months will be of use as they step forth into a more physically active part of their lives.

Along with this, there is a celebration of the great potency of the youth of the year, symbolized by the Mabon – the solar hero Arthur, with all the wild and budding world before him. Yet this power is nothing without the blessing of Sovereignty, the goddess of the Land. To her, both Winter and Summer owe allegiance. Moreover, although they contend one with the other to be her champion, their reigns are complementary – providing a balanced whole throughout the course of each year.

BELTANE

The original meaning of the name of this ceremony is 'lost', although it probably meant the 'fires of Bíle'. No surprise then that the major feature of Beltane is fire. It was a time for the renewal of the perpetual hearth fires that were to be found in every home. These would be extinguished, the hearths cleared, cauldrons scoured, fire dogs cleaned, the house generally tidied, and all set new and fresh. The fire would then be relit by Druids from torches carrying flame from the ceremonial bonfire – each household thereby receiving a blessing from sun and Druid alike.

The lighting of the ceremonial bonfires and the rekindling of the hearth fires probably marked the beginning and end of the formal parts of Beltane.

However, much else went on, both formal and informal, that centred on the Bel Fires. Leaping through flames (or over the embers at the edge for the less nimble and adventurous) was one of these.

Leaping was done for many reasons, but it was essentially to bring good fortune. This practice was not confined to Beltane, however, as there are well-documented descriptions from Ireland that folk leapt the summer solstice bonfires there in the late eighteenth century. Leaping was based on the belief that the fires destroyed those powers hostile to humanity, purified the air, and allowed people, animals, and plants to thrive and become fertile. In some areas, it was the custom to build two fires and drive livestock between them. It must have been a frightening prospect for the animals but there is evidence to suggest that it was an effective way of killing the parasites that would have thrived on beasts confined during the winter.

Another theme of this final spring ceremony is fertility in its widest sense – the generative light and heat of the sun symbolized by the fires. In later centuries, this became part of folk culture in the May dances that evolved from the less formal aspects of the Beltane celebrations. May dancing, when looked at carefully, reveals a very complex pattern of movement and ritual, producing spiral patterns on the ground pierced through the centre by the pole. The circles and cycles that are set out by the dance provide conduits through which the energies that lay within the earth could rise to the surface. These dances occurred in the last of the three ceremonies associated with spring, as it was essential that everything should have been prepared and ready to accept the energies that were raised. Fields would have been ploughed and sown, animals turned out to pasture, houses spring cleaned, and so on. This first burst of activity in the agricultural cycle would have been more or less complete by Beltane – a bit like cleaning the grate and laying a new fire. Everything would then be ready and waiting for the spark of energy provided by the match.

Life has changed a great deal since the prevalence of the Beltane festivals and the May celebrations. Beltane now works on a deeper level with energies of the spirit, rather than with the earthy energies of the past. Fertility and the rising powers of spring are now celebrated, honoured, and harnessed in the context of a spiritual quest to restore something of the old ways of working with the Land, honouring Sovereignty, and maintaining vitality.

SUMMER SOLSTICE

Although the solstice is an astronomical event that takes place at a particular instant in time, the celebration of summer solstice is generally held on the longest day of the year. This is the time when the sun, born anew at the winter solstice, reaches the very peak of its strength. In the symbolic struggle between the Light and the Dark, the powers of growth and decay, the Kings of Winter and Summer, this is the point of greatest brightness and vigour in the annual cycle.

The Mabon, child of the Goddess, has now reached his full powers. The realm of Arthur is finally at peace. Druids celebrate that potency and that potential because, in combination with the Goddess, it has given us all life and will ripen us all to maturity. In that lies one of the deep truths of the Druid Way: that nothing is constant except, perhaps, the constancy with which the cycles turn. For Druids know and accept that just as the sun reaches its greatest strength, its powers will now fade until the Winter King gains the upper hand and reaches his full strength at the time of the winter solstice. And just as Arthur's realm comes to know peace, its powers are scattered in the quest for the Grail. Ultimately, however, Arthur embodied both summer and winter. His reign was one of transformation in which opposing forces, rather than competing for the right to represent Sovereignty, were subsumed within it.

Druids celebrate their personal sovereignty. They cannot, they believe, rely on others to run their lives; they cannot rely on others to be guardians of the Land. They feel they must take up these entwined responsibilities for themselves. Sovereignty is to be bestowed on each of them if they prove themselves worthy, and they must stand in the full spiritual glare of the midsummer sun and know their own hearts. They must embrace all the aspects of their selves, and integrate them so that they may use them in service of the Land, as well as in service of the Goddess and the God.

LUGHNASAD

Lughnasad means 'the remembrance of Lug'. The name is ambiguous. It does not commemorate Lug, as one might think, but was instigated by him in memory of his foster mother, Tailtiu. Lughnasad became a great festival lasting many weeks and featured athletics events as well as displays of skill and artisanship. The last official contests were held in August of 1169 under the jurisdiction of Ruraidh Ó Conchobhar, the last High King of Ireland.

This was also traditionally a time when farmhands were hired for the coming year, when animals were sold, when far-flung communities came together, and when temporary marriages were made (to be ended after a year and a day if the couple did not get along under the same roof). It also marked the beginning of the cereal harvest, the period that ends with the autumn equinox.

Tailtiu was a daughter of the Fir Bolg king of the Great Plain. She became foster mother to Lug. That Lug should establish a great festival in honour of Tailtiu says much about his affection for her. That it should be kept to this day betokens the importance of what she did – single-handed, clearing the forest of Breg for use as agricultural land, dying as a result of her labours. The Great Goddess allowed an aspect of herself to be sacrificed in order that her new children could settle and feed themselves with skills passed on to them by her foster-child Lug. The principal connection between Lug and Tailtiu is, therefore, one of agriculture in its widest sense – a use of all skills to tend the earth without abusing her.

It is a feature of the Celts, and of Druids today, that a festival of life and a time of celebration should mark the death of one as beloved as Tailtiu. This is a recognition of death in life, of the cycle that sustains us all, and of the sacrifice made by so many on our behalf. Without the harvest, without the mowing down of the grain and grass, there can be no sustenance and no renewal. Druids believe it is right, therefore, that the fertility and life of the Land and all its creatures should be celebrated and their unity recognized, even at the time of the cutting of the corn when thoughts turn to the decay and death of the year.

AUTUMN EQUINOX

The autumn equinox is a mirror image of the spring equinox. It marks the end of the dominance of the Summer King and the move toward Winter's rule. Once again, all is equally balanced. Summer has gone. Winter has yet to be. Everything moves inexorably from the Light to the Dark. Light should not, however, be equated with goodness and the Dark with evil. Those are largely Abrahamic notions and have no relevance to the way in which ancestral Celts saw the world. The Dark is as important to Druids as the Light, but it requires a different way of working and a different strategy for managing.

The inspiration for this is in the natural world. As summer gives way to winter, we see that plants and animals are preparing themselves for the coming season. Most trees begin to shed their leaves – and those that do not have leaves that are adapted to the cold and the stronger winds. Plants start to die back and retreat beneath the ground where they are protected from frosts and over-grazing. Animals stock up with food either by hoarding it or by eating more to put on extra layers of fat. Some animals will later hibernate. Everything is preparing itself for a period of quiescence when little happens in the outer world.

In the past, it was second nature for our ancestors to start building up their stores of firewood and food, to make sure their dwellings were capable of withstanding the storms of winter, to see the outer world put in order before retreating within their dwellings and their selves. There, they would take up work that could be done indoors, just as they would take up work that could be done within themselves. It was a time of weaving and repairing, a time of storytelling, a time when they were forced together and had to learn to get along. It was a time to sit quietly and think, a time of patience.

Modern conveniences isolate us from the need to respond to the changing seasons. Nonetheless, Druids respond in other ways and think carefully about the changes and what they mean to them in both material and spiritual terms. This is reflected in the ceremony itself, which celebrates a mature strength that will carry the Druid forward. They cross into the inner realm of the Winter King ready to meditate upon the experiences gained from their more practical work in the outer world.

SAMHAIN

Samhain is not about death, as many suppose; it is about the dead. There is a difference. If there is a place on the wheel of the year for death, it is the autumn equinox, but death is so much a part of the process of living, so much a part of the ongoing cycle, that it is accorded no special status. The dead, however, do have their own festival, for they are the ancestors, the loved ones now gone. Druids believe it is only right that they pay their respects to the dead, and set aside a special time to honour them. This coincides with what ancestral Celts considered the end of summer and the end of the agricultural year. It is indicative of their attitude to death that the end of the cycle is not death itself (the harvest) but the state of being dead (fields cleared and ready for the next year).

With all the work of the year done and everything ready for the coming cycle, there would be time then for Celts to tidy up their past lives, time to settle differences, time to pay debts, and time to remember. Samhain is a recognition of the fact that when the time comes, we should embrace death as readily as we embrace the rest of life.

This attitude applies equally to relationships and associations, be it the end of a marriage, leaving school, or leaving home. It is, Druids believe, part of the natural order of our lives, part of the cycle of our being, and like any part of the cycle, it marks a transition from one phase of being to another.

Originally, this was a time for guising (going masked). Men would disguise themselves as women, women as men, young as old, old as young, living as dead, and dead as living. This custom has its roots in a belief that the dead return to commune with the living at a time when the normal boundaries between this world and the Otherworld are dissolved. There is nothing sinister in this – none of the ghosts, monsters, or rotting corpses implied by Hallowe'en. It was simply a time to make a final reckoning of what had been lost, to honour and give thanks for the time that had been shared, to settle debts (from which trick or treat has probably evolved), and to say a final goodbye so that both the living and the departed could move on in their respective worlds.

WINTER SOLSTICE

The time of the winter solstice has been marked and celebrated by many peoples for thousands of years. It was traditionally an open-air ceremony on sites with orientations toward the solstice sunrise and, in some cases, the sunset as well. Newgrange in County Meath, Ireland (built some 4,500 years ago) was carefully constructed so that the light of the rising midwinter sun passes along the upper gallery of the approach passageway, straight into the central chamber. At Stonehenge, the rising sun on midwinter's day can be seen through the south-east trilithon.

Druids, of course, did not build these monuments, although they doubtless knew of their existence and function. However, these monuments do establish the antiquity and importance of the event. And we know the winter solstice was still supremely important through into the historical era because the Christian Church appropriated it at the end of the third century AD as the moment of the nativity of the Christ.

During the ceremony, the cycle of death and rebirth is observed, the apparent death of the sun is mourned, the lights extinguished, the greatest dark of the year embraced. It is in this deepest darkness that each person is alone. However, the moment is not endless, for the fire is lit and the sun returns. It is not yet strong, but its light is the hope and promise of a new year and a new reign. All this is embodied in the ceremony in the person of the Mabon, the sacred child. As his birth is always on the shortest day (and feasted after he has survived for three days), he is clearly a solar deity. Much of the myth cycle of the Mabon has been lost to us in direct form, but we can glimpse some of it from the early Arthurian tales.

Arthur, too, is a solar deity. He comes into his own on the shortest day, drawing the sword from the stone and thereby demonstrating his unique power over the two great symbols of summer and winter, the symbols of the Land and of Sovereignty. With him and aiding him in his quest to unite and heal the Land is Gawain in his guise as a green man, who achieves his own quest for Sovereignty in Arthur's name, bringing renewed fertility. Morgan, too, is present, watching over Arthur, protecting him from harm, bestowing further symbols of her power upon him. And, when he has broken his mortal self in her name by protecting the Land, she bears him away to be healed in Avalon.

For many Druids, the ceremony at winter solstice is by far the most important of the annual celebrations. It is the turning point of the whole year, where one inner cycle ends and the next begins. The ritual celebrates birth and rebirth, healing, sovereignty, and a commitment to the Land. It is also the most personal of the ceremonies, for whereas the others treat equally with the relationship between the material and spiritual, the winter solstice ceremony is almost entirely inward. It revolves around the relationship that a Druid has with the self – the place where each must stand alone in the dark.

There is nothing maleficent in this. At its most exoteric, it is about coping with the problems that life throws at us, especially those for which we have a genuine responsibility. Esoterically, it is the moment when a Druid reaches the centre of the spiral and at that place has to come to terms with their true self, perhaps the hardest task of all on any spiritual journey.

Darkness is to be found at the heart of all mystery traditions, and there, if you are spiritually ready, you will find two things. The first is that no matter who or what you may be, there are certain things in life which can only be done by you, and for which you alone have responsibility. The second is that in the very heart of darkness there is light. It is the light of birth, rebirth, and, for Druids, a commitment to the Druid Way.

RITES OF PASSAGE

The ceremonies of the eightfold year are to be found reflected in the ceremonies that are referred to here as rituals of the Land. This is true on both literal and metaphorical levels. The varying positions of the sun and moon provide, as we have seen, the timetable for the Sky rituals. However, this relationship with the Sky is also indicative of the scope and tenor of those ceremonies. They mark the pattern of a Druid's relationship with the wider community of life, the universe itself, and the universal aspect of spirit.

Rites of passage are governed by the Land. They follow the same cycle of birth, growth, maturity, death, and rebirth that is to be found in the ceremonies of the eightfold year, but the emphasis is different and the focus is much narrower. What is more, the turning of the earth does not dictate the times at which these ceremonies occur. Rather, they are linked to the self and mark the pivotal occasions of a Druid's life.

There is a connection, however, albeit far less overt. The rites of passage connect with the Land in that just as a Druid's relationship with the Land is personal, so the rites celebrate a personal journey and the relationships a Druid makes and breaks with others and the Land along the way. The focus, too, is more on the material aspect of being, not only recognizing that people have a material as well as a spiritual dimension, but also acting as a reminder that we all live very firmly in that material dimension.

Druid rituals, as Druids are the first to admit, are not ancient. No one knows how ancestral Celts made formal celebration of the major events of their lives. We do not even know for certain which events they considered important, although it is possible to make an educated guess. For example, people who live by a lunar calendar do not calculate or celebrate their birthdays in the same way as people who live by a solar calendar. They tend to have a collective 'birthday' when they celebrate their new year.

We do know one thing and that is that ancestral Celts were a highly spiritual people who loved to party. Moreover, there are tantalizing glimpses in the old tales of certain rites of passage. It is not possible to say whether these were the norm or whether they were included in these tales because they were out of the ordinary. However, from a study of law texts and other sources more prosaic than the myths and legends, it is possible to derive a list of eight important events that modern Druids believe should be marked by ceremony and, where appropriate, by celebration. This is by no means an exhaustive list of such rites – the personal nature of what is celebrated prompts many Druids to add others that are personally significant – but those discussed here are held more or less in common.

Druids believe these rites of passage are all too often neglected. This is not to say that they are ignored. They are neglected in the sense that they have become both devalued and disconnected. The reasons given for this are complex, but, in essence, it is that we have forgotten why these events are so important. Attempts to mark them in modern society have become entirely self-referential – we celebrate an event because it is that event and for no other reason. In losing any connectedness with other aspects of life, the deeper reason for celebrating such events and their value to people and their community has diminished.

For Druids, all living things follow a cycle through the duration of a lifetime. Moreover, in each cycle each of us undergoes a number of essential transitions that shape us as social beings. In human society, there are a number of these transitions that are common to us all. We are born, so making a full transition into this world from the Other; we are named and thus recognized as people in our own right; most of us reach an age when we become capable of taking full responsibility for our actions; we assert our independence and make our own way in the world; we commit ourselves to relationships beyond those to which we were born; relationships end; we die and make our return to the Otherworld; our material remains are disposed of.

These events occur and recur in complex cycles, more so today as the structure of society is more complicated than ever it was. They also run one into another and each contains elements of the others. Dying, for example, brings relationships to an end in this world, just as it is asserts a form of independence. This is one of the ways in which Druids see these events, these rites of passage, making a connection. They are the experiences of a single cycle of life that help to give it unity and mark its evolution. This alone invests them with enormous value for the Druid and makes them worth celebrating in a coherent fashion. There is more, however. Not only are these experiences seen as events that unify each life, but they are also the experiences of others, in which all can share. In whatever culture or religion you consider, these events are held to be of great importance. They highlight the key moments, not only in personal development, but also in social development. As such, they are marked with formal ritual, no matter how intimately.

Because ancestral Celtic society was tribal, personal and social development were one and the same thing. It is only in comparatively recent times that these have been considered separate, rather than distinct. The whole question of connectedness is fundamental to the Celtic metaphysic and to being Druid. Such rites of passage were likely to have been moments of communal celebration in the widest sense of the phrase. They were rituals that bound the person to the community, the community to the person, community with community, and the person to themselves.

Communion is essential. It is no use expressing a belief in the connectedness of all things if we do not actively participate. Nor can the connection solely be receptive. It has to be two-way, otherwise our existence first becomes selfish and then progresses toward psychosis. Connection must also be constant. It cannot be turned on and off, no matter how guarded and careful we might be in order to protect ourselves. Everybody filters their experiences, especially now that the pain of the whole world is so easily brought into our homes on an hourly basis. To cut one's self off from that altogether, however, is to allow one's spirit and compassion to die.

Part of the filtering process is ritual. Each time a Druid enacts a ritual properly, no matter how trivial seeming or brief, they create a sacred space, a protected place in which they can explore, understand, and reaffirm their connectedness. In the rituals of the eightfold year, they commune with the larger world. During their rites of passage (and at other times), they commune with themselves and with their fellow travellers.

Communing with the self is, Druids believe, often neglected, even though most people recognize that the ancient saying, 'Know thyself', is one of great wisdom. This is not an easy path to travel, but Druids believe that if it is not done, then a large portion of what it is to be Druid is neglected, for being Druid is just that – it is something they are, not something they do in addition to what they are. Rites of passage offer pointers to the rough shape of their being, and are one means by which they define the parameters of what they are. Druid communion, however, extends beyond the self and the Way followed by each Druid. No matter how intensely they are Druid, they know they are part of a larger community of both spirit and matter. Their actions bind them to that community in all its complexity, and the nature of their actions helps to shape it, as well as their place within it.

Each of the rites of passage also marks the completion of a cycle within a cycle. They are transitions, initiations, the moments of rebirth (and often of revelation) that all Druids experience when they open themselves to the sacred. Certain of these have, perforce, to be conducted by others on their behalf, but that neither lessens nor invalidates their importance. This highlights the absolute duty of care Druids have when performing these rites for others. That is also why these rites are not about binding people to anything unless they have specifically given their consent (as in marriage).

Because they are personal, relating to the self and to immediate family and friends, the shape and texture of these rituals are different from those of the eightfold year. They are certainly less formal. Formality is not always convenient or, indeed, appropriate. Most of the rites are marked by the kind of informality one expects of close relationships, for the focus is on people and the family rather than on deity. Even with solemn occasions such as marriage and burial where a degree of formality dignifies the events, the emphasis is always on the personal.

Taken together, these rituals are seen as the circle of our lives, constructed as we live. They are an integral part of our material and spiritual existence. In these rituals, Druids are not attempting to connect with or celebrate the wider existence of the universe (although that connection exists in that we are all part of that wider existence). Rather, they are celebrating their selves. This is in no way egotistical. It is an acknowledgment of their personal being in a way that links them with the universe, nurtures their spirit, and brings balance into everyday existence.

This is all too often ignored by those who seek a spiritual path. Their whole focus is on the Sky, on the mystical experience, on the glamour of the big ritual. Druids are certainly aware of the larger picture, but, as already mentioned, they do not believe they can successfully explore that larger domain unless they have an understanding of their own being in its normal, everyday existence.

This does not mean that one set of rituals is considered more important than the other. They are different interpretations of a single theme. Winter solstice, for example, is a celebration of the birth and rebirth of the sun, which is symbolic of life on a large scale. It is a powerful and important time. So, too, is the birth of a child. Yet that is to be celebrated on an intimate scale, in keeping with the fragility of the newly arrived soul. The intent is no less powerful or reverential, simply in scale with and appropriate for the event.

THE PERSONAL

The eightfold year, we have seen, is a ritual manifestation of the Sky and is concerned with the world. Rites of passage relate to the Land and are concerned with community. The final set of rites discussed here is concerned with the personal and relates to the Sea. We have already discussed how the Sea relates to the largest of our personal spiritual concerns – the journey of the soul to the Otherworld. Here we are concerned with the spiritual in the everyday world and how the self deals with its self and with that immediate experience of the world in which we all live.

Celts through the ages have had a prayer and a blessing for every conceivable occasion. In fact, they have had many prayers for each occasion, and where they lacked one their nature was such that they could easily extemporize. With short rhymes and lengthy pieces, they invoked the goddesses, gods, and spirits to weave together the everyday world with the world of the spirit.

Prayer is a constant act of renewal. Druids see creation, not as a far distant and one-off event, but as a continuous process in which all must play their part and for which all must accept their responsibilities. Getting that part right, acting correctly, and fulfilling responsibilities toward the rest of creation is helped by constant appeal to those higher powers that are willing to help as long as we are willing to accept our place. This should not be taken in a hierarchical sense. The concept of a chain of being does not accord with the way in which the real world works. Accepting our place means knowing where, in the vast web of life, we properly belong. It also means not doing things that would distort or cut the strands of the web. After all, if we disturb too many, our own sources of sustenance will be denied us.

Everyday life is guided by the rhythm of the day and the month. From this, we derive the other natural unit of time – the fortnight.[87] It is, therefore, the full moon and the new moon that help to govern the shape of the everyday. In following a solar calendar, it is all too easy to lose touch with the rhythm of the moon. Ancestral Celts lived their lives quite naturally by the lunar cycle and Druids try to ensure that they do the same. This is not just a matter of staying in tune with ancestral practice. Druids believe it also makes sense materially, psychologically, and spiritually. Materially, it tunes the physical body to one of the major cycles of existence and with the one planetary body that has a significant effect on the earth and all life thereon. Human beings tend, for example, to be more sexually active around the time of the full moon. Birth rates are, unsurprisingly, thought to peak in a similar cycle.

Psychologically, people are affected by the lunar cycle. Accidents, crimes, and irrational behaviour follow a lunar cycle, reaching their peaks around the time of the full moon – hence the term lunacy. Although this is largely a statistical effect to be discerned in large populations, it is recognized as a genuine phenomenon.

Spiritually, following the cycles of the moon is an important and ongoing link with the Goddess. Although much of Celtic lunar lore has been lost, it is clear that the moon was important to ancestral Celts. The lunar cycle represents the cycle of fertility of the Goddess and much agricultural work, such as sowing and ploughing, may well have been governed by phases of the moon as well as other factors. Some people still tend their gardens in like fashion and Druids are generally aware of the phases and position of the moon. Indeed, many celebrate the full and new moons in addition to the other rituals they perform.

This is not worship of the moon, any more than the rituals of the eightfold year are performed to worship the sun. These acts are celebrations of the way in which the universe works and of the way in which this working affects people in their material and spiritual being. They are also a means by which Druids try to attune themselves to the cycles and rhythms of the natural world, believing that this will benefit their material being and act as a form of meditation that will help calm and mature the spirit.

MEDITATION

Meditation is an essential part of any spiritual path and is practised worldwide. The earliest known mention of 'meditative ecstasy' is in the *Rig Veda*, which is thought to have been composed around three thousand years ago in northern India. In the fifth century BC, Siddhārtha Gautama found enlightenment whilst meditating under a Bodhi tree, and so the Buddhist path of deliverance is via meditation. It was in the fourth century BC that formalized meditation became known. This was through the teaching of Taoism, which emphasized the importance of breath control within meditation. Many Eastern techniques involve attempts at mental control that allow the meditator to move beyond normal experience into a void that has absence of all thought. In the West, by contrast, we usually only hear of the Christian custom of silent prayer and reflection.

Because of all this, and because of the popularity of some forms of Eastern meditation, people have been led to believe that meditation is primarily an Eastern discipline. There is, however, a long and well-established tradition of meditation within pre-Christian Celtic religious and spiritual practice.

Druids do sometimes practise an Eastern style of meditation as an exercise in calming. Primarily, however, they use a different form of meditation. Rather than clearing the mind of all thought and images to achieve a higher state of consciousness, the Druid will use carefully chosen images and visual narratives. That is because Druids do not meditate in order to transcend this world, but in order to become more in tune with it. Rather than divorcing their self from the universe, they seek clearer states of consciousness in order to open their self to the world and better integrate it with the matrix of existence from which they feel we have become divorced.

Becoming absorbed by the sunset colours across the sky, feeling the grass with bare feet after a shower of rain, holding a peach-coloured shell, or sitting on a windy hilltop simply to experience the wind, are all states of meditation best described in the later poems attributed to Taliesin. Although a clear and settled mind is necessary for this, the belief that all meditation is done in an uncomfortable full-lotus yoga position while trying to empty the mind of thought and emotion is unfounded.

The techniques practised by Druids today may or may not have a long history. It cannot be denied, however, that ancestral Druids practised certain forms of meditation. This is partly because they believed in an inner and outer world – as we do today. However, it is also because the training of Druids involved techniques that cut them off from trivial distractions of the World to enable them to concentrate on their inner being and open them up to their awen.[88] These and other activities suggestive of meditative and trance states are found in many of the old tales. Whether these states were achieved with the aid of hallucinogenic substances is a matter of debate.[89] Modern Druids, however, do not use them, believing it is better to practise meditation when one's system is clear of all pollutants, including alcohol.

Meditation is often referred to as visualization or pathworking. In visualization, images are chosen (be they imagined or observed in the world) for their symbolic or elemental quality in order to allow the Druid to synthesize their self with the world. This kind of meditation is usually done alone. With pathworking, paths or journeys are constructed (usually from Celtic mythology) to introduce Druids to narrative forms, to deities, and to ideas. These are often used as teaching tools and a Druid will narrate the journey whilst others listen and explore the images they are given. Pathworking is especially useful with those who are new to the Druid Way as an experienced practitioner can guide them safely through the journey and back to where they started. Insightful discussions often follow such sessions.

There is one other type of visualization technique – the Inner Grove. This is, in effect, an inner sanctuary that all Druids have. The nature of the sanctuary varies with the Druid. It can be a stone circle or a forest grove, a cave or a hilltop, a roundhouse or a spring. Whatever it is, the Inner Grove is the personal domain of the Druid. It is a place of rest, a calm centre in a hectic world, a spiritual hearth where Druids can centre themselves. From this place, they can make journeys into the deeper reaches of the Forest in the knowledge that there is somewhere secure to which they can return.

Many people dismiss as mere imagination the notion of other dimensions to our life. As those who do not have the conventional five senses can testify, however, there are many ways of understanding the world. One way is imagination – a faculty that should not be dismissed as mere make-believe. It is much more than that. Imagination is the ability to experience the world other than by our five senses; it is the ability to experience aspects of the world we would not normally be able to encounter. Without imagination, a Druid will say, we cannot have compassion. Without imagination, we cannot transcend our material existence.

13

BEING DRUID
IN THE WORLD

BEING DRUID IN THE WORLD

Being Druid is not just about ceremonial and ritual practice. It is an entire way of life, expressed in everything that a Druid does. This is because becoming Druid involves adopting a new outlook on the world. For many, the change is gradual and, in itself, does not cause problems. However, living true to the Druid Way can be difficult. Pagans in general and Druids in particular face prejudice for their beliefs and practices. In the extreme, this has involved people losing their jobs, having their children taken away by social service departments, and more vulnerable members of the pagan community being driven to suicide. It is ignorance of the Druid Way, however, rather than outright prejudice, that is the main problem encountered by Druids when dealing with the rest of the world.

The popular image of Druids is derived from highly distorted media portrayals, along with passing reference to the Druid Way in works of fiction where it is used to add a hint of exoticism and menace. It is no wonder that when Druids feel it necessary to let others know what their religion is, they are met with confusion. Few Druids, therefore, go out of their way to announce their beliefs to the outside world. Indeed, most Druids would find such behaviour at odds with their beliefs, for the Druid Way is a quiet and private relationship between a person and the world of spirit.

For all that these problems do occur, they are atypical. The major problem faced by Druids is how they organize their ordinary everyday lives in a world where the prevailing metaphysic is at odds with their own. All Druids, of course, are different. On the whole, however, they aim for simplicity. The notion of simplicity is related to the Celtic metaphysic and may best be described as the practical application of the Celtic vision of the world to everyday life.

Simplicity is the art of finding the least complicated route. All things are relative, however. Living simply is a complex matter – a reflection of the complexity of the world. Where life is involved, the natural order of things is toward increasingly complex systems. Yet no matter how complex, it is all necessary. The World, on the other hand, is complicated. Human endeavour has taken what is complex and elegant and complicated it for no obvious good reason.

When things become complicated, they all too easily obscure what is needful. This is true at all levels, from the most basic of material requirements to the highest of spiritual aspirations. In order to support the complicated structures that are erected, the World behaves mendaciously, creates problems that did not exist and wastes resources solving them, avoids or ignores the problems that do exist, destroys life, and promulgates war. Indeed, violence and war are supreme expressions of the complications upon which the World is built.

Simplicity shuns what is complicated. It is a search for the complex, a search for the most natural way in which to express one's self, and conduct the mundane activities of one's life. It means learning to see through the complications of the World so that we manage our lives in ways that sidestep those entanglements.

There are those who would call this opting out. In a sense, this is true. It is opting out of a system that Druids see as materialistic, violent, and destructive, a system that has abjured the truth and has no moral basis. Druids try to minimize their support of such an arrangement. In the first instance, this involves looking at every aspect of how they live their day-to-day lives and embracing that which is simple. Simplicity, however, requires trust and it requires honour. Much of what is complicated about the World derives from the fact that we live in a system based on a lack of trust – not just between individuals, but also in the world about us. The more complicated the World becomes, the easier it is for people to exploit any trust that does exist and to foster doubt in what is merely complex.

Trust is an expression of truth. Druids believe that we each need to assess our lives to remove all the complicated clutter that has built up around us like a dead weight. This is not simply a matter of ridding ourselves of all those material things we do not actually need. Every part of life should come under scrutiny so that our whole approach is simplified and attuned to the way in which the world works. To do this, it is necessary to trust in the Land, trust in the Sea, and trust in the Sky – trust that these can and will provide for all the genuine needs of humankind.

Simplicity is, of course, comparative. There are no absolutes, not least because each person has their own relationship with the world. It is not possible to make hard and fast rules about what is simple, because such rules belong to the domain of the World. They complicate matters. In order to cover all eventualities, they are endlessly long and can wrap people up in arguments about what is and what is not appropriate, removing responsibility from the person and placing it in some nebulous elsewhere – be that society, State, Church, or deity.

For Druids, balance is the key and that, they believe, begins within each of us. Whether we like it or not, we are all part of the material world. If we are fortunate, we have jobs, buy food, wear clothes, own cars and houses, watch television, and go on holiday. Unfortunately, however, many people are caught up in the material side of life. They become so unbalanced by the merry-go-round of a money-orientated material life that all other forms of thought and action are considered strictly out-of-bounds.

The Druid Way is a spiritual path that accepts that we have a material existence, accepts that the material is essential to our wellbeing. It is not a path of deprivation where one must give up all possessions and become parasitic on others in order to find personal salvation. Indeed, it is not even a path of personal salvation. The Druid Way is a path of balance between, and integration of, the material and the spiritual in order to effect healing. Failure to integrate the material and the spiritual means they cannot be kept in balance. Without balance, we end up with extremism. Go too far down the material road and the spirit withers, along with compassion and love. Go too far or too obsessively with the spiritual and the spectre of fundamentalism rears its ugly head. A fundamentalist Druid[90] is every bit as unpleasant and dangerous as a fundamentalist who claims affiliation with any other religion.

There are fine distinctions that a Druid has to learn. Acknowledging the relative nature of simplicity – the need for integration and balance – means placing trust in our intuitive faculties. This is not easy. We are taught from a very early age that there is something not quite right about doing that. But this scepticism is because purely rational and analytical minds have insufficient tools with which to distinguish between intuitive decision-making and a purely egotistical and emotional response to one's surroundings.

Each decision about life has to be taken on its merits. It has to be done openly with complete acceptance of one's responsibility for what one does, says, and thinks. Taking such responsibility is another aspect of simplicity that many find difficult to accommodate. Although we do not have absolute control over our lives (for even simple lives are complex and involve other people, as well as social, economic, and natural environments), acting responsibly and in full knowledge of what we do and what effect that has is part and parcel of what we are as self-aware beings. We cannot claim self-awareness as part of what makes us human and then turn our backs on what that implies.

Inherent in the idea of simplicity is the Druid's rejection of conventional ideas of 'progress'. This is a term that is invariably used to mean increased material complication and it rarely coincides with any true improvement in our lives – materially or spiritually. It is also tied inexorably to the linear view of the world, which polarizes all things. Yet for the Druid, the world is cyclical. Improvement in our lives, therefore, is achieved by lessening the complications and realizing that each point on the cycle (just as each season of the year and each time of the day) will provide for what is needed in our lives.

Rejection of conventional ideas of progress and the linear allows the Druid to forge a different relationship with time. Many of the complications in our lives and in the World as a whole come from the distorted vision we have of time. A simple life is based in the now. That does not mean it has no regard for the past or the future. Indeed, those who live simply pay more heed to those things than do those who live linear lives. However, those who live in linear fashion are always trying to live their lives in the future – and it cannot be done.

Simplicity is also an acknowledgment that we cannot control the natural world. Accepting that is another aspect of the trust that is required. Stepping back from the notion of control also means accepting that humans are not superior beings with an innate right to do as they wish with the planet and its inhabitants. Druids believe that we do not and cannot own the world any more than we can control it. We have a place in the world, and our particular form of intelligence may have a role in its preservation. We may even be arrogant enough to call ourselves stewards, and perhaps we may be, providing we are genuinely prepared to accept the responsibilities of such a position. However, we are no more than stewards and never can be.

To find their place in the world, Druids will act appropriately. In the things they do and the things they make, they try for the minimum level of refinement. Materials that they use are as close to natural as possible and are biodegradable or, at the least, recyclable. Their actions accord with systems that use least energy most efficiently, that do not waste materials, and that do not tie them up in meaningless activity.

All of this requires that Druids become aware of the true cost of things. Not just the price on the ticket stuck to the box, but the social and environmental costs of production, as well as the miles travelled between sourcing raw material, getting the finished product into their homes, and disposing of all the waste material the product produces. This also applies to their relationships and all the other non-material aspects of their lives. They look at them all carefully and find that there are invariably simpler, truer, and less destructive ways of doing things.

It is obvious that there is a high degree of ambiguity and paradox within the notion of simplicity being found by embracing the complex. Ambiguity and paradox, however, are part of the world. They belong in life and are great teachers for they provide a timeless means by which to explore the mysteries of the world and human existence within it. To embrace simplicity, as Druids embrace it, is to embrace the complexity of the world, recognizing that that complexity is not in any way alien. Indeed, it is recognizing that they are but a part of that complexity and that the complications of the World are unnecessary. It is a declaration that in their everyday lives, in their thoughts and actions, in their whole being, the material and the spiritual, they are a part of the whole.

14

CONCLUSION

CONCLUSION

A ncestral Druids inherited, were guardians of, and further developed a wisdom tradition of enormous antiquity. The origins, form, and most of the content are lost to us because they predate written records by thousands of years. It is possible, however, to piece some of the tradition together and explore the earliest of understandings of some of the great mysteries of being – the perception of natural law, the mystery of life, the divine origin of the universe, and the relation of human beings to these things. These principles remain an immutable depth, no matter how much the surface of life may alter. They apply to all people at all times and they have been the theme of the teachings of all great teachers. They are a common thread running through all religions.

This statement is often questioned. If it is so, why do we have so many different religions? If it is so, why are there such things as religious conflicts and wars? The answers are simple. Conflict and wars may be conducted in the name of this, that, or some other religion, but that is merely a pretext. No conflict can be called religious, no matter how just it may seem to some. A religious conflict is a contradiction in terms. Religion is to do with becoming one; conflict is to do with fragmenting the one. The pretext is made by those who do not understand what religion is, most often those blinded by a fanatical adherence to something that gives them a feeling of power over others. These are souls in torment who wish to inflict their own pain on others.

As to why there are so many religions when they are all derived from a common source – it is simply because people are different. We each understand the world in different ways, as individual persons and as groups of people shaped by our environment. The journey of the spirit may be toward the same goal, but we each start from a different place and must travel, therefore, by a different route. Those brought up in cultures in which reincarnation is a recognized fact, have no difficulty in accepting this. Each life will give us the opportunity to explore a different route, and each route can be explored from many perspectives.

The body of inner knowledge, the ancient wisdom, is retained by us all at an unconscious level. It cannot be retrieved by intellectual effort, although we can go a long way to uncovering it by that route – laying the foundations, as it were, for what will follow. Access to this wisdom is through intuitive processes that have to be nurtured within those who are receptive. This goes beyond the rational – which is why academics and rationalists often dismiss the very notion of its existence.

There are a few, in each generation, who carry this wisdom at a conscious level and who guide those of us who seek to unlock it from within ourselves. They function beyond the confines of time and space, are ageless and deathless, are human and more. Once in every thousand years or so, one of them will step forward and make their presence known to the wider world in order to remind us of our greater destiny and illuminate our path, which may have grown dark.

As with any tradition that passes from generation to generation, some is lost, some is corrupted. Nevertheless, it is possible to recover enough to keep it renewed. It is hard work, but that is part of the task. The wisdom, in its ultimate form, may be simple, but the getting of wisdom must be difficult so that when the goal is finally reached we are mature enough to manage what we have learned.

Each people has its own way of entering into the search for this wisdom. The Celtic peoples inherited and refined a way that has a stronger continuity than many others. Much has happened to dilute it over the years, but that has also acted to strengthen what is left. For the Celts, it was wood-sense, tree knowledge, forest lore, an understanding of the natural world, that provided a surface system with which to train the mind to the point where the mystical apprehension of the wisdom was possible.

Although details of this ancient wisdom are obscure, there is little doubt about the basic tenets, and these are still integral to being Druid today. This wisdom comprises a deep understanding of natural law, of the patterns that underlie and bind together all life and all spirit. The natural law is a reflection of the divine and through an understanding of the world about us it is possible to come to an understanding of what is hallowed. This does not happen in one great leap. There are many stages and levels of understanding, each contingent upon the one before. We are many steps away from being one. For Druids, the goal is the next step, not the final one.

The principle of reflection – in which the divine is mirrored in the natural world – applies also to the way in which wisdom can be won. The wisdom is within us as much as it is around us. Druids believe we must understand ourselves as much as we must understand all that is about us. Everything is connected. The whole is to be found in each part. Their search therefore begins within and without at the same time.

This is succinctly symbolized by the spiral maze known since prehistoric times, which has been adopted by modern Druids. Also known as a septenary spiral, this form (and its variations) can be found in many places – including St Nectan's Kieve near Tintagel in Cornwall. Carved on to megaliths, cut into turf, even laid out on Christian church floors – it takes you inward and leads you out. It is a journey of mystical death taken by Druids into the dark centre that is the womb from which they will be reborn.

Many treat this maze as a form of temple, concentrating only on its material aspect. Although it is satisfying to create it in physical form and to walk the path, all such configurations are symbols and must be understood in this light. They are the key to the entrance to the mystery that lies beyond.

The only true temple of the Druid is Life. From the human perspective, this resides in the form of our bodies. However, our bodies, our selves, our being – all have many aspects. Moreover, the self is not isolated from the rest of Life. Humans are an integral part of the universe. One of the quests of Druids is to overcome the deficiencies of their material senses in order to understand this. It is one of the wisdoms they work to win.

That we are one with the universe is a wisdom that is easy to accept on an intellectual level. It is far harder to accept emotionally, harder still to absorb into the very core of the self so that it becomes instinctive. The entrance to this innermost mystery is in the narrowest confine of our being. The spiral must be followed to its centre before one can return, reborn. In this journey, the Druid learns to put aside their consciousness. This has been conditioned by our many environments, which today bear little or no resemblance to the environments of early times when the wisdom was more fully appreciated. Not only has the physical world changed, but so too has the very psychological make-up of humanity. This is another of the things that Druids work to change within themselves.

In this journey, the Druid must also put aside the intellect. There are dire limitations to our knowledge, conditioned as it is by centuries of thought based on materialistic and analytical patterns. What is more, knowledge is delivered through the use of the alphabet, an invention that hinders the development of the right side of the brain. Druids do not reject these things – they simply recognize their limitations.

Among the many accomplishments of Druids in the past was the ability of their adepts to understand, evolve, and make use of the ancient wisdom that they had inherited. Not all Druids worked directly on this. Many were content to be healers or lawyers, singers and seers, but even their skills were derived from and attuned to the natural laws that form part of the wisdom tradition. Druids had knowledge, they were literate, but they recognized and were skilled at many additional ways of knowing and understanding the world. The same is true of Druids today. There is more to this, however, than simply a search for understanding, wisdom, and spiritual enlightenment. There is a purpose in the search itself, a purpose in the goal, for the goal is just the beginning. Druids seek this wisdom so that they might use it in the world.

If you read between the lines of even the most Christianized of the Grail stories, you will see that attaining the Grail is not the ultimate purpose of the quest. The Grail is sought so that it can serve, heal, and bring fruitfulness to the Wasteland. And in that, Druids see the purpose of their journey.

Druids must make themselves fit for the journey – and most seekers, having improved themselves, stop there. As far as they and the teachers they have found are concerned, that was their whole purpose. It is a step in the right direction, but it is only a step. Having made themselves fit, Druids use that strength to seek out their Grail, to seek out the Light. For many seekers who have continued to this point, the journey ends here. They have satisfied their own ends and feel they may bask in the Light they have discovered.

However, there is more. As far as Druids are concerned, the journey has a third part, in which they let go of their own desires and ends and make themselves a vessel for the Light that they may carry it back and radiate it for the benefit of others.

For all that we have talked here of ancient wisdom, it is important to remember that it is ancient only inasmuch as it has been with us for a great length of time. It is not ancient in the sense of being out of date. It is timeless, dynamic, evolving – a living tradition. Nor should it be thought that this wisdom is 'hidden' or 'secret'. It is there in plain sight for all who are prepared to seek it out. The discipline involved in seeking it out and making sense of it once we have learned to apprehend it, however, *is* difficult. That is often mistaken as a way of hiding things. But as we seek, we learn the one real secret – that there is no secret and that nothing is hidden.

The ancient wisdom is alive, it is vibrant, and it is right in front of our eyes. Indeed, it is to be found in every blade of grass, every flower, every tree, every mouse, dog, cat, cow, hawk, and fish, in every cloud and star, in every book, every song, every dream, and in every human being. It is written in huge letters in the world about us. What Druids finally apprehend, no matter how profound it is in one sense, is exceedingly simple in another. What Druids seek is not the wisdom itself because it is ever changing, but the wherewithal to recognize it where it is, the wherewithal to recognize the great simplicity, the wherewithal to understand the profundity within the simplicity. Moreover, in so doing they seek to bring balance and healing to a world that is damaged and suffering.

That, in essence, is the truth about Druids. There are variations. Some practise in slightly different ways; some use different terminology; others would argue over matters of detail. But there is no more than this. No hidden agenda, no desire to destroy other religions, no 'evil' intent, no peculiar practices, no sorcery, or sexual predation. This is the truth and the whole of the truth.

For some, of course, the truth is never enough. Yet it is they who imagine the things that are not actually there, they who would invent the mysterious. Druids, on the other hand, prefer to investigate the ordinary, the everyday, the real world around them, and reveal the mysterious and miraculous that is therein.

NOTES

Notes

1. Pagan religions are a worldwide phenomenon, occurring in many different forms, and currently adhered to by approximately 5 per cent of the world's population. Only a small proportion of that percentage represents the resurgent forms of paganism to be found in modern Western society. These are sometimes referred to as neopaganism, recopaganism (for reconstructionist paganism), and geopaganism (a tautology if ever there was one). Other terms, such as mesopaganism (referring to eighteenth-century revivalists of paganism), are also used. They are not used in this text, not least because someone is either pagan or they are not. Distinct and specific forms of paganism, such as the Druid Way, Wicca, Bön, and the many nameless varieties practised across the globe, deserve to be treated seriously and on an equal basis. For a breakdown of figures and a more comprehensive description of the world's pagan religions, see York (2003).

2. Whilst there are a number of Druid Orders and Fellowships with quantifiable memberships, they constitute only a part of the whole. Many adherents do not belong to formal groups. They work alone or in small informal groups as this better suits their temperament and understanding of their faith. Some estimates actually put the proportion of 'lone' Druids in excess of 50 per cent of the total.

In total, conservative estimates based on the information available, including census returns and membership of formal groups, suggest that there may be 20,000 Druids in Britain and Ireland with at least a further 50,000 elsewhere in the world (principally western Europe, North America, and Australasia). These figures exclude those Mutual Societies and charitable organizations that make use of the title Druid, as well as those individuals involved solely with cultural events such as *eisteddfodau* (an *eisteddfod* is a Welsh-language competitive festival of the arts, principally the language arts and music – the plural is *eisteddfodau*).

3. The fast growth rate is actually for paganism as a whole. Within this, the Druid Way is growing at a slower pace than, for example, Witchcraft, although none of these figures takes into account the drop-out rate, which is higher for Witchcraft than it is for the Druid Way.

4. The Abrahamic tradition consists of Judaism, Christianity, and Islam.

5. BC and AD will be used throughout in preference to BCE and CE. There is no genuine 'Common Era', just one imagined by predominantly western Christian theologians, taken up by scientists, and imposed on other cultures. To disguise a dating system based on Christianity as a common dating system is dishonest. Furthermore, as Celts and their Druids lived in a part of the world that became Christian (in name if nothing else) it seems only right to stay with the dating system most applicable to that area.

6. Throughout this book, the term 'ancestral Celts' is used to refer to the Celts of pre-Christian times. It is not just a matter of convenience, but reflects the importance of the ancestors and ancestral practice to Celtic thought and religion.

7. The point is adequately made in this alone. 'Europe' is a Greek name for a region barely settled and never conquered by the Greeks.

8. The time span in itself presents an enormous problem when we talk of 'the Celts'. In the archaeological record alone there are two distinct periods of cultural development, each subdivided into a number of periods – and that is just the first thousand years. Care has to be taken to be specific and to understand clearly what people mean when they talk of the Celts.

9. There has been debate about the current use of the word on the grounds that 'Celt' bears little relation to the specific term used in archaeology. Although, clearly, legitimate concerns are being raised, not least about what seems to be a very profitable hijacking of the word 'Celtic' to sell all manner of books and craftwork that bear as much relation to the Celts as dreamcatchers do to Native Americans, arguments are also being put forward that seem driven by some agenda other than correct use of archaeological terminology.

A number of straw men have certainly been raised in this debate. Simon James, for example, in his *The Atlantic Celts: Ancient People or Modern Invention* (1999), makes some interesting points about the use of terminology that are far from contentious, but then seems to draw conclusions that go well beyond the premises he has set out. Indeed, he seems to be making a distinction between reality (that which exists) and our perception of reality. Although this may be valid for physical objects, it is on shakier ground (if any ground at all) when applied to concepts – all of which are derived from our perceptions of reality. That no one is recorded as having called themselves a Celt before 1700 (itself a shaky claim) is an insufficient premise from which to begin to argue that the whole idea of insular Celts is a modern interpretation.

Each age makes its own interpretation of the past and invents new terminology that seems more suited to current understanding. However, we should not confuse the name with the actuality. When we talk of the Iron Age, for example, we use modern terminology. It is simply a convenient label to attach to a given period. No one at the time used it. It does not follow from that, that Iron Age culture did not exist. Indeed, when it comes to terminology, 'Celt' and 'Celtic' are probably more useful and more accurate than 'Iron Age'. The former describes a people and their cultural development. The latter describes a technology. I am not sure that in the future we would be flattered to be lumped together with everyone else on the planet as belonging to the Silicon Age – or whatever name future archaeologists choose to give to our times – not least because it ignores the fact that only a small proportion of people on the planet use computer technology, and some still use stone tools.

One of the most vociferous contributors to this debate is John Collis. He has rightly condemned some authors who use

> ...a mishmash of information from different times and different places which is often of little value for understanding the societies being described.
>
> *pp 75-80 in Arnold, B. & Gibson,D. B. [eds] (1995)*

However, this is nothing new, nor is it a problem confined to the Celts. The very same complaint could be made about the Greeks, the Egyptians, or the Meso-Americans, to name just a few. Collis, however, is worried about more than intellectual rigour in the writing of books. He seems concerned that the concept of Celts is being used to political ends and feels that archaeologists should be duty bound to warn the public of this 'hidden agenda'.

In one regard, the concern may seem to be valid. Archaeology can be a political battleground of the most violent kind – intellectually and physically. Ask any archaeologist working on biblical archaeology. The stance that Collis takes, however, presupposes two things. The first is that the past should somehow be kept separate from the present. The second is that archaeologists could and should engage in such activity, that they are the sole and rightful gatekeepers to the past.

They certainly have every right to engage in debate about the meaning of their findings and the use to which that might be put. They have every right to make sure that what is reported about their work is correct. They do not, however, have exclusive rights over the past. Nor is the past divorced from the present. That is neither desirable nor possible. Indeed, as David Lowenthal concludes in *The Past is a Foreign Country* (1985):

> The past remains integral to us all, individually and collectively. We must concede the ancients their place... But their place is not simply back there, in a separate and foreign country; it is assimilated in ourselves, and resurrected into an ever-changing present.

That is, after all, one of the reasons why we study the past. Our world and its people have been shaped from it. Knowing that and understanding it are recognized as important, and not just by those who seek to establish (or re-establish) national identity in a world of increasing homogeneity. There is a great deal of rootlessness and a hunger to find a past. Archaeologists alone cannot feed that hunger for they are bound by the conventions of their field of study. Many quite rightly refuse to make claims and statements that are unsupported by the facts. Moreover, there are some that are notorious for not publishing their findings. The past, however, is not understood by archaeology alone and if people look elsewhere for information and understanding, then archaeologists have to accept this as part of a wider debate to which they contribute. Conversely, this places a responsibility on those who look to the past – for whatever reason – to get their facts right. They may speculate, but speculation must be based on hard evidence and on reliable sources. Wild claims, no matter who makes them, do a disservice to us all.

10. Urnfield culture appeared in west central Europe in the Late Bronze Age and is distinguished by hillfort building and the large number of cremations buried in urns in cemeteries (urn fields). Elite burials included grave goods, one class of which are the bits and side pieces of horse harnesses.

11. It is thought that Celtic languages descended from a Common Celtic, which in turn was descended from a hypothetical common Indo-European language from which all the languages of Europe (except Finnish, Estonian, Magyar, and Basque) are said to have evolved. Numerals are commonly cited as evidence of this early language.

English	*one*	*two*	*three*
Welsh	*un*	*dau*	*tri*
Irish	*aon*	*dó*	*tri*
German	*eins*	*zwei*	*drei*
Latin	*unus*	*duo*	*tres*
Greek	*énas*	*duo*	*treis*
Russian	*odin*	*dva*	*tri*

Although there is no direct evidence for such a language, it does fit the known facts and helps to explain clear cultural and linguistic similarities between peoples as far apart as Ireland and India.

12. This migration accounts, in part, for the fact that tribes separated by hundreds of miles have the same name. This does not apply universally, as some tribe names are derived from deities and location.

13. Ancient Greeks used the name *Keltoi* (the Latin is *Celtae*) as a general designation. At the beginning of the third century BC another name appears, *Galatai* (Galatai). Hieronymos of Cardia used this word to describe the people who invaded Macedonia and Greece and then went on to settle in Asia Minor. The Latin *Galli* came into use at about the same time.

In each case, these seem to be general terms rather than specific tribal names. Further, they are clearly derived from names or words that the Celts used themselves. The name of the *Celtici* (a Celtic people) and personal names from Iberia like *Celtigum, Celtus,* and *Celticus* are evidence that the root word is native to the Celts. Beyond that, we run into all the usual problems that surround the naming of things when two cultures meet, although we can reasonably assume that if the root was used to derive personal names it was nothing too wayward.

A number of explanations have been offered to accommodate the different names. Perhaps the simplest is that suggested by Julius Caesar. The Celts call them themselves Celts; the Romans call them Gauls. It might even be a simple matter of a difference in pronunciation. We are, after all, inclined to pronounce 'Caesar' as 'see-zur' whereas the man himself would probably have pronounced it something like 'ky-sar'.

As to the meaning of the word, much ingenuity has been brought to bear on this. Many suggestions have been attempts to derive a meaning that suits the etymologists' particular view of the Celts. Thus, we have been offered an Indo-European root word, *quel*, meaning 'elevated'. Whether that is meant to imply nobility or some such form of superiority or merely to denote that Celts were highlanders or mountain dwellers is not made clear. Another root, *kel*, means 'to strike', implying that the Celts were a warlike people. This, in particular, seems to be an attempt to make the name fit some classical descriptions, although the Celts were no more warlike than any other people were at the time.

Perhaps the most sensible suggestion is that the word 'Celt' derives from an early root that gives us the Sanskrit *cárati* and the Latin *cultura*. There are many shades of meaning here, from the notion of 'walking together' through to 'care' (both appropriate to the Celts). The Latin points us to the nearest modern English word, 'culture'. In other words, 'Celt' probably means 'the people'. Given the number of cultures worldwide whose name for themselves means just that, it is perhaps the safest meaning to stick with for the time being.

14. Given that a number of war leaders were called Brennus, it is just as likely to have been a title meaning 'chieftain' as it was to have been a personal name.

15. With its large number of Legions, Britain was also, on occasion, the launching pad for attempts by various individuals to become Roman emperor.

16. Inspired by Greek currency (and probably arising out of prolonged trade with them), the Celts had developed their own distinctive coinage by the late

fourth century BC. Coins are found across the entire Celtic world with the exception of Ireland, which appears not to have adopted money until the Christian period was well established. Like all other examples of Celtic artisanship, the coins are well made and in some cases extremely detailed.

Most coins follow a basic pattern with a head or figure on one side and an animal on the other. The animal is very often a horse, sometimes with a chariot. The next most popular animal is the boar and there are also to be found bears, cattle, ravens, and goats. Early coins contain easily identifiable representations of deities, whereas later examples have portraits of men and women who may well be actual tribal chieftains.

17. *Oppidum* is Latin for town, and is the word that best defines the defended settlements of the Celts. Their own word for such places is unknown. Although the majority of Celts were rural dwellers, they built settlements of considerable size. Most of these developed out of defended sites like hillforts. The *oppidum* at Los Cogotas near Avila in Spain is a wonderful example, with a defended upper enclosure built across two hilltops and enclosed by a wall. Access is through heavily defensive gates. A lower enclosure on the western side seems to have been less heavily built up and there were a number of gates in the wall. Although the whole enclosure covered some 14.5 hectares, it is small in comparison with other *oppida*.

18. At least, this is the case in the late La Tène. We do not know if this was the practice earlier, but given the continuity of development we find in other areas of Celtic culture, it seems highly likely that there was a formal structure to the education system – one that may even predate the Celts.

The colleges may just have been groups of pupils attached to a teacher, but given the numbers involved, logistics may have dictated that there were campuses at a number of locations. None has been identified by archaeology, although it is difficult to know how they would be distinguished from other settlements.

19. This is another term of which we must be wary. Druids were undoubtedly highly educated, but we cannot say that what they taught to others was a set of teachings in the sense that these constituted a coherent body of principles in a system of belief. There may have been teachings of

this kind in what they learned (and there is some evidence that this is so), but largely Druids taught the skills and knowledge by which to carry out the tasks in which they chose to specialize.

20. The Gundestrup Cauldron or Bowl, discovered in 1891 near Gundestrup, Jutland, is one of the most celebrated of the pieces of Celtic artisanship that we have. Measuring 14 inches (42 cms) in height and 25fi inches (69 cms) in diameter, it is 96 per cent pure silver (originally gilded) and weighs 20 pounds (nearly 9 kilos). It is made up from a base plate, five inner plates, and seven outer plates. Whether it was ever used as a cauldron is debatable.

What marks it out as special is the way in which the panels are decorated. The exterior panels show the faces of deities surrounded by symbols associated with them. The interior panels have more complex scenes that would appear to illustrate incidents from Celtic myth.

Examination of the cauldron suggests that several silversmiths were involved in its manufacture; stylistic details indicate an origin in Thrace or Romania. Its journey to Jutland is, therefore, a vexed question. A number of routes have been suggested, but perhaps the most convincing is that it was made for or traded to a Gaulish chieftain or Druid from whom it was later taken by Teutonic raiders.

21. Fostering was a strong tradition in Celtic culture. Although not universal (and it is uncertain when it developed), young people would be fostered with patrons to help build bonds with other tribes and families, to allow them to experience more of the world than would be open to them by staying with their own families, and to receive an education. The practice continued in Gaelic Scotland until the eighteenth century.

22. The importance of the triune nature of the world proved to have a major influence on a new religion that was embraced by many Celts. Hilary, Bishop of Poitiers (c. AD 315–c.367), was a Gaulish Celt whose work *De Trinitate* was highly influential in defining the concept of the Holy Trinity in Christianity.

23. The Celtic love of threes was put to good use in creating a mnemonic system to aid learning. Druids spent in the region of twenty years

memorizing traditions, verse forms, genealogies, precepts, law, and all the other methods and facts they would require to function effectively in society. Any aid to help them learn and remember this prodigious quantity of material would no doubt have been welcome. By far the major part of the system has been lost to us. Happily, however, we do still have a small collection of triads from both Britain and Ireland. These consist of a title, followed by three brief references and, occasionally, a brief explanation.

Welsh Triad 1, for example, goes as follows:

> *Teir Lleithiclvyth Ynys Prydein:*
>
> *Arthur yn Pen Teyrned ym Mynyv, a Dewi yn Pen Esgyb, a Maelgvn Gvyned yn Pen Hyneif;*
> *Arthur yn Pen Teyrned yg Kelli Wic yg Kernyw, a Bytwini Esgob yn Ben Esgyb, a Charadavc Vreichuras yn Ben Henyf;*
>
> *Arthur yn Ben Teyrned ym Penn Ryonyd yn y Gogled, a Gerthmul Wledic yn Benn Hyneif, a Chyndeyrn Garthwys yn Benn Esgyb.*

Which means:

> Three Tribal Thrones of the Island of Britain:
>
> Arthur as Chief Prince in Mynyw, and Dewi as Chief Bishop, and Maelgwn Gwynedd as Chief Elder;
>
> Arthur as Chief Prince in Celliwig in Cornwall, and Bishop Bytwini as Chief Bishop, and Caradawg Strong-Arm as Chief Elder;
>
> Arthur as Chief Prince in Pen Rhionydd in the North, and Gerthmwl Wledig as Chief Elder, and Cyndeyrn Garthwys as Chief Bishop.

This would have been used (like all other triads) as a key to unlock more comprehensive amounts of information – in this case about the places and people to whom reference is made. Much of this information has also been lost and we are left with tantalizing hints of a vast mythological, historical, and cultural vista – a bit like having the index of an atlas from which all the maps have been removed. For all that, the triads are extremely important to our understanding of Celtic culture.

24.

> *...quos memoria proditum est pecunias mutuas, quae his apud inferos redderentur, dare, quia persuasum habuerint animas hominum immortales esse.*

> *Valerius Maximus, II, 6, 10*

25. Celtic society worked by a lunar calendar, so the time of Samhain would have been fixed by other means, probably by counting off forty-five days from the autumn equinox.

26.

> Oide faskontez apo barbarwn arxai filosofian kai ton tropon par ekastoiz authz ektiqenai fasi touz men gumnosofistaz kai Drnidaz ainigmatwdwz apofqeggomenouz filosofhsai sebein qeouz kai mhden kakon dran kai andreian askein

> *Diogenes Laertius,* Vitae, *Intro. 6*

27. Poseidonius (c. 135–c. 50 BC) of Apamea in Syria was a philosopher and historian. Although he is thought to have travelled widely (including parts of Gaul), he spent most of his life on the island of Rhodes. In spite of being Greek, his writings were strongly coloured by his ardent pro-Roman stance and he took every opportunity to laud Roman imperial attitudes whilst presenting all other cultures in an unsympathetic light. This makes him an unreliable source of information on the Celts.

28. The labyrinthine investigations of those who wanted to prove a connection between the Druids and Judaism (and thus Christianity) are fascinating, but they throw little light on the history of the Druids. What they do illuminate is a deep desire (constrained by the mores of the time) to reclaim a British past. Those interested in this should read Owen (1962), which provides an excellent introduction to the subject and a structure for further study.

29.

Iam per se roburum eligunt lucos, nec ulla sacra sine earum fronde conficiunt, ut inde appellati quoque interpretatione Graeca possint Druidae videri.

Pliny the Elder, Nat. Hist., *XVI, 249*

Now, they [Druids] choose groves of oak for the tree itself, and never complete any worship without a garland of leaves there, so that from an interpretation of this the Greeks are able to know the name of the Druids.

30. A word preceded by an asterisk denotes a reconstructed or conjectural form based on linguistic evidence.

31. This is pushing things to their extreme limit, but archaeological evidence is more and more supporting the idea that the various cultures that have flourished through the millennia did not come about as the result of migration or invasion, but by a diffusion of ideas through a vast trading network.

32.

Disciplina in Britannia reperta atque inde in Galliam translata existimatur...

(Julius Caesar, *De Bello Gallica*, VI 13)

33. These studies are in their infancy, but they are already showing remarkable results and are helping to add to various debates. For example, it has been fashionable in the last fifty years to claim that the Saxon entry into Britain was not so much an invasion as a gentle settlement followed by friendly integration of the populations. Place names have long run counter to this idea. Now it is clear from genetic information that much of England was 'ethnically cleansed' by the Saxons, and the native population were pushed westward.

34. Strabo, *Geographia*, IV, 4, c.197, 4.

35.

Per haec loca hominibus paulatim excultis viguere studia laudabilium doctrinarum, inchoata per bardos et euhagis et drasidas. Et bardi quidem fortia virorum illustrium facta heroicis composita versibus cum dulcibus lyrae modulis cantitarunt, euhages vero scrutantes seriem et sublimia naturae pandere conabantur. Inter eos dryaridae ingeniis celsiores, ut auctoritas Pythagorae decrevit, sodaliciis adstricti consortiis, quaestionibus occultarum rerum altarumque erecti sunt et depectantes humana pronuntiarunt animas immortales.

Ammianus Marcellinus, XV, 9, 8

In these regions, as the people gradually became civilized, attention to the gentler arts became commoner, a study introduced by the Bards, and the Euhages, and the Druids. It was the custom of the Bards to celebrate the heroic deeds of their famous men in epic verse accompanied by the sweet strains of the lyre, while the Euhages strove to explain the high mysteries of nature. Between them came the Druids, men of greater talent, members of the intimate fellowship of the Pythagorean faith; they were uplifted by searchings into secret and sublime things, and with grand contempt for mortal lot they professed the immortality of the soul.

36. Diodorus Siculus, *Histories*, V, 31, 2-5.

37. Eugene O'Curry, in his *On the Manners and Customs of the Ancient Irish*, offers the following 'curriculum' for the training of a Bard. This represents what was happening during the early medieval period in Ireland after Druids had faded somewhat from the scene, so it may reflect a change that incorporates Druidic lore.

Year 1 – 50 Ogams or alphabets. Elementary Grammar. Twenty tales.
Year 2 – 50 Ogams. Six easy lessons in Philosophy. Some specified poems. Thirty tales.
Year 3 – 50 Ogams. Six minor lessons of Philosophy. Certain specified poems. Grammar. Forty poems.
Year 4 – *The Bretha Nemed* or Law of Privileges. Twenty poems of the species called *Eman* (Births). Fifty tales.
Year 5 – Grammar. Sixty tales.
Year 6 – The secret language of the Poets. Forty poems of the species *Nuath* (Twins). Seventy or eighty tales.

Year 7 – *Brosnacha* (Miscellanies). The Laws of Bardism.

Year 8 – Prosody. Glosses (the meaning of obscure words). *Teinm Laeghda* (Illumination of Song). *Imbas Forosnai* (Light of Foresight). *Dicheltel do Chennibh* (Extempore Incantation). *Dindsenchas* (Land Lore).

Year 9 – Specified number of compositions of the kind called *Sennet* (?), *Luasca* (?), *Nena* (?), *Eochraid* (Keys), *Sruith* (Streams), and *Duili Feda* (Wisdom Tales). To master 175 tales in this and the next two years.

Year 10 – A further number of the compositions listed above (part of the 175 tales).

Year 11 – 100 of the compositions known as *Anamuin*.

Year 12 – 120 *Cetals* (Orations). The Four Arts of Poetry. During this and the two years previous to master 175 tales, along with 175 of the tales learned by the Annruth – 350 tales in all.

Some of these terms cannot easily be translated. Nonetheless, it is clear that being a poet was taken seriously and involved a great deal more than simply learning a few poems. Remember that everything set out here would have been memorized by rote.

38. Dion Chrysostum, *Orations*, XLIX.

39. To be precise, 235 lunar months are equal to 19 years, 125 minutes, and 10fi seconds — a reckoning that would advance by one day every 228 years.

40.

> *Celi christe deus quid agam~ qua parte morari*
> *Terrarum potero~ cum nil quo uescar adesse:*
> *Inspicio~ nec gramen humi~ nec in arbore glandes*
> *Tres quater et iuges septene poma ferentes*
> *Hic steterant mali~ nunc non stant ergo quis illas*
> *Quis michi surripuit~ quo deuenere repente:*
> *Nunc illas uideo~ nec non sic fata repugnant*
> *Sic quoque concordant cum dant prohibent que uidere*
> *Deficiunt nunc poma michi~ nunc cetera queque*
> *Stat sine fronde nemus~ sine fructu plector utroque*

Cum neque fronde tegi ualeo~ neque fructibus uti:
Singula bruma tulit~ pluuiisque cadentibus auster
Jnuenio si forte napes tellure sub ima
Concurrunt auideque sues~ aprique voraces
Eripiunt que napes michi quas de cespite vello

Christ, God of heaven, what shall I do? In what part of the world can I stay, since I see nothing here I can live on, neither grass on the ground nor acorns on the trees? Here once there stood nineteen apple trees bearing apples every year; now they are not standing. Who has taken them away from me? Whither have they gone all of a sudden? Now I see them — now I do not! Thus the fates fight against me and for me, since they both permit and forbid me to see. Now I lack the apples and everything else. The trees stand without leaves, without fruit; I am afflicted by both circumstances since I cannot cover myself with the leaves or eat the fruit. Winter and the south wind with its falling rain have taken them all away. If by chance I find some navews [turnips] deep in the ground the hungry swine and the voracious boars rush up and snatch them away from me as I dig them up from the turf.

Geoffrey of Monmouth, Vita Merlini, *translated by J. J. Parry*

41. My knowledge of Welsh is limited; my knowledge of Gaelic more so. I am indebted, therefore, to Eleasaid Ní h'Eibhin for allowing me to reproduce the following from *The Celtic Metaphysic* (2003).

In both Irish Gaelic (Gaeilge) and Scottish Gaelic (Gàidhlig), there are two words that are used for the verb 'to be'. These are: *Is* and *Tá* (*Tha* in Scots Gaelic). I will concentrate on Irish, since that is my native tongue, however, Scottish is essentially similar since it developed from Irish, specifically from Gaedhilg-Uladh (Ulster Gaelic) with which it still shares many commonalities.

Tá:
The verb *Tá*, which is literally the verb 'to stand', is used to describe where someone or something is, or what state a person or thing is in.

That is to say, where something is temporary and thus *not* innate in something, for example:

Tá mé anseo – 'I am here' (Literally 'I *stand* here').

Tá Loch nEathach fuar – 'Lough Neagh is cold' (Literally 'Loch Neagh *tands* cold').

Tábreá inniu – 'It is fine today' (Literally 'It *stands* fine today').

Where *Tá* is used on its own it translates as 'there is', for example:

Tá bord ansin – 'There is a table there'.

Tá duine anseo – 'There is a man here'.

We see a similar construction in Scottish:

Tha mi sgith – 'I am tired'.

Tha iad a' tighinn – 'They are coming'.

Is:

The word *Is* is used to refer to the permanent qualities of something (that is, what is innate within something). The nearest meaning of *Is* in English would be 'it is', hence it is not quite strictly purely a verb per se and is thus traditionally referred to as the 'copula', for example:

Is mise Eleasaid – 'I am Eleasaid'.

It is an innate part of my being that I am Eleasaid – it is *who* I am.

Is Ban-Draoi mé – 'I am a (female) Druid'.

It is an innate part of my being that I am a Druid – it is *what* I am.

Is maith an scéalai an aimsir – 'Time (history) is a great storyteller'.

It is an innate quality of history that it tells us the stories of old.

Similarly in Scottish Gaelic, *Is* is used in statements which link two nouns or a noun and a pronoun.

Thus, we can see two concepts here – that which is innate within something, that is its innate *being* as well as that which is occurring, yet which is not innate. That is, *there is an identity of self (the individual) within the identity of (what is) the greater whole.*

If we turn now to the idea of possession of something, we see two linguistic constructional forms:

Mo:

In Gaelic the word for the possessive pronoun 'my' is *Mo*, for example:

Mo cheann – 'My head'.

Mo bhráthair – 'My brother'.

In both these cases we are back to the idea of innateness, that is, it is innate that it is my head; it is innate that he is my brother (because of blood).

The *Tá ... Ag* (*Tha ... aig*) construction:

This is the more common way of expressing ownership of something, for example:

Tá an cú agam – 'My dog' or 'I have a dog' (Literally 'The dog stands at me').

An teach s'agam – 'My house' (Literally 'It is a house at me').

Tá deich bpunt agam – 'I have two pounds'.

Similarly in Scots:

Tha càr aig Niall – 'Neil's car' or 'Neil has a car'.

From this, we see that the idea of *ownership* of items (as espoused in the Post Classical Western Scientific Materialistic metaphysic) is anathema. That is to say, one *cannot* own something that is not innate to the self – one is merely its lessor or steward. (Note that in modern standard Irish – *An Caighdeán Oifigiúil* – this distinction has disappeared and the word *Mo* is used to indicate ownership, since it has become a direct equivalent of the English 'my').

42. Morann mac Cairbre was a Brehon (lawgiver and therefore Druid) who left instructions for the High King, Feradach Finn Fachtnach (r. AD 95-117) in his will. These instructions are to be found recorded in *Leabhar na Nuachonghbala* (Book of Leinster). A translation can be found in Koch & Carey (2003).

43. See, for example, the *Carmina Gadelica*, a collection made in the Highlands and Islands of Scotland during the nineteenth century by Alexander Carmichael.

44. Anyone who is interested in reading further on this subject should look at the work of the Druid, Greywind. Others, such as Brendan Myers, Eleasaid Ní h'Eibhin, and Erynn Rowan Laurie, are also exploring the Celtic metaphysic and the theology of the Druid Way.

45. Ronald Hutton (1991), for example, states unequivocally that no pagan religions have survived the advent of Christianity. Conversely, Jones & Pennick (1995) produce a great deal of evidence to the contrary, as does Squire (1905).

46. For a full and intriguing account of Boudicca's campaign, Hunt (2003) is highly recommended. As he points out, Boudicca's demise probably had a great deal to do with the fact that she conducted a major military campaign in the months directly following a severe flogging.

47. Kentigern's *Life*, like that of many early Celtic saints, is a wonderful mixture of pagan wonder tale and Christian homily. This is indicative of the problems surrounding the idea of Celtic Christianity. At times, it is difficult to know if it is a genuine blending of cultures and beliefs or a subtle form of Pope Gregory's instruction to Abbot Mellitus to appropriate pagan customs and places of worship in order to draw pagans to the new faith.

48. Arderydd is Arthuret near Carlisle. In the *Trioedd Ynys Prydein*, Triad 84 tells us that Arderydd was one of the three futile battles of Britain, fought over a trivial matter and between British kings.

> *Tri Ouergat Ynys Prydein:*
>
> *Vn onaddunt a vu Gat Godeu. Sef y gwnaethpvyt, o achavs yr Ast y ar ivrch fechvys a Chornvgil;*
>
> *Yr eil a vu y Gweith Arderydd, a wnaethpvyt o achavs nyth yr Ychedydd;*
>
> *A'r drydydd oedd waethaf. Sef oedd honno, Camlan. A honno a wnaethpvyt o gywryssedd Gwenhwyuar a Gwennhvyvach. Sef achaws y gelwit y rei hynny yn ouer: vrth y gwneuthur o achavs mor ddiffrvyth a hvnnv.*

Three Futile Battles of the Island of Britain:

One of them was the Battle of Goddeu. It was brought about by the cause of the bitch, together with the roebuck and the plover;

The second was the Action of Arderydd, which was brought about by the cause of the lark's nest;

And the third was the worst. That was Camlan. It was brought about because of a quarrel between Gwenhwyfar and Gwennhwyfach. This is why those were called futile: because they were brought about by such a barren cause as that.

Bromwich (1961)

49.

Since we hold the same Faith, why do customs vary in different Churches? Why, for instance, does the method of saying Mass differ in the holy Roman Church and in the Church of Gaul?

Bede (1990), I, 27

50. The Druidic tonsure was also known as the Celtic tonsure. The front part of the head was shaved up to a line that ran from ear to ear over the crown. Quite why Druids should have adopted a tonsure of any kind (and this one in particular) is uncertain, although the shaving of the head of priests is common to many religions. Celtic Christians claimed their authority in this (and other matters) as St John, whose Gospel has a distinctly Celtic tone. The Church in Rome cited their authority as St Peter and they shaved the crowns of their heads so that a circle of hair remained, symbolizing the crown of thorns.

51.

Among the Welsh there are certain individuals called *awenyddion* who behave as if they were possessed by devils. You will not find them anywhere else. When you consult them about some problem, they immediately go into a trance and lose control of their senses, as if they were possessed. They do not answer the question you put to them in any logical way. Words stream from their mouths, incoherently and apparently meaningless and without any sense at all, but all the same well expressed: and if you listen carefully to what they say you will receive the solution to your problem.

Gerald of Wales tr. Thorpe, L. (1978), I, 16

52. The earliest extant version is in *The Red Book of Hergest*, which dates from 1375 to 1425. However, studies of the language used in *The Red Book of Hergest*, along with other motifs and fragments of these tales found in older manuscripts, suggest that they were first written down around the time of the Norman invasion.

53. A literal translation of 'Gwen Teirbron' is 'White three breast' and she was, indeed, a three-breasted deity. Gwen also means 'holy' and once meant 'prayer'.

54. Doctor William Price of Llantrisant is a perfect example. Obsessed by the Druids, he cremated his young son when he died. Since cremation was not then a legal method for the disposal of corpses, he was tried at Cardiff assizes, but was acquitted and was himself cremated in 1893.

55. Those who are interested in this complex and controversial contribution to our understanding of ancestral Druids and pagan Celtic religious practice would do well to start with Owen (1962) and Jones (1998). These two books provide a good overview as well as excellent bibliographies.

56. The counter-culture was not just sex and drugs and rock and roll, as many would now have us believe. It was a period that saw an extraordinary flowering of ideas and ideals. Although we may now be living through the establishment backlash, these ideas are now in the public domain, and are maturing, and gaining strength – attempts to commercialize them notwithstanding.

57. Stonehenge is the obvious example, yet there are many other sites, such as Avebury, Glastonbury, and Parliament Hill, that are inundated on a regular basis with requests for the conducting of ceremonies that bear scant resemblance to what little we actually know of ancestral practice. It is these events that attract the media, especially if the sites have been proscribed by the authorities, as Stonehenge was for a number of years. In some cases, a genuine political point is being made by such gatherings, but they are often rather embarrassing affairs with different groups vying for space and with little sense of divinity or mystery.

58. This is not to deny that the stages of moral and spiritual development cannot be identified. The works of James Fowler and Lawrence Kohlberg, for example, are eloquent testimony to that. These are, however, frameworks to aid our understanding, not stages to which we must conform.

59. See pages 11-33 of Smart (1969) for his own account of this description. There are many other ways of describing religion. This model was chosen partly because it is the one with which I am most familiar, but largely because it is relatively free of jargon and easy to understand.

60. Most Druids are rightly reluctant to try to define what they are and what they believe in a few sentences. This is partly a recognition of the organic nature of the Druid Way, but also a recognition of the fact that any definition will inevitably require much further explanation. Perhaps the best short definition is that given by Brendan Myers:

> If I had to summarize what a Druid is in one sentence, the sentence might be:
>
> *A Druid is a professional invigilator of living spiritual mysteries as expressed by Celtic cultural forms.*
>
> This is the most precise and yet fully encompassing definition that I can conceive of at this time. It does not employ vague metaphor, but uses analysable language, and it does not harken back to a claim about history which means that this definition may serve contemporary people. But even so, perhaps it deserves further elaboration.
>
> 'professional'
> because being a Druid is a responsibility for one's tribe, not only for one's own self. Being a professional means having a skilled capacity that not everyone has yet everyone needs; it is the investment in you

by one's tribe so that you could acquire that skilled capacity that grounds you in responsibility to that tribe. Being a Druid requires one to be accessible and available to people whose scope of spiritual vision is not as wide as yours. Among one's responsibilities to such people is to aid them to widen their scope of vision. Being a Druid is even a responsibility to the world itself, for as the ancient Druids said, 'we created the world', and without Druids to bring about the renewal of the seasons with their rituals, the world might end. So go the myths. But even contemporary Druids have responsibilities to the world for our Earth is dying. She is being poisoned by the excrement of human industry.

'invigilator'
a word encompassing a range of ideas, including steward, investigator, watcher, even 'knower', but also operator and user. An invigilator is a person who keeps a vigil, which means watchful and mindful and attentive over something. And so to say that a Druid is an invigilator is to say that a Druid is watchful and mindful of something.

'living'
to emphasize that the spiritual mysteries are real and accessible, and not locked in an unknowable, unreachable heaven but manifest and realized in our embodied world.

'spiritual mysteries'
universal principles of animation that emerge from all environmental life. Spiritual mysteries exist everywhere and always, and are knowable by everyone. They are the life-experiences and world-forces that give shape to reality and meaning to our existence. Yet there needs to be something more saying that there is a particularly Druidic way of knowing them. Hence the last part of the definition, which reads:

'as expressed by Celtic cultural forms'
being the culturally specific content of my definition, so to include poetry, art, archaeology, architecture, literature, mythology, language, and folklore, and so to require Druids to have comprehensive knowledge of most of these features of Celtic culture. This is also a

strictly epistemic issue, for it touches on ways of knowing about things, which is different from the issue of what things essentially *are* (that's metaphysics).

[and]

Druidism is the revival of the ancient Celtic religion which holds the Earth and the environment as sacred, and promotes a morality based on truth, honour, strength, and justice.

I believe this is simple enough to be understood by all, and is fairly representative of both ancient Druidism and modern revival Druidism.

Brendan Myers (2004)

61. Language is one of the essentials that define a culture. Celtic languages are also expressions of the Celtic metaphysic, and certain concepts cannot easily be expressed without knowledge of such languages. Celtic languages still in use are Irish, Scottish Gaelic, Welsh, and Breton. Manx (from the Goidelic) and Cornish (from the Brythonic) are considered extinct although efforts are being made to reconstruct and revive them.

62. Talk of biological or any other kind of evolution cannot be taken as an endorsement of the classical Darwinian view exemplified by the notion of 'survival of the fittest'. There are other models for evolution, including the idea that the basic driving force of increasing complexity is co-operation (both conscious and unconscious).

63. Magic, as already discussed, being an approach to understanding and working with the world that is akin to science, but is synthetic, rather than analytical, and deals with the whole of the universe, rather than just its material aspect.

64. Söderblom, N. (1913), 'Holiness', *Encyclopaedia of Religion and Ethics*, vol 6. (eds, Hastings, J., Selbie, J. A. & Gray, L. H.), Clark, Edinburgh.

65. On this matter, see Jackson (1964). Although some of the detail of this study is open to question, the general thesis that the epic tales of Ireland (and

to some extent Wales) throw a great deal of illumination on the customs and thought of pre-Christian Iron Age peoples of Europe is now generally accepted.

66. These are the Irish Brehon Law system and the Welsh Laws of Hywel Dda. There are also references to other Celtic legal systems. The Molmutine Law of Cornwall is mentioned by Geoffrey of Monmouth as having a role in protecting the weak against oppression. The ancient laws of Dàl Riada (a version of the Brehon Laws) were proclaimed by Domnuil I of Alba in the ninth century AD. In the eleventh century AD, an expanded Alba required new laws that reconciled those of the kingdoms it had absorbed and these were drawn up in the *Leger inter Bretonnes et Scotos*. Comparison of the Irish and Welsh systems, along with what we know of other systems now lost, suggests that there may have been a law system common to insular Celts, if not all Celts, for the principles on which the laws are based are identical.

67. This point is ably made at length by Professor Louis Arnaud Reid in his book *Philosophy and Education – An Introduction* (Heinemann, 1962). Whilst this is clearly a book about the uses of philosophical enquiry to and in education, it explores matters that are basic to an understanding of human existence in all aspects of being.

68. I realize that this is a device that works only in print. Capital letters are difficult (though not impossible) to hear in discussion. In this, however, I am following a usage derived from the phrase 'the Truth against the World', which can be taken to mean that what people do by choice should be measured by a single standard – truth.

69. To a Druid, neither good nor evil are absolutes. They are not abstracts, nor are they resident in, or personified as, a form of deity or anti-deity. There is no devil or Satan and there are no demons. Sin as a transgression against God is also a concept alien to pagans, for their relationship with deity is of a different kind from that of those within the Abrahamic tradition. It is also worth noting that those who worship Satan are *not* pagans. They are firmly within the Abrahamic tradition.

70. Situation Ethics was first clearly stated in modern times by the Anglican theologian Joseph Fletcher in his book *Situation Ethics: The New Morality* (SCM, 1966). His position is summed in the following:

> The situationist enters into every decision-making situation fully
> armed with the ethical maxims of his community and its heritage,
> and he treats them with respect as illuminators of his problems. Just
> the same he is prepared in any situation to compromise them or set
> them aside in the situation if love seems better served by doing so.

Save that Druids would substitute 'truth' for 'love', this is a reasonable
summary of how they approach ethical problems.

71. For example, in the *Lebor Gabála Érenn* (the Irish Book of Invasions),
Amairgin Glúnmar, on setting foot on Irish soil, makes a declaration that
begins:

> I am a wind in the sea
> I am a sea-wave upon the land
> I am the sound of the sea
> I am a stag of seven combats
> I am a hawk on a cliff
> I am a teardrop of the sun...

Poems in the Taliesin tradition (that is, poems attributed to Taliesin but
unlikely to have been written by him) also contain such direct statements.
They are not comparisons in which the poet claims to be *like* the wind, or
like a teardrop of the sun. He *is* those things, he is the essential unity
underlying all things, and his is the ability of the adept to experience that
unity.

72. This is not the heaven of Abrahamic tradition, merely an epithet
meaning the Sky. The Sky, the Land, and the Sea are the three elements of
Celtic cosmology.

73. The *Mabinogi*, more properly known as the *Pedair Cainc y Mabinogi*
(Four Branches of the Mabinogi), is one of the greatest works of medieval
literature. Drawn extensively from oral tradition, these tales were collected
into four books or branches and written in the mid-twelfth century AD,
possibly by a single person. The fourth branch is called, in English, *Math,
Son of Mathonwy*. A complex tale with mythological and magical elements,

it is clearly composed of fragments that relate the adventures and relationships of the British deities. The *Mabinogi* invariably appear in print under the title *The Mabinogion* with seven or eight other tales, including heroic age episodes from the life of Arthur.

74. The Romans, Julius Caesar in particular, have for ever muddied our understanding of the nature of many of the Celtic deities by making somewhat arbitrary comparisons between Graeco-Roman gods and goddesses and those of the Celts. This was further compounded by the somewhat patronizing attitude of Romans to other religions. They tolerated them (where they presented no threat to Rome), but they imposed their own imperfect understanding of them on the people they had conquered.

75. The *Lebor Gabála Érenn* is a twelfth-century text in which are collected pseudo-historical tales arranged as a chronology of successive invasions of Ireland. Although the subject is Celtic, the chronological framework and some of the commentary are clearly biblical in origin, which suggests Christian redaction. There are even attempts to insert Hebrew mythology. All that notwithstanding, it is still a masterpiece of literature and, along with *The Mabinogion*, is one of the major sources of information and inspiration for modern Druids.

76. Beltane is now conventionally celebrated on the first day of May and heralds the summer half of the year. Fires are lit and it is considered an auspicious time to begin large-scale projects. It was perhaps smoke from the Beltane fires of the Tuatha Dé Danaan that obscured the sun for three days.

77. Ogham are the only known form of native Celtic letters. They probably originated in south-west Ireland and have never been found outside Ireland and Great Britain – despite claims that they have been discovered in America.
The ogham 'alphabet' – more properly the 'beth-luis-nuin' – consists of twenty letters, to which a further five (representing diphthongs) were added at a much later date to accommodate Latinate introductions to the language.

Many people think of the ogham as nothing more than a tree alphabet, but this is not strictly true. Part of the confusion stems from the fact that most (though not all) of the names of the letters are also the names of trees.

Although in one system the letters do represent trees, ogham were also attached to many other systems and name lists. There are body ogham, hound ogham, cow ogham, work ogham, place ogham, and so on. However, the link with trees is early and deep, as ogham were considered to be branches of the Tree of Wisdom, and were probably used as a means of teaching.

The original twenty ogham are divided into four groups or *aicme*. These consist of anything from one to five straight lines or notches cut to, or across, a stem line. This stem could be either vertical or horizontal. Where the line is horizontal, the letters are to be read from left to right. Where the line is vertical, it was the usual practice to write from top to bottom. Inscriptions that followed the outer edge of a stone slab or the inner line of an arch were generally written from bottom left, upward, across the top and then down the right-hand side.

Claims about the great antiquity of the ogham should be treated with some caution, although they are probably a good few centuries older than any of the extant examples. Their use for divination has no direct support in ancient texts. There is, however, circumstantial evidence that Druids considered them to have magical properties. If that were the case, they would undoubtedly have been employed as tools for understanding the future course of events.

78. This may also make him the archetype for the Lancelot of the Arthurian tales. Lancelot, meaning, 'the one who holds the spear', is probably the title of an office held by one of Arthur's trusted companions. In the early Christian tales, this was probably Bedwyr, a warrior with only one hand who was skilled in the use of the spear and was given the task of returning the sword to the Lady of the Lake – a logical duty, given that we know from later tales that the Lancelot was known as the Lancelot of the Lake.

79. *Fidchell*, and its Welsh equivalent *gwyddbwyll* (both meaning 'wood sense'), are board games that have a sacred aspect connected with kingship and sovereignty. Sometimes described as chess (perhaps because one player has a piece called a King), it predates that game by centuries. We do not know the exact rules, although it is clear from what evidence we do have that it is similar to the Scandinavian games of *Tablut* and *Hnefatafl*.

The board is square with a grid of nine holes by nine (the playing pieces being elaborate pegs). One player has a King and eight soldiers; the other has sixteen soldiers. At the beginning of the game, the pieces are set out with the King at the centre and his own men forming a cross about him. The other pieces are arranged four to each side of the board. The object of the game for the King's force is to enable the King to reach any one of the four corner squares; for the Enemy, it is to trap the King.

All moves are made orthogonally, one hole at a time. The King's force has first move. A player captures his opponent's soldiers by trapping them between two of his own. The captured piece is removed from the board. The King is captured only when he is surrounded on all four sides.

80. A Grove (with a capital 'G') is either a collection of Druids who meet together on a regular basis or, as in this case, the working space of a Druid, whether internal or in the 'real' world.

81. The 'Nobles of the Wood' were the oak, hazel, holly, yew, ash, Scots pine, and wild apple; the 'Commoners of the Wood' were the alder, willow, hawthorn, rowan, birch, elm, and wild cherry; 'Lower Divisions of the Wood' were the blackthorn, elder, spindle, whitebeam, strawberry tree, aspen, and juniper; and 'Bushes of the Wood' were the bracken, bog-myrtle, gorse, bramble, heather, broom, and wild rose.

Compare this list with the thirty-three native trees of Britain and Ireland (that is, those trees that colonized Britain and Ireland between the end of the last Ice Age and the severing of the land from continental Europe by rising sea levels): alder (*alnus glutinosa*), ash (*fraxinus excelsior*), aspen (*populus tremula*), bay willow (*salix pentandra*), beech (*fagus sylvatica*), bird cherry (*prunus padus*), black poplar (*populus nigra*), box (*buxus sempervirens*), common oak (*quercus robur*), crab apple (*malus sylvestris*), crack willow (*salix fragilis*), downy birch (*betula pubescens*), field maple (*acer campestre*), pussy willow (*salix caprea*), hawthorn (*crataegus monogyna*), hazel (*corylus avellana*), hornbeam (*carpinus betulus*), holly (*ilex aquifolium*), juniper (*juniperus communis*), large leaved lime (*tilia platyphyllos*), midland thorn (*crataegus laevigata*), rowan (*sorbus aucuparia*), Scots pine (*pinus sylvestris*), sessile oak (*quercus petraea*), silver birch (*betula pendula*), small leaved lime (*tilia cordata*), strawberry tree (*arbutus unedo*), whitebeam (*sorbus aria*), white willow (*salix alba*), wild cherry (*prunus avium*), wild service tree (*sorbus torminalis*), wych elm (*ulmus glabra*), yew (*taxus baccata*);

and the twenty trees represented by the ogham:

birch, rowan, alder, willow, ash, hawthorn, oak, holly, hazel, apple, bramble, ivy, broom, blackthorn, elder, elm, gorse, heather, aspen, yew.

82. There is no ancient manuscript telling us what Druids wore. Native texts tend to suggest that the higher up the social scale, the greater the number of colours you were allowed to wear. Some have suggested this may refer to complexities of plaid. Druids, being at the top, may have had resplendent ceremonial and formal robes. The only possible reference to robes is in Pliny (*Nat. Hist.*, XVI, 249) and the translation can be made in a number of ways. Pliny writes:

> *Sacerdos candida veste cultus arborem scandit, falce aurea demetit, candido id excipitut sago.*

This is usually translated along the lines of:

> A priest in white clothing climbs the tree, cuts [the mistletoe] with a golden sickle, and it is caught in a white cloak.

The context, however, allows equally for the following translation:

> A well-dressed priest in beautiful clothes climbs the tree, harvests [the mistletoe] with a gilded pruning hook, and it is caught in a beautiful cloak.

83. The eightfold year of festivals and ceremonies is disputed by some Druids and many academics who claim that it is a relatively modern invention. Although the name may be, there is plenty of evidence that ancestral Celts celebrated eight annual festivals. The lunar festivals (also referred to as the fire festivals) are not in any dispute. These take place at times roughly midway between the solstices and equinoxes. Known as Samhain, Imbolc, Beltane, and Lughnasad, they are well documented and have been celebrated for thousands of years. They were open festivals in which the public participated, and they were presided over by Druids who performed their priestly and legal functions.

These days, the lunar festivals are usually celebrated on a single day, using conventional dates from the Gregorian calendar. Thus, Imbolc falls on 1 February, Beltane on 1 May, Lughnasad on 1 August, and Samhain on 1

November. The Gregorian calendar is, however, a solar calendar and to hold the festivals on these days tends to undermine their nature. As they are lunar festivals, they probably followed a lunar cycle and were celebrated at specific phases of the moon. Samhain, as the time when the doorway between the worlds is open, is the time of the dark moon. Imbolc is celebrated on the first quarter of the moon, Beltane at the full moon, and Lughnasad at the third quarter.

The solar festivals take place on the solstices and the equinoxes. The evidence for the recognition of these days as sacred and worthy of celebration is based on several points that are often overlooked. The first is that the Celts had numerous and important solar deities in their pantheon, including Mabon, the sacred child. To suggest that they would not have acknowledged the importance of these deities and the sun to which they were linked is absurd. The second point is that the sun itself was an object of esteem and was recognized as essential to the agricultural life of the Celts. The third is that what little we know of calendars is that they were based on lunar cycles that were adjusted in order to stay in step with the solar cycle. This required Celts to know how the year was progressing. Marking the equinoxes and solstices was by far the easiest way to calculate the approximate time of the lunar or fire festivals. The fourth point is that a great deal of later Celtic myth embodies tales based on a solar cycle. The fifth is that when Christianity appropriated pagan festivals, the Church did not subsume the lunar festivals. Rather, they took over the solar festivals, which suggests these were far more important to the Celts as spiritual rituals.

In contrast with the lunar festivals, which were public and open celebrations of the outer mysteries, the solar festivals were quiet and contemplative affairs during which the inner mysteries were probably celebrated. It is likely that the Druids retreated at these times and undertook private ceremonies in their groves as well as presiding over whatever public ceremonies were held.

The progress of the festivals (and all their names) are marked on the chart below, showing how they fall against the Gregorian calendar and the lunar periods of the Coligny calendar (a bronze artefact of the first century AD discovered in France in 1897).

Coligny Month	Gregorian Period	Festivals
Samonios	Oct./Nov.	Samhain
Dumannios	Nov./Dec.	
Riuros	Dec./Jan.	winter solstice
Anagantios	Jan./Feb.	Imbolc
Ogronios	Feb./Mar.	
Cutios	Mar./Apr.	spring equinox
Giamonios	Apr./May	Beltane
Simivisonios	May/June	
Equos	June/July	summer solstice
Elembiuos	July/Aug.	Lughnasad
Edrinios	Aug./Sept.	
Cantlos	Sept./Oct.	autumn equinox

The names given to the festivals by modern Druids vary according to how they were taught. Nearly all use the Irish names for the lunar festivals. Others balance this by using the modern Welsh names for the solar festivals. A few (quite often those who have come to the Druid Way from Wicca) make use of Old English (and sometimes Christian) terminology.

Irrespective of the historical veracity of the eightfold year, Druids today celebrate the turning of the year with eight ceremonies. The Druid Way, after all, is not an academic reconstruction of the past but a living spiritual tradition.

84. This nomenclature is not common to all Druids, but is used here to demonstrate the underlying unity of Druid spiritual practice and thought.

85. A note on terminology. The reason for calling the solar festivals 'solar' is obvious: they mark the passage of the sun in relation to the horizon and thus delineate the cycle of the year (the period in which the earth moves once around the sun). The other ceremonies, in contrast, are referred to as lunar festivals. This is a convenience. The choice of the term 'lunar' has much more to do with symbolism than with using the moon to gauge when the ceremonies should be held. Moreover, whilst everyone celebrated the event at hand, there was a deeper recognition of the aspects involved in this

communion with the way in which the universe worked. The lunar and solar cycles wove together as part of a greater unity and this, too, was celebrated.

86. Stonehenge, although undoubtedly imbued with a great sense of the sacred, is not Druidic. Its choice as a gathering place on the summer solstice is rooted in the beliefs of the eighteenth-century Druid Revivalists.

87. The seven-day week may be considered as natural as it falls (more or less) on each of the lunar quarters, but it does not feature in ancestral timekeeping.

88. Awen is difficult to define, but contexts suggest meanings such as 'creative inspiration', 'connection with spirit', 'oracular voice'. The first mention of it is in the eighth century *Historia Brittonum*, conventionally ascribed to Nennius, a work based on earlier texts. There are later references by Giraldus Cambrensis (Gerald of Wales) in his twelfth-century *Description of Wales*. Later texts, such as the *Book of Taliesin* also include the word 'awen'.

A Druid today may think of awen as inspiration or divine power – an energy flow or communion. It is also the poetic muse, the breath of creativity, even the reins that bind them to the source of all inspiration. The word is extant in the Welsh language, and has the meaning 'poetic gift'.

89. It is popular at present to claim that Druids were shamans. Certainly, some areas of shamanic practice were similar to ancestral Druidic practice. There were similarities, however, between Druidic practice and very early Christianity (which is why it was tolerated by some of them), just as there were similarities to Buddhism and a number of other religions. This does not make Druids Christian, any more than it makes them Buddhist. It merely illustrates the fact that the spiritual quest of humankind is one that is common to all. Different religions are therefore bound to have aspects in common.

90. Fundamentalist Druid is, in fact, a contradiction of terms. The Druid Way is marked by the need for balance and tolerance. There are, however, those who claim to be Druid who display an alarming intolerance toward other religions of all traditions. Paganism has long had to contend with certain fascist and racist organizations that claim erroneously to be pagan. It is not a unique experience.

SELECT BIBLIOGRAPHY

Not all the research for this book was derived from other books. Conversations, lectures, workshops, and direct experience over the years have provided a large proportion of my understanding of the subject. Besides which, a bibliography of books on the Celts, the Druids (past and present), and related matters would fill a book in its own right.

The texts below are listed for two reasons. The first is that they are the ones I referred to most in researching this book. Many of them have excellent and more comprehensive bibliographies of their own. The second is that they are, with a few exceptions, easily available to the general reader.

Adkins, L. & R., 1982, *The Handbook of British Archaeology*, David & Charles, Newton Abbot.

Anon, 1989, *Two Celtic Saints – The Lives of Ninian and Kentigern*, Llanerch, Felinfach.

Arnold, B. & Gibson, D. B. (eds), 1995, *Celtic Chiefdom, Celtic State: The Evolution of Complex Social Systems*, Cambridge University Press, Cambridge.

Augros, R. & Stanciu, G., 1987, *The New Biology – Discovering the Wisdom in Nature*, Shambhala, Boston.

Barber, R., 2004, *The Holy Grail*, Allen Lane, London.

Barham, L., Priestley, P. & Targett, A., 1999, *In Search of Cheddar Man*, Tempus, Stroud.

Bede (tr. Sherley-Price, L.), 1990, *Ecclesiastical History of the English People*, Penguin, London.

Bord, J. & C., 1982, *Earth Rites*, Granada, London.

Bord, J. & C., 1985, *Sacred Waters*, Granada, London.

Bradley, I., 1993, *The Celtic Way*, Darton Longman & Todd, London.

Bromwich, R., 1961, *Trioedd Ynys Prydein: The Welsh Triads*, University of Wales Press, Cardiff.

Chadwick, N. K., 1966, *The Druids*, University of Wales Press, Cardiff.

Chadwick, N. K., 1971, *The Celts*, Penguin, London.

Chapman, M., 1992, *The Celts – The Construction of a Myth*, St Martin's Press, New York.

Chetan, A. & Brueton, D., 1994, *The Sacred Yew*, Penguin, London.

Coe, J. B. & Young, S., 1995, *The Celtic Sources for the Arthurian Legend*, Llanerch, Felinfach.

Cole, P., 1999, *Philosophy of Religion*, Hodder & Stoughton, London.

Collingwood, R. G., 1945, *The Idea of Nature*, Oxford University Press, Oxford.

Cook, R., 1974, *The Tree of Life*, Thames & Hudson, London.

Cunliffe, B., 1997, *The Ancient Celts*, Oxford University Press, Oxford.

Cunliffe, B., 2001, *Facing the Ocean: The Atlantic and its Peoples*, Oxford University Press, Oxford.

Cunliffe, B., 2003, *The Celts – A Very Short Introduction*, Oxford University Press, Oxford.

Darrah, J., 1994, *Paganism in Arthurian Romance*, Boydell, Woodbridge.

Davies, B., 2003, *An Introduction to the Philosophy of Religion*, Oxford University Press, Oxford.

Devereux, P., 1992, *Symbolic Landscapes*, Gothic Image, Glastonbury.

Dillon, M., 1948, *Early Irish Literature*, University of Chicago Press, Chicago.

Dillon, M., 1973, *Celt and Hindu*, University College, Dublin.

Dillon, M. & Chadwick, N., 1967, *The Celtic Realms*, Weidenfeld & Nicolson, London.

Eliade, M., 1958, *Patterns in Comparative Religion*, Sheed & Ward, London.

Ellis, P. B., 1990, *The Celtic Empire – The First Millennium of Celtic History*, Constable, London.

Ellis, P. B., 1992, *Celtic Inheritance*, Constable, London.

Ellis, P. B., 1992, *Dictionary of Celtic Mythology*, Constable, London.

Ellis, P. B., 1993, *Celt and Saxon*, Constable, London.

Ellis, P. B., 1994, *The Druids*, Constable, London.

Ellis, P. B., 1995, *Celtic Women*, Constable, London.

Ellis, P. B., 1997, *Celt and Greek*, Constable, London.

Ellis, P. B., 1998, *The Ancient World of the Celts*, Constable, London.

Ellis, P. B., 1998, *Celt and Roman*, Constable, London.

Fowler, J., 1981, *Stages of Faith: The Psychology of Human Development and the Quest for Meaning*, Harper & Row, San Francisco.

Gantz, J. (tr.), 1976, *The Mabinogion*, Penguin, London.

Gantz, J. (tr.), 1981, *Early Irish Myths and Sagas*, Penguin, London.

Gerald of Wales (tr. Thorpe, L.), 1978, *The Journey Through Wales & The Description of Wales*, Penguin, London.

Gerald of Wales (tr. O'Meara, J.), 1982, *The History and Topography of Ireland*, Penguin, London.

Gildas, (tr. Winterbottam, M.), 1978, *The Ruin of Britain and other documents*, Phillimore, Chichester.

Graves, T., 1990, *Inventing Reality: Towards a Magical Technology*, Gateway, Bath.

Green, M., 1968, *The Gods of the Celts*, Alan Sutton, Stroud.

Green, M. J. (ed.), 1995, *The Celtic World*, Routledge, London.

Greywind, 2001, *the Voice within the Wind – of Becoming and the Druid Way*, Grey House in the Woods, Ballantrae.

Greywind, 2005, *the Light beyond the Forest – of Seeing and the Druid Way*, Grey House in the Woods, Ballantrae.

Greywind, tba, *the Truth against the World – of Being and the Druid Way*, Grey House in the Woods, Ballantrae.

Haywood, J., 2001, *The Historical Atlas of the Celtic World*, Thames & Hudson, London.

Hood, A. B. E. (tr.), 1978, *St Patrick – His Writings and Muirchiu's Life*, Phillimore, Chichester.

Hubert, H., 1992, *The History of the Celtic People*, Bracken Books, London.

Hunt, R., 2003, *Queen Bouddica's Battle of Britain*, Spellmount, Staplehurst.

Hutton, R., 1991, *The Pagan Religions of the Ancient British Isles*, Blackwell, Oxford.

Jackson, K. H., 1964, *The Oldest Irish Tradition: A Window on the Iron Age*, Cambridge University Press, Cambridge.

James, S., 1999, *The Atlantic Celts: Ancient People or Modern Invention*, British Museum Press, London.

Jones, L. E., 1998, *Druid Shaman Priest*, Hisarlik Press, Enfield Lock.

Jones, P. & Pennick, N., 1995, *A History of Pagan Europe*, Routledge, London.

Kelly, F., 1983, *The Book of Leinster*, Dublin Institute for Advanced Studies, Dublin.

Kelly, F., 1988, *A Guide to Early Irish Law*, Dublin Institute for Advanced Studies, Dublin.

Kendrick, T. D., 1927, *The Druids: A Study in Keltic Prehistory*, Methuen & Co Ltd, London.

Kinsella, T., 1969, *The Tain*, Dolmen Press, Dublin.

Koch, J. T. & Carey, J., 2003, *The Celtic Heroic Age*, Celtic Studies Publications, Aberystwyth.

Kohlberg, L., 1984, *Psychology of Moral Development*, Harper & Row, New York.

Kropotkin, P., 1914, *Mutual Aid – A Factor of Evolution*, Porter Sargent, Boston.

Laing, L., 1979, *Celtic Britain*, Granada, London.

Laing, L. & J., 1980, *The Origins of Britain*, Granada, London.

Laurie, E. R., 1995, *A Circle of Stones – Journeys & Meditations for Celts*, Eschaton, Chicago.

Levy, G. R., 1948, *The Gate of Horn*, Faber & Faber, London.

Loomis, R. S., 1993, *Celtic Myth and Arthurian Romance*, Constable, London.

Low, M., 1996, *Celtic Christianity and Nature*, Polygon, Edinburgh.

Lowenthal, D., 1985, *The Past is a Foreign Country*, Cambridge University Press, Cambridge.

MacCana, P., 1983, *Celtic Mythology*, Newnes, Feltham.

MacCulloch, J. A., 1911, *The Religion of the Ancient Celts*, T & T Clark, Edinburgh.

MacCulloch, J. A., 1992, *Celtic Mythology*, Constable, London.

MacKillop, J., 1998, *Dictionary of Celtic Mythology*, Oxford University Press, Oxford.

MacMurray, J., 1957, *Persons in Relation*, Faber, London.

MacMurray, J., 1957, *The Self as Agent*, Faber, London.

Maier, B. (tr. Edwards, C.), 1997, *Dictionary of Celtic Religion and Culture*, Boydell, Woodbridge.

Marcel, G., 1951, *The Mystery of Being*, Harvill Press, London.

Markale, J. (tr. Burke, B. N.), 1981, *Merlin – Priest of Nature*, Inner Traditions, Rochester, Vermont.

Markale, J. (tr. Graham, J.), 1985, *The Druids,* Inner Traditions, Rochester, Vermont.

Markale, J. (tr. Hauch, C.), 1976, *King of the Celts*, Inner Traditions, Rochester, Vermont.

Markale, J. (tr. Hauch, C.), 1976, *The Celts*, Inner Traditions, Rochester, Vermont.

Markale, J. (tr. Mygind, A., Hauch, C., & Henry, P.), 1972, *Women of the Celts*, Inner Traditions, Rochester, Vermont.

Matthews, C., 1987, *Mabon and the Mysteries of Britain – an Exploration of the Mabinogion*, Arkana, London.

Matthews, C., 1989, *Arthur and the Sovereignty of Britain – King and Goddess in the Mabinogion*, Arkana, London.

Matthews, C., 1989, *The Celtic Tradition*, Element, Shaftesbury.

Matthews, C. & J., 1994, *The Western Way*, Arkana, London.

Meehan, A., 1991, *Knotwork – The Secret Method of the Scribes*, Thames & Hudson, London.

Meehan, A., 1995, *The Tree of Life*, Thames & Hudson, London.

Megaw, R. & V., 2001, *Celtic Art: From its Beginning to the Book of Kells*, Thames & Hudson, London.

Milis, L. J. R. (ed.) (tr. Guest, T.), 1998, *The Pagan Middle Ages*, Boydell & Brewer, Woodbridge.

Mounier, E. (tr. Mairet, P.), 1952, *Personalism*, Routledge,London.

Myers, B., 2004, *Dangerous Religion*, Earth Religions Press, Nyack, NY.

Nasr, S. H., 1968, *Man and Nature – The Spiritual Crisis in Modern Man*, George Allen & Unwin, London.

Nennius (tr. Morris, J.), 1980, *British History and The Welsh Annals*, Phillimore, Chichester.

Ni h'Eibhin, E., 2003, *The Celtic Metaphysic*, unpublished paper.

O hOgain, D., 1999, *The Sacred Isle – Belief and Religion in Pre-Christian Ireland*, Boydell & Collins, Woodbridge.

O'Curry, E. (ed. Sullivan, W. K.), 1873, *On the Manners and Customs of the Ancient Irish*, Williams Northgate, Dublin.

O'Donohue, J., 1997, *Anam Cara – Spiritual Wisdom from the Celtic World*, Bantam Press, London.

Owen, A. L., 1962, *The Famous Druids*, Oxford University Press, Oxford.

Paterson, J. M., 1996, *Tree Wisdom*, Thorsons, London.

Pennick, N., 1996, *Celtic Sacred Landscapes*, Thames & Hudson, London.

Piggott, S., 1975, *The Druids*, Thames & Hudson, London.

Rankin, H. D., 1987, *Celts and the Classical World*, Croom Helm, London.

Rees, A. & B., 1961, *Celtic Heritage – Ancient Tradition in Ireland and Wales*, Thames & Hudson, London.

Rees, B. R., 1998, *Pelagius – Life and Letters*, Boydell, Woodbridge.

Rhys, J., 1904, *Celtic Britain*, SPCK, London.

Richards, G., 1991, *The Philosophy of Gandhi*, Curzon Press, Richmond.

Richards, J. R., 1980, *The Sceptical Feminist*, Pelican, London.

Rolleston, T. W., 1985, *Myths and Legends of the Celtic Race*, Constable, London.

Ross, A., 1967, *Pagan Celtic Britain*, Constable, London.

Ross, A., 1999, *Druids*, Tempus, Stroud.

Roszak, T., 1979, *Person/Planet*, Victor Gollancz, London.

Russell, B., 1961, *A History of Western Philosophy*, Unwin, London.

Russell, P., 1982, *The Awakening Earth*, Penguin, London.

Russell, P., 1995, *An Introduction to the Celtic Languages*, Longmans, London.

Rutherford, W., 1987, *Celtic Mythology*, Thorsons, London.

Rutherford, W., 1993, *Celtic Lore – The History of the Druids and their Timeless Traditions*, Aquarian Press, London.

Seddon, R., 1990, *The Mystery of Arthur at Tintagel*, Rudolf Steiner Press, London.

Seymour, J., 1989, *The Ultimate Heresy*, Green Books, Bideford.

Shlain, L., 1998, *The Alphabet Versus The Goddess*, Allen Lane, London.

Sjoestedt, M-L. (tr. Dillon, M.), 1949, *Gods and Heroes of the Celts*, Methuen & Co Ltd, London.

Skolimowski, H., 1985, *Eco-Theology*, Vasanta Press, Madras.

Skolimowski, H., 1992, *Living Philosophy*, Arkana, London.

Skolimowski, H., 1993, *A Sacred Place to Dwell*, Element Books, Shaftesbury.

Smart, N., 1969, *The Religious Experience of Mankind*, Charles Scribner's Sons, New York.

Spence, L., 1981, *British Fairy Origins*, Aquarian Press, Wellingborough.

Squire, C., 1905, *The Mythology of the British Islands*, Gresham, London.

Stewart, R. J., 1986, *Merlin: Prophetic Life and The Mystic Vision*, Penguin, London.

Stewart, R. J., 1990, *Celtic Gods Celtic Goddesses*, Blandford, London.

Strachan, G., 1998, *Jesus the Master Builder – Druid Mysteries and the Dawn of Christianity*, Floris, Edinburgh.

Streit, J. (tr. Latham, H.), 1984, *Sun and Cross*, Floris, Edinburgh.

Tagore, R., 1931, *The Religion of Man*, George Allen & Unwin, London.

Taylor, T. (tr.), 1925, *The Life of St Samson of Dol*, Llanerch, Felinfach.

Thompson, M., 1997, *Philosophy of Religion*, Teach Yourself Books, London.

Tolstoy, N., 1985, *The Quest for Merlin*, Hamish Hamilton, London.

Travers, P. L., 1989, *What the Bee Knows*, Aquarian, London.

Underhill, E., 1993, *Mysticism*, Oneworld, Oxford.

Underhill, E., 1993, *The Spiritual Life*, Oneworld, Oxford.

Versluis, A., 1986, *The Philosophy of Magic*, Arkana, London.

Waite, A. E., 1933, *The Holy Grail – Its Legends and Symbolism*, Rider & Co, London.

Wentz, W. Y. Evans, 1911, *The Fairy-Faith in Celtic Countries*, Oxford University Press, Oxford.

White, J. & Talboys, G. K., 2002, *the Path through the Forest – a Druid Guidebook*, Grey House in the Woods, Ballantrae.

White, J. & Talboys, G. K., 2004, *Arianrhod's Dance – a Druid Ritual Handbook*, Grey House in the Woods, Ballantrae.

Williams, H., 1899, *Two Lives of Gildas*, Llanerch, Felinfach.

Winner, A. K., 1970, *The Basic Ideas of Occult Wisdom*, Theosophical Publishing, Wheaton, Illinois.

Wood, J., 1998, *The Celts – Life, Myth and Art*, Duncan Baird, London.

Wood, J., 2000, *The Celtic Book of Living and Dying*, Duncan Baird, London.

York, M., 2003, *Pagan Theology – Paganism as a World Religion*, New York University Press, New York.

INDEX

agricultural 233
hydrological 185
inner 244
lunar 188, 250-251
social 246
solar 188
spiritual 233
cyclical, see Celtic metaphysic

Dagda, the 31, 173, 174
  as Cernunnos 174
  as guardian of the Land 174-175
  as Lord of the Animals 174
Danu 32, 92, 171, 172, 174
dark 172, 238, 240, 244
day 188
  longest 238
  shortest 243
  start of 188
death 35, 71, 134, 186, 189,
  196-197, 240, 241-242, 243, 246
deities, see Celtic deities
Dian Cécht 173
Diodorus Siculus 51, 281
Diogenes Laertius 38, 43, 279
Dion Chrysostum 52, 281
discipline 136
divination 208, 292
divine principle
  female xiv, xv
  male xiv, xv
  manifest in nature xiv
Divine Youth, see Mabon
doctrinal writings 144
doctrine 144, 146
Domnu 172
Don, see Danu
Druid
  Celtic word 44
  meaning of word 42-46
Druid Fellowships 97
Druid Orders 96, 97, 212, 214-217,
  220
  as community 217
  as modern invention 214-215
  organization of 215
  size of 215
  teaching 215
  threefold path 215-216
Druid Revivalists 96
Druids xvi, 50, 51, 116, 124, 135,
  212, 215, 217
  ancestral
    as central 225

as Christian priests 90
clothing 293-294
colleges 24, 30, 55, 89, 90, 277
education 53, 55-56
literacy 54
meditation 252-253
memory 54
origin of 46-50
organization of 50-57
religion 30
role 24, 46, 50-57, 84
schools, see colleges
teachings 54, 90, 96, 277
threefold division 50-53
women 56
as teachers 135, 137
becoming 214
definition of 287-288
development
  personal 247
  social 247
education of 124
history of 125
image of 136
meditation 251-254
numbers of xii, 272
name, present day use of xvi
oaks 44, 45
personal circumstances 161-162
see also Hedge Druids
teachings 31, 130, 144-169
  sources of 144
truth 45
work of 125
Druid Way
  as celebration 128-129
  as intellectual activity 116-117
  as living tradition xvii, 128
  as mystery tradition 142
  as organism 117
  as pagan religion xiii
  as religion xiii, 100, 140
  as service 138-139, 158
  as spiritual path 142, 258
  as spiritual tradition 142
  as way of life 256
  defined 116-142, 287-288
  dimensions of 137-139
    craft 137
    healing 137
    metaphysical 137
    natural philosophy 138
    ritual 138
    seeing 138

magical, see Celtic metaphysic
Maiden Castle 28
Manannán mac Lir 173
Maponus, see Mabon
Martin of Tours 86
Matter of Britain 144, 173, 178
Matter of Ireland 144
May Day 93, 238
meditation 138, 227, 251-254
    Buddhist 251
    Druid 252
        purpose of 252
    eastern techniques 252
    pathworking 253
    Taoist 252
    visualization 253
megalithic monuments 4
    builders of 49
memory 125-126
Mesolithic 48
metal-working 4, 5
metaphysics 137, 166
mistletoe 202-203, 209
mnemonic keys 54, 278
Modron 177
monism xv
month 188
moon 187, 188, 232, 250
Morgan 209, 244
Mór Rí 92
Mórrígan 173
mourning 134, 196-197
Myrddin 32, 56, 88, 91, 209
mystery 103
mystical experience 108
mythology 109

naming 246
natural 72
    law 264, 266, 268
    order 152
    philosophy 138
    world 145, 182, 188, 241, 260
    knowledge of 128, 265
naturalism 72
nature 152-153
    as manifestation of divine xiv
Neolithic 49
Newgrange 243
night 188
number 34
    nine 57, 209
    thirty-three 171
    three 34, 278

oak 44-45, 203, 207-208
    groves 208, 280
    sacred 32, 93
O'Curry, Eugene 281
ogham 174, 206, 291-292
    trees 293
Ogma 173-174
ollam 52
Onomaris 56
oppidum 277
order 69, 158
Orders, see Druid Orders
organicistic, see Celtic metaphysic
Otherworld 35, 57, 71, 122, 173,
    185, 189-198, 209, 242, 249
    as place of balance 195
    journey to 36-37, 197
    location 36
    names of 36
    not supernatural 193
other worlds 193
Ovates, see Vates

pagan
    derivation of word xiii
    metaphysic 97
    spirituality 214
    theology 101
paganism xii, 91, 94, 95, 100, 101,
    141, 146, 272
    definition of xiii-xvi
    Celtic 96, 214
    informal expression of xvi
    resurgence of xvi
pagans 101, 145, 188
    numbers of xii
panentheism 118
pantheism, animistic 118
past 72, 134-135, 260
pathworking, see meditation
pax Romana 18
Pelagius 39
    heresy 87
        as Druid philosophy 77
pentagram 207, 209
person 166-168
    cult of 114
    definition of 79
personalism 79
personalist, see Celtic metaphysic
personal possessions 191-192
    disposal of 192
    endowed with spirit 191
philosophy 105